RELIGIOUS AND SECULAR

RELIGIOUS AND SECULAR

Conflict and Accommodation between Jews in Israel

Edited by Charles S. Liebman

A Project of

KETER PUBLISHING HOUSE
JERUSALEM LTD.

Library of Congress Catalog Number 89–85371
ISBN 0–9623723–1–5

Manufactured in the United States of America
Produced by The Bookmakers, Incorporated, Wilkes-Barre, Pennsylvania
Copies of this book may be obtained from AVI CHAI
509 Madison Avenue, New York, New York 10022

Contents

Foreword

During the summer of 1986 the Chairman and Executive Director of AVI CHAI met with forty-five individuals whose knowledge of Israeli society spans a wide range of professional disciplines and personal philosophies. This was the first step in our endeavor to learn whether the Foundation could play a constructive role in increasing the understanding and sensitivity in Israel among Jews of different levels of religious commitment and observance.

Based on these meetings our Trustees concluded that, while our goal was to make a meaningful contribution to Israeli society, we did not possess a sufficient understanding of these complex societal problems to develop philanthropic initiatives. Therefore, the Board decided to deepen its insights into how possibly to bring Jews closer to an appreciation and understanding of one another, which is intended to be our primary focus in Israel.

First consideration was given to a comprehensive sociological study in order to define attitudes and actual behavior among diverse populations in Israeli society. Upon exploration, we found this would entail both practical and technical problems.

We, therefore, embarked on two approaches to gaining information about behavior in Israel among those perceived as "religious" and "non-religious." As a first step we sought to identify what was known already and enlisted a researcher who conducted a literature search of published studies of interaction between these two broad groups. His survey included both Hebrew and English sources and academic as well as governmental papers. It became evident that few studies have focused seriously on the theme of religious/non-religious relations. The conclusion drawn was that little factual basis exists for understanding the nature of daily interaction among Israelis of different levels of religious commitment. What is clear is the awareness of Israelis across the spectrum of the increasing number of public issues which cause or reflect conflict, at times, exacerbated by the media.

Parallel to the literature review we commissioned a series of societal case studies designed to offer anecdotal insights into the dynamics of religious/non-religious relations. The project, under the direction of Dr. Charles S. Liebman, engaged researchers and journalists to examine in specific settings the manner of interactions, specific causes of tension, and some ways in which the tensions are overcome. Some settings illustrate instances of conflict; others demonstrate different modes of accommodation and conflict resolution.

As we reviewed these studies, our Trustees realized that the insights gained into the complexity of these situations can be important beyond our own internal use. We believe that this material can be helpful to leaders in Israel and the Diaspora in their struggle to understand the problems which have arisen in recent years over these issues. Therefore, our Board decided to publish these studies in both Hebrew and English. We were pleased that Keter Publishing House recognized the value of this material and is presenting it in book form. We hope that others will find this work to be a valuable contribution to their understanding.

We want to acknowledge with appreciation the important contributions made by each of the authors of these articles to a further understanding of the dynamics of these issues. Our special thanks go to Dr. Charles S. Liebman, a world renowned scholar, who husbanded this project from its conceptualization to successful completion. His commitment to the quality of these studies went beyond mere professionalism and reflected his personal concern and dedication to the improvement of relations among Jews in Israel. We also wish to acknowledge the fine workmanship of John Beck and his team at The Bookmakers, Incorporated who produced the volume, and Marcia Pacht, the AVI CHAI staff member who coordinated the process.

The Trustees of AVI CHAI, like many other Jews in Israel and the Diaspora, have been deeply troubled in recent years by the tensions which have beclouded the atmosphere of relations among Jews of different levels of religious commitment and observance. Our Foundation is committed to efforts to ameliorate some of these tensions by the sound philanthropic role it can play.

We will continue to develop information which can serve as a basis for further attempts to diffuse these societal tensions. Opinions expressed in this book and the facts upon which they are based are solely those of the respective contributors. It is the hope of the Foundation that the insights which can be gained from these articles will not only stimulate scholarly research but will lead to constructive programmatic responses toward improving the current state of affairs, both by AVI CHAI and by others.

AVI CHAI
A Philanthropic Foundation
Shevat, 5750
February, 1990

Charles S. Liebman

Introduction

ISRAELIS ARE concerned with the problem of tension between religious and non-religious Jews. It is deemed second only to the problem of Arab–Jewish relations as a cause for civil conflict. In fact, in March 1988, 58 percent of a random sample of Jews in Jerusalem identified religious–secular relations as the most serious problem in the city, whereas only 23 percent stated that Jewish–Arab relations were the most critical problem. In 1985 the majority of Israelis described relations between religious and non-religious Jews in Israel as "bad." Almost one-quarter of the total Jewish population in Israel reported an "unfavorable" impression of religious Jews in a 1986 survey, 66 percent reporting an unfavorable impression of the *haredim* (sing. *haredi,* a type of Orthodox Jew to be described below). Nevertheless, as the author of Chapter Six indicates, the vast majority of religious and non-religious interact with one another under peaceful conditions.

This volume comprises a series of case studies, written especially for this volume, focusing on relationships between religious and non-religious Jews in Israel in a variety of settings. Some settings were chosen because they illustrate instances of conflict, others because they demonstrate different modes of accommodation and resolution of conflict. In Chapter One, Amnon Levi, reporter for the Israeli newspaper *Hadashot,* describes one segment of the Israeli religious public, the *haredim*. The term *haredi* literally means fearful, recalling the scriptural reference to the righteous person who fears the word of God. In the nineteenth century the term was a synonym for an Orthodox Jew. Today, in Israel, religious (Orthodox) Jews are divided into religious-Zionists, also called national-religious, and *haredim,* whom the press refers to as "ultra-Orthodox." *Haredim* are generally categorized by their strict interpretation of Jewish law, their rejection of secular culture, and their ambivalent attitude to the present Jewish State. In the case of some *haredim* this attitude is hostile. *Haredim* tend to insulate themselves from non-*haredim*. Levi discusses the interrelationship of different types of *haredim* with religious as well as with non-religious Jews. In Chapter Two, he describes the *haredi* press and the image of the non-*haredi* world which it projects to its readers. In Chapter Three Samuel Heilman, a professor of sociology and an authority on Jewish religious life, examines the image of the religious in the secular press. In Chapter Four, Naomi Golan, reporter for the religious daily *Hatzofeh,* describes the conflict over the opening of a movie theater on *Shabbat* (the Sabbath) in one Israeli city, and in Chapter Five she discusses the successes and failures of mixed religious and non-religious settlements in Judea and Samaria. Chapter Six, written by Ephraim Tabory, a senior lecturer in sociology at Bar-Ilan University, describes relations between religious and non-religious Jews in an upper-middle-class neighborhood. In Chapter Seven, Asher Cohen, a doctoral student and political activist, describes the most successful effort to integrate religious and non-religious Jews in one political party, the right-wing Tehiyah party. In Chapter Eight, Tamar Hermann, another doctoral student, and David Newman, a lecturer in geography at Ben-Gurion University, look at the opposite end of the political spectrum, the Israeli peace movement: they explain why the unification of the religious with the non-religious peace groups has never even been seriously attempted. In Chapter Nine, Leonard Weller, professor of sociology at Bar-Ilan University, and his wife Sonia, librarian and social researcher, report on their interviews of "mixed" married couples—one spouse religious and one not religious. In Chapter Ten, Yisrael Wollman, night editor for the daily newspaper *Yediot Aharonot* and editor of the religious-Zionist monthly *Emdah,* describes the organizations in Israel which deal, directly and indirectly, with the problem of relations between religious and non-religious Jews. The final chapter, written by the editor, offers some observations on the relationships between religious and non-religious Jews in Israel, based on these studies and some additional material.

Before turning to the case studies themselves we want briefly to introduce the main characters in our book—the religious and non-religious Jews of Israel.

When one seeks to identify the religious orientations of Israeli Jews it is commonplace to divide them into *dati* ("religious," pl. *datiim*), *masorati* ("traditional") and *lo dati* ("not religious"). Sometimes survey researchers substitute the term *hiloni* ("secular") for *lo dati.* These terms, however, can be misleading. The term "non-religious" suggests that one lacks any religious belief or observes no Jewish ritual or ceremonial. But, as we shall see, that is not true even of all secular Jews and certainly not true of the *masoratiim.* It would therefore be closer to the truth if we thought of the *dati* as an Orthodox Jew, i.e. one who accepts the binding nature of Jewish law in the belief that this law reflects, either through revelation or rabbinic interpretation, the will of God. Traditional and secular Jews should then be thought of as non-Orthodox rather than as non-religious.

There is no official census in Israel which asks Jews to define themselves in accordance with their religious orientation. But the categories of *dati,* traditional, and secular are commonly used by survey researchers, and Israelis don't seem to have much trouble locating themselves in one of these three groups. The early surveys also used a fourth category, "anti-religious," but this was dropped since less than five percent of the Jewish population so defined themselves.

Since the 1960s the proportion of the population who report themselves as *dati* has remained fairly constant—around twenty percent of the adult Jewish population. In all fairness, twenty percent is an estimate arrived at by overweighting the actual number of *dati* respondents, a procedure deemed necessary because the *haredim* are under-represented in sample surveys. (As we noted above, we discuss the *haredim* in greater detail in Chapters One and Two.) There are a variety of types of *dati* Jews in Israel. The major distinction is between *haredim* and national-religious (or religious-Zionists), but there are sub-categories within both *haredim* and religious-Zionists. Some of these are discussed in greater detail in the chapters that follow. But all *dati* Jews in Israel are conscious of themselves as constituting a separate sector within Israeli society. This consciousness is reinforced by symbols of dress. *Haredim* dress in a very distinctive manner, but even those national-religious Jews who dress in accordance with the norms of the non-religious public are identifiable, if they are males, by their *kippah* (head covering). And it is not without significance that religious women increasingly dress in a distinctive style: this is partly out of their desire to identify themselves as religious and partly because contemporary styles for women automatically mark off the female who feels bound by Jewish law to dress more modestly than these styles dictate. The attitude of virtually all the *datiim* toward the non-*dati* Jews is one of "us" and "them." Attitudes toward "them" vary. Among some *dati* Jews the attitude is one of hostility, among others one of paternalism with even a sense of obligation to convince "them" it is better to be like "us," among others it consists of a desire to overcome barriers for the sake of greater Jewish unity, and among still others there is an attitude of inferiority. Among most, attitudes are probably mixed. But whatever the attitude toward the non-*datiim, dati* Jews sense their own distinctiveness.

This is not true of the other two groups, for the simple reason that, at least until recently, the non-*datiim* were not continually sensitive to the presence of the *dati* segment of the society. Of course they knew of the existence of the *datiim,* but these were perceived as a minority with whom one might, perhaps, have to come to some kind of accommodation in particular situations, rather than as a group with which one must continually contend. This is a rather typical position for any majority group which tends to be sensitive to a minority only when some particular circumstance brings that minority to its attention. One outcome of the recent rise in tension between the *dati* and non-*dati* public is a growing self-consciousness among non-*datiim,* the secular ones in particular, about their identity as non-*dati* Jews. One might thus say that non-*dati* Israelis are also increasingly adopting an "us" and "them" mentality.

Those who define themselves as *masorati* (traditional) constitute about 35 percent of the Jewish population. This figure has declined slightly but steadily in the last ten to twenty years. The traditional Jew is the most difficult to categorize. Disproportionately high numbers, but by no means all of them, are of Sephardic origin, which means that they or their fathers were born in Asian or African, generally Islamic, societies, in contrast to Ashkenazi Jews, most of whom come from Europe or the United States. The *masorati* Jew observes quite a few Jewish traditions. He is likely to attend synagogue on most, if not all, Sabbaths. He or she not only maintains a kosher home but is likely to insist on keeping Jewish dietary laws outside the home. The traditional Jew, especially if Sephardic, is likely to be very strict in observing Jewish tradition relating to burial and mourning. But unlike the religious Jew, the *masorati* Jew is consciously selective about his or her observance and may take certain liberties unthinkable to the *dati*. The traditional Jew is likely to turn on television or ride to the beach or attend a soccer game on the Sabbath. Moreover, unlike the religious Jew, the traditional Jew observes the tradition out of a sense of commitment to the customs of his parents or perhaps even the history of the Jewish people, but not because of a belief that this is what God has commanded.

The reader familiar with American Jewish life might now ask where this description of *dati* and *masorati* leaves the Conservative or Reform Jew in Israel. There is no adequate answer to this question. Although the Conservative movement in Israel calls itself the *Masorti* Movement, seeking perhaps to capitalize on the fact that a large number of Israelis identify themselves as "traditional," the fact is that neither the Conservative nor the Reform movement easily fits under the rubric of *dati* or *masorati*. However, neither plays any role in any of our case studies. At the present time, both groups combined number less than ten thousand families and the difficulty of locating them within our map of religious identifiers presents no problem for this study.

The proportion of Israeli Jews who define themselves as *hiloni* ("secular") is estimated at about 45 percent and has been rising slightly over the past two decades. Many secular Jews observe quite a few rituals of the Jewish tradition. This is especially true of those who were raised in *dati* homes. In fact, some of those who define themselves as secular, but who say that they were raised in *dati* homes, observe more Jewish ritual than some Jews who define themselves as traditional. At least, that is what might be concluded from a comparison of the data on "Sura" in Chapter Six with surveys of the religious behavior of Jews who define themselves as traditional. "Sira" is a predominantly Ashkenazic middle-class neighborhood in a large Israeli metropolis. The author of Chapter Six notes that, of all those who define themselves as secular, ten percent report that they recite kiddush on Friday evening and 32 percent that they fast on Yom Kippur, 22 percent claim they maintain a kosher home, and 32 percent light Shabbat candles. On the other hand, the percentages fall virtually to zero among secular Jews who state they were raised in secular homes. But despite the evidence that the level of religious observance of Jews who define themselves as traditional overlaps the level of ritual observance of those who define themselves as secular, the definition itself remains significant. It seems likely that at least some of those Israelis who call themselves "secular" rather than "traditional" are signaling their wish to distance themselves from the *dati* Jew and the Orthodox understanding of Judaism.

Any mention of secular Jews in Israel requires that a distinction be made between secularism as a way of life and secularism as an ideology. Secularism as life-style, that is, the decline in Jewish observance on the one hand, increasing ignorance of the Jewish tradition and greater public acceptance of the violation of traditional Jewish norms on the other, is growing. This is true despite the phenomenon of *hazara b'tshuva,* the decision by thousands and perhaps even tens of thousands of young men and women who were raised in non-*dati* homes to become observant. I know of no reliable estimates, much less precise figures, on the number of *hozrim b'tshuva* (those who have embraced Orthodox Judaism), but I suspect it is no greater than the number of those raised in religious homes who abandon observance of *halakha* (Jewish law). The latter group receive much less notice. On the other hand, certain religious practices—circumcision, bar-mitzvah, conducting a seder, not riding on Yom Kippur, etc.—have become national norms and show no sign of declining.

In contrast to secularism as a way of life, secularism as an ideology—that is, secularism as a philosophy and a program of living and not simply an absence of religious observance—is the province of a small minority of the population. Nevertheless, there *are* ideological secularists in Israel, and they play an important part in our story, both as actors in some of the case studies that follow (especially Chapters Four and Five) and because, in the minds of some religious Jews, their image looms larger than their numbers would justify—in the minds of the *haredim* in particular, as we note in Chapter Two.

There are two types of ideological secularists. The first might best be labeled nationalist-secularists. They understand the Jewish people as a nation, and Judaism as a national culture rather than a religion. Nationalist-secularism in the form of Zionist-socialism was once the dominant ideology in Israeli life. In the last twenty to thirty years, nationalist-secularism, posing as an alternative to the Jewish religion, has declined. This is acknowledged by the secularists themselves who speak of an "ideological vacuum" or, in Amos Oz's phrase, stutter defensively that their own brand of Judaism is really not inferior to that of the *dati.* Their political influence is most pronounced within the left-wing Zionist party, Mapam. A distinguished representative of the nationalist-secularists was the late Abba Kovner, who spoke about the secular Jews' need for the *datiim* in order to orient themselves Jewishly and the *dati* Jews' need for the secularists because religious Jews have lost their sense of responsibility to the Jewish public. The extent to which nationalist-secularists are rooted in the Jewish tradition is reflected in the statement of Yaacov Hazan, the grand old man of Mapam, that *yerida* (emigration from Israel) by kibbutz members is attributable to the absence of Jewish education. Ideologically close to the nationalist-secularists, yet so positive toward religious elements in the tradition that they hardly merit the label "secularist," are groups such as the kibbutz movement's Oranim (see Chapter Ten) that seek to bridge the distance between humanist and universalist ideals of secular Zionism and the religious tradition.

The second brand of ideological secularism is no longer in retreat and in the last few years has taken to the offensive. Indeed, some of the tension between the secular and religious sectors is attributable to its champions' sense of their numerical strength and yet of their political impotence. They are best described by the label universalist-secularist and best represented by the political party Ratz (the Citizens Rights Movement). Their adherents are to be found in disproportionate numbers among Israeli academics and most prominently in the literary-intellectural world. They dominate the Israeli theater. Universalist-secularists object to any manifestations of Judaism in the public domain other than symbolic vestiges. The writer Aharon Megged characterizes them as those who would remove the Zionist scaffolding that was once necessary in creating the state but now stands as an obstacle to a truly democratic society. They favor a liberal democratic state, in which, according to their understanding, the individual rather than the group stands at the center of concern. They do not attribute any moral or ideological role to the state, indeed they fear its coercive powers, and they therefore heartily favor separation of religion and state.

There are no accurate measures of the number of universalist-secularists among Israeli Jews. It is unlikely that they constitute as much as five percent of the population. But their disproportionate representation among academics and artists and in the media means that their ideas carry great weight, and they themselves believe that as time passes more and more Israeli secularists will adopt their position. Their own frustration with their lack of influence within the political system and their sense of the growing weight of the religious element in the public sphere feeds their belief that a backlash of the secularists in their favor is bound to occur in the near future.

This brings us to the final point in our sketch of the socio-religious landscape. Whereas Israelis have not become more religiously observant in the last twenty years, they have become more conscious of their Jewish identity and more anxious to affirm the connection between the Jewish tradition and the Jewish state. This is attributable to many factors. It has to do with the legitimation that religion provides to the State of Israel, including the occupation of the Greater Land of Israel (i.e. Judea and Samaria); it has to do with the enmity of the Arabs, which is directed at Israelis by virtue of their Jewish identity and thereby reinforces the Israeli's Jewish consciousness; it has to do with the failure of secular Jewish alternatives to which we alluded above; with the growing influence of the Sephardic element of the population who, even if they are not *dati,* are more deferential to the Jewish tradition than are Ashkenazi secularists; and, finally, with a coincidence of political factors that lends political weight to the religious parties out of all proportion to the number of their voters. Although there is no evidence that Israelis are more observant of Jewish law today than they were in the past, many commentators have noted the increased penetration of religious symbols into the public domain in the past twenty years. Hence, both religious and secular Israelis, the extremists among them in particular, might easily be misled about developments in Israeli society. There is a fear on the part of some secularists that the future is one of increasing religious domination and oppression by a minority who have somehow managed to gain control of the society. Some *dati* Jews have been no less misled: believing that the future is in their hands, they have become less considerate of others and less sensitive to the social fact of their own minority status.

With this background information we will now look more carefully at specific instances of interaction between the *dati* and the non-*dati* Jews.

Amnon Levi **I**

Anglo-Saxon *Haredim*

Can They Serve as a Bridge between Haredim *and Non-Religious?*

THE TERM *haredi* (pl. *haredim*) literally means fearful and recalls the scriptural reference to the righteous person who fears the word of God. In the nineteenth century the term was a synonym for an Orthodox Jew. Today, in Israel, religious (Orthodox) Jews are divided into religious-Zionists, also called national-religious, and *haredim,* whom the press refers to as "ultra-Orthodox." *Haredim,* as noted in the Introduction, are categorized by their strict interpretation of Jewish law and their ambivalent attitude to the Jewish State—which in the case of some *haredim* is hostile. *Haredim* tend to insulate themselves from non-*haredim.*

It is difficult to determine precisely how many *haredim* there are in Israel. No single organization encompasses all of them. Lines between *haredim* and religious-Zionists are not always as neatly drawn as outsiders sometimes believe. Nevertheless, the great majority of religious Jews in Israel have no trouble in locating themselves in one camp or the other. *Haredim* comprise roughly 25 percent of all religious Jews in Israel. In other words, roughly five percent of the Israeli Jewish population.

The *Haredim,* in turn, are composed of many sub-groups. The broadest distinction is between *hasidim* and *misnagdim.* The traditional world of late eighteenth- and early nineteenth-century Eastern European Jewry was the scene of a bitter struggle between *hasidim* and *misnagdim.* While that struggle has since abated, it remains significant because, within the *haredi* world, Jews continue to identify themselves with one side or the other, and certain differences in custom and religious practice continue to distinguish them. *Hasidim* are organized into a variety of groups, each of which is aligned with a different dynasty of charismatic leaders, called *rebbis* (sing. *rebbi*). *Misnagdim* tend to be primarily of Lithuanian origin (the term *misnaged* literally means "opponent"), and the labels *misnaged* or "Lithuanian" are used interchangeably to refer to that portion of the *haredi* world which is spiritually descended from rabbinic leaders who vigorously rejected hasidism. They rejected hasidism as too mystical, excessively centered on the personality of the *rebbi,* and insufficiently oriented to the study of traditional sacred texts. The *haredi* world, therefore, comprises different groups of *hasidim,* each loyal to a different *rebbi,* and *misnagdim.* Both sides find that more unites than divides them. They are all opposed to secularism and to many manifestations of modernity. Hence the term *haredi* is not simply a generic classification, but suggests a common way of life and world-view. However, as we shall see, a new group of *haredim* has emerged in Israel which challenges many stereotypes about them.

Immigrants from English-speaking countries are referred to as "Anglo-Saxons" in Israel. The relatively large influx of *haredi* immigrants from English-speaking countries in the last few years, especially from the United States, accounts for a new category, Anglo-Saxon *haredim.* We wish to examine what influence, if any, they have exercised over *haredi* society, and what impact, if any, they have had on *haredi*–non-religious relations.

The Ministry of Absorption does not keep data on the religiosity of new immigrants. In spite of this, the spokesman for the Ministry stated that the majority of new immigrants, especially from the United States, are religious, and that a not inconsiderable number of them were *haredi.* How many are they? The best we can do is arrive at some rough estimates. Agudat Israel sees itself as the representative party of Israeli *haredim.* Its office in Jerusalem seeks to maintain an accurate listing of the *haredi* potential. It has a record of roughly 4,000 English-speaking families in Jerusalem and a similar number in the Tel-Aviv suburb of Bnei Brak. Smaller concentrations of Anglo-Saxon *haredim* are to be found in other cities (Ashdod, for example). Rabbi Yirmiyahu Abramov, an immigrant from South Africa and one of the heads of the Ohr Somayach Yeshiva, who established an organization named "A'aleh" to aid Anglo-Saxon immigrants, states that in Jerusalem alone about 5,000 families have registered with his organization. From these inexact and partial figures it seems reasonable to conclude that there are somewhere in the neighborhood of 10,000 Anglo-Saxon *haredi* families in Israel. This is quite a large group for the *haredi*—a group which has the power, in view of its size, to make a significant impact on *haredi* society.

In what manner, if any, does this group of Anglo-Saxon *haredim* differ from the rest of *haredi* society? At first glance, differences appear so pronounced that the very term *haredi* seems inappropriate. Shimon Messer, for example, is a Dublin-born businessman who recently immigrated to Israel and settled in a mixed community of *haredi* and religious-Zionists, Har Nof, on the outskirts of Jerusalem. Messer himself is unsure how to define himself and his fellow Anglo-Saxons. "I wear a black *kippa* [skullcap, a symbol of *haredi* identity], but do not define myself as either haredi or as national-religious." He says he is somewhere in between what Israelis call *haredi* and what they call national-religious. Another Anglo-Saxon resident of Har Nof, P.Y. (he prefers to remain anonymous), explains that the Anglo-Saxon *haredi* doesn't require a label until he moves to Israel. Outside of Israel, he says, these labels are far less meaningful:

> There you don't need to be identified as a *haredi* or as a member of the national-religious camp. You are defined as *shomer mitvzot* [one who observes the commandments], as a *ben Torah* [a Jew who is both personally observant as well as familiar with the classical religious texts], as one who is as punctilious in the observance of the most minor religous laws as he is in the observance of the major ones. [The descriptive phrase which the respondent uses is derived from rabbinic texts]. That is enough. One does not need a more exact definition than that.

The Anglo-Saxon, predominantly American, *haredim* recognize that they are different from Israeli *haredim,* and this feeling is reciprocated. While these differences stem from the backgrounds of the Anglo-Saxon *haredim,* they are also accounted for by the fact that the Anglo-Saxons do not represent a cross-section of *haredim* in the United States or other English-speaking countries. For example,

Satmar *hasidim* and those close to Satmar, i.e. the *haredim* who bitterly oppose the very existence of the State of Israel (seeing in its establishment the work of the Devil), do not immigrate. *Haredim* who immigrate from Anglo-Saxon countries are identified with more moderate *haredi* factions.

A second group of Anglo-Saxon *haredim* are those who initially came here to study with no intention of immigrating. They are the sons (and in fewer cases daughters) of parents who sent them to one of the more prestigious *yeshivot* (sing. *yeshivah,* academies for advanced Talmudic study) or girls' colleges and teachers' seminaries in Israel. These are generally Lithuanian institutions, but there are some hasidic institutions of this type as well. Such schools are held in high regard by Western *haredim* and their isolated environment is deemed preferable to the more open environment that necessarily prevails in any institution in the West. Sending one's teenage son (and in some cases a daughter) to Israel is comparable in some respects to sending one's child to a finishing school abroad. Afterwards, they are expected to return to their parents' home. But some remain in Israel, marry (often a partner of Anglo-Saxon origin), and establish their home there.

Socio-economically, one can divide Anglo-Saxon *haredim* into two groups. Ricki Shushan, a *haredi* journalist who works for a non-religious newspaper, was born in Israel but lived in the United States for many years. She returned to Israel a few years ago and chose to settle among the American *haredim* in Har Nof. According to Shushan, some of the new *haredi* immigrants are very wealthy. They have in fact built a second home in Israel but continue to conduct business outside the country. If they live in Jerusalem they are attracted to the wealthier neighborhoods such as Rehaviah, Bayit Vegan, and Har Nof. The less wealthy—those who came to Israel primarily to study—live elsewhere.

One may understand the profile of the Anglo-Saxon *haredi* community in Israel by identifying its source of income, its patterns of consumption, and its style of life. All these items contribute to the unique character of the Anglo-Saxon *haredi.*

Anglo-Saxon *haredim* are work-oriented, and the kind of work they do often involves them directly with the non-religious world. They make their living as merchants, stockbrokers, diamond dealers, and members of the free trades. One of the largest electronics stores on 47th Street in New York belongs to Chaim Yudel Goldstein, a Satmar *hasid.* It is said that the present Satmar *rebbi,* prior to his selection as *rebbi,* had a computer terminal in his home linked to the New York stock exchange. This kind of work-orientation is somewhat unusual among the *haredi* elite in Israel, and the professional activity of Anglo-Saxon *haredim* borders on the bizarre in their eyes. The ideologue of Neturei Karta (probably the most extreme of all *haredi* groups), Rabbi Yerahmiel Domb, lives in London and is engaged in the gold-jewelry trade. It is rumored that the items he offers for sale include gold crucifixes. Domb did not deny the accusation during an interview, suggesting instead that there was nothing wrong with selling such items.

After their arrival in Israel, the *haredim* continue to engage in their previous occupations. The A'aleh organization, which is concerned with Anglo-Saxon *haredi* immigrants, published three issues of its journal in the first months of its existence. The purpose of the journal was to aid in the adjustment of the new *haredi* immigrant. The three issues were not concerned with identifying and locating the best yeshivot, or *mikvaot* (ritual baths), or rabbinical courts. Instead, the first issue explained the principles of the Israeli banking system, the second dealt with the Israeli National Insurance system, and the third with methods of obtaining loans and mortgages.

Patterns of consumption are also unique. Most of the new *haredi* immigrants, as we indicated, are wealthier than the average Israeli. (In addition, they benefit from the right of new immigrants to import household items free of tax for two years). Both their purchasing power and their consumption patterns account for the fact that their homes are different from the homes of other Israeli *haredim.* It is not only the microwave oven in which they bake their *kugel* that identifies them, it is the sophisticated stereo system in their living-rooms, from which one can hear the latest *haredi* hit songs or even classical music and light kitsch music such as Golden Guitar. Many of these *haredim* had a television set in their living-rooms in the West. This is considered taboo within the Israeli *haredi* community, and those who choose to own such an appliance in Israel will generally keep it in the privacy of their bedrooms. Most accept local *haredi* norms (widespread among the stricter *haredim* in the West as well), and they will forgo television. But in many instances they will replace the television set with a video equipped with a special monitor to enable them to see films of *haredi* singers and other more acceptable forms of entertainment.

The relative affluence brings with it characteristic behavior associated with leisure culture. *Haredim* in the United States, for example, are more oriented to this-worldly pleasures. They relax. One might even find the extremist Satmar *hasidim* in the most exclusive vacation areas. The kinds of questions which the rabbis of the American *haredi* community are asked, questions like whether one's wife may take ski lessons, or how a woman can dress modestly in a ski resort (since a woman is forbidden to wear pants), would sound bizarre to the ear of an Israeli *haredi* rabbi.

Practices associated with leisure culture are retained after the *haredim* immigrate. In Har Nof, in Bayit Vegan, and in other Anglo-Saxon *haredi* concentrations, one can find invitations to home parties and to bazaars where American-style clothing is sold, announcements of various therapy groups which interest Anglo-Saxon *haredim* and notices of women's evenings, dinners with speeches and slides, and spectacular fashion shows. Unlike the locals, Anglo-Saxon *haredi* women generally do not work, and this allows them much more time for "self-improvement." Futhermore, their husband comes home late from work and their children take their main meal, lunch, at school. Thus the women have a great deal of free time.

Anglo-Saxon *haredi* women, from the United States in particular, have organized a variety of women's groups. One can find in *Hamodia* and *Yated Ne'eman,* the two Haredi dailies, announcements of music and cooking groups, lectures on various topics, and even a massage institute under the supervision of Torah sages, where, of course, there is total separation between men and women. Hotels located close to neighborhoods with Anglo-Saxon *haredi* concentrations have sought to attract this potential clientele. The luxury Ramada Renaissance hotel in Jerusalem, for example, has allocated separate hours for men and women at its swimming-pool in order to draw *haredim*—and they have succeeded.

For the outsider who observes the Anglo-Saxon *haredim* and compares them to the Israeli haredim, it appears that the status of women diverges greatly. The local paper in Har Nof is edited by a *haredi* woman from the United States, a role most unusual for an Israeli *haredi.* There are other signs that point to the difference in the status of Anglo-Saxon *haredi* women. Most *haredi* groups in Israel are opposed to women driving a car: this is considered immodest conduct. Posters in Meah Shearim periodically warn against the brazen conduct of women who drive cars, but *haredim* from the United States see nothing wrong in this. (*Haredi* women do stop smoking, at least in public. Even outside Israel, *haredim* find smoking by women objectionable, and in Israel it is considered detestable.) Anglo-Saxon *haredi* women continue to dress according to overseas fashions. Their clothes are more attractive, they have more jewelry, and they are responsible for a veritable revolution in women's wigs.

In addition to the idea of beautifying oneself, Anglo-Saxon *haredim* have also introduced or created a market for a series of products which were heretofore unobtainable in the *haredi* community. This includes Italian pizza and pancakes under the strictest rabbinical supervision, a butcher's store specializing in American cuts of meat, steak houses, take-home foods, and finally various "do-it-yourself" stores. This has created a measure of bitterness among the most sectarian of the *haredim*. *Hahomah,* the Neturei Karta journal, published a bitter denunciation of the *haredi* rabbinical court for granting its supervision to such products. "Did we come to the Holy Land to eat *haredi* pancakes?" the paper enquired.

Anglo-Saxon *haredim* also differ in their external appearance. Many of them are clean-shaven. When Rabbi Moshe Sherer was appointed to his post as chairman of the World Executive Committee of Agudat Israel, the *rebbi* of Gur said that he had to grow a beard since it was inconceivable to have so senior a representative of Agudat Israel clean-shaven. Sherer, however, refused. When Anglo-Saxon *haredim* do grow beards they are trimmed. They wear stylish suits instead of the long black coats typical of Israeli *hasidim*. When they are still new in Israel, one can see some wearing, for example, a light blue blazer, a style very different than that of Israeli *haredim*.

But the differences between Israeli and Anglo-Saxon *haredim* extend beyond the matter of dress or standard of living or style of life. There are differences that touch upon the core of *haredi* ideology—for example, education. Anglo-Saxon *haredim* wish to add secular subjects to the school curricula. *Haredi* yeshivot eschew such material. Hence, the Anglo-Saxon *haredi* is forced to face a very significant decision in regard to the education of his children—to send them to the local *haredi* school and forgo secular studies, or to enroll them in a religious but non-*haredi* school and thereby deprive them of a classical *haredi* education. An attempt to resolve the problem by establishing a school which combines *haredi* emphasis on the study of sacred texts with the addition of secular studies met vehement opposition. An American immigrant, Rabbi Baruch Chait, established the Maaravah school along such lines. Chait's students were graduates of the Chinuch Atzmai *(haredi)* school system, and this rendered his institution particularly threatening to many *haredi* leaders. Maaravah has been in existence for three years. In March

1988, the Haredi newspapers *Hamodia* and *Yated Ne'eman* published a letter by Rabbi Eliezer Menahem Shach, the preeminent leader of Lithuanian *haredim,* condemning this yeshivah and calling upon parents to withdraw their children from it.

Girls from Anglo-Saxon *haredi* homes also have problems adjusting to the *haredi* school system in Israel. For example, *haredi* girls in Israel must wear school uniforms. The Anglo-Saxon girls object to the idea and the lack of style in the cut of the uniform. In Israel girls are forbidden to read secular literature, whereas in the United States no objections are raised, even in some of the strictest *haredi* schools, to reading the novels of, for example, Charles Dickens. In Israel girls are forbidden to listen to most kinds of music whereas in America this is not prohibited. In order to lessen the friction, special schools, such as Mevo Yerushalayim in Bayit Vegan, were established for Anglo-Saxon girls.

An interesting compromise has been reached in regard to sports. The Americans regard participation in sport as self-evidently desirable and necessary for the child's development. Many Israeli *haredim* regard sport, or at least any form of organized sport, as a sign of decadent Hellenism. In the Sanhedrin school of the Chinuch Atzmai network, in Har Nof, the majority of the students in the school were Anglo-Saxons who insisted on sport activity, but the Israeli *haredi* minority objected. The unofficial compromise was to have the children engage in sport during recess, but to eliminate athletics from the official school program.

The language in the Anglo-Saxon immigrant *haredi* schools is also distinct, with all the cultural consequences generated by language differences. Most Anglo-Saxon *haredim* speak English rather than the Yiddish customary among Israeli *haredim.* Among the *misnagdim* one can even find *haredim* who don't understand Yiddish. Among the Boston *hasidim* in Har Nof, a group to whom we shall return, classes for women are held in English, there is a private elementary school conducted in English, and a "Havurat Tehillim" (a group of youth who meet on Saturday afternoon to recite the Psalms) where discussions take place in English.

Consumption patterns, attitudes toward western culture, occupations and sources of income, leisure activities and relative affluence, all make the Anglo-Saxon *haredim* different. They themselves become aware of this when they move to Israel. They live among concentrations of their own people, preferring neighbors with a mentality similar to their own. One can even find *hasidim* who originally moved to Israel in order to be close to their *rebbi,* relocating after a short while in order to live closer to other Anglo-Saxon *haredim.*

This description of the Anglo-Saxon *haredi* suggests someone much closer to the non-religious Jew than is the Israeli *haredi.* The question is whether this difference extends to the relations of the Anglo-Saxon *haredi* with the non-religious and to attitudes toward Zionism and the State of Israel.

The answer seems to be that they do. Rabbi Yirmiyahu Abramov, who immigrated from South Africa some time ago, attempts to explain the difference between the Anglo-Saxon and the Israeli *haredi.*

> There is no difference in general world-view. We are bound to the same Torah sages and accept their direction. The difference is in the way matters are implemented. We have a different approach to matters; for example, in regard to the struggles between *haredim* and non-religious in Jerusalem. The sensitivity of those who come from abroad to these struggles is identical to that of the local *haredim,* but we would like to solve them in a different fashion. It is difficult for a person from the West to accept throwing stones [at cars which travel on the Sabbath] and violence. The matter [of Sabbath violation] is very painful, but this group [the Anglo-Saxon *haredim*] cannot come to terms with this form of the struggle.

Generally speaking, Anglo-Saxon *haredim* are much more moderate in their attitudes toward non-religious society. Secondly, and no doubt related to this, their identification with the State of Israel is stronger than that of the Israeli *haredim.* While still living abroad they may have contributed money to philanthropic campaigns in support of Israel and they no doubt followed developments within the State with sympathy. Furthermore, unlike those Israeli *haredim* who may be sympathetic to the State or its institutions but feel they must conceal this fact, Anglo-Saxon *haredim* express their support openly.

When they do immigrate, the Anglo-Saxon *haredim,* as we suggested, are far less hostile to the non-religious Jews in Israel than are the local *haredim.* When they lived abroad many of them had frequent contact with non-religious Jews. They were involved in business ties of various kinds and may have formed social or at least quasi-social ties as well. They find it painful, they say, to see a Jew violate the Sabbath or eat non-kosher food, but those who behave in such a manner are not strangers to them. Having lived abroad, their religiosity is more internal. A senior official of Agudat Israel in Jerusalem commented on this with considerable bitterness:

> They do not live the struggles in the country. They are detached from our struggle here. They don't understand it. They are more moderate, and see the State of Israel with all its components as the State of the Jewish people.

The Anglo-Saxon *haredim* are proud of their moderation. Rabbi Meir Horowitz, the son of the Bostoner *Rebbi,* leader of a large group of American *haredim* in the Har Nof suburb of Jerusalem, explains this in the following way:

> One who lives among non-Jews must think in democratic terms. Just as I have rights, so do others. Consideration for the other person is democracy. I would have preferred that there be no religious parties in Israel, for then all the parties would know that they had obligations toward the religious. I am disturbed by the intense commitments that exist here to the political parties.

This attitude to the non-religious and the State may be the most important distinguishing characteristic of Anglo-Saxon *haredim.*

Is there any reason to hope that the Anglo-Saxon *haredim* will moderate the attitudes and behavior of *haredi* society in Israel in its relations with the non-religious? Will the Anglo-Saxon influence lead to better relations between the *haredim* and the non-religious in the country? The majority opinion among *haredi* leaders and among knowledgeable non-religious figures who were interviewed on this topic is that the influence of the American *haredim* is very slight. The *haredi* community is guided by a small and closed group of rabbis, and this group is not interested in bringing others into its ranks. The Bostoner *Rebbi,* who immigrated to Israel, was not invited to become a member of the Moetzet Gedolei Hatorah, the Council of Torah Sages which directs Agudat Israel, even though some of its members include hasidic *rebbis* of lesser stature. Rabbi Mordechai Elephant, who came from the United States and heads the Itri Yeshivah in Jerusalem, is considered by many to be an outstanding Torah sage. But he has not been included in the inner circle of heads of yeshivot in Israel. The same is true of Rabbi Sheinberg, head of the Torah Ohr Yeshivah. Thus the Anglo-Saxon *haredim* are deprived of influence at the elite levels; and this is of particular significance for, as we shall see, those are the levels at which so many basic decisions within the *haredi* community are made.

Not only is the Moetzet Gedolei Hatorah closed to the American *haredim,* but they are generally excluded from *haredi* politics as well. Agudat Israel is built on factions: hasidic groups such as Vizhnitz, Belz, Gur, the members of the Old Yishuv in Jerusalem, and the Lithuanians, but it does not include, nor does it welcome, the formation of an Anglo-Saxon faction. It remains very suspicious of this innovative group of *haredim* from Anglo-Saxon countries with its idiosyncratic variant of *haredi* culture. Rabbi Yirmiyahu Abramov says that the heads of Agudat Israel in Jerusalem consult with him on many issues, and he is delighted about that, but he cannot point to any matter in which his opinion on matters was accepted.

A *haredi* Knesset member, who is well-aware of *haredi* politics in Israel, offers support for this general appraisal. Avraham Verdiger, leader of Poalei Agudat Israel, lives in Kiryat Mattesdorf, a *haredi* neighborhood in Jerusalem with many Anglo-Saxon immigrants. He does not believe that the latter have any influence on *haredi* life here. The second generation, he says, already look like the local *haredim.* In America, the parents went to a university after having studied in yeshivot for many years. In Israel, their children remain in a yeshivah and forgo secular studies. In America, the *haredim* work after they are married. Here, the second generation studies in a Kolel (a framework in which married men pursue advanced Talmudic study) and is supported through stipends and gifts. (In all fairness it should be noted that this practice is becoming increasingly common in the United States as well.) An American *haredi* from Jerusalem, P.Y., found that by choosing a *haredi* school for his son he had in fact determined that his son would become an Israeli rather than an American-style *haredi.*

Verdiger believes that the Americans are more influenced than influential. The majority of American *haredim* also believe this to be true. We can explore the accuracy of this assessment by a more careful look at developments in Har Nof.

Har Nof, a new suburb at the western edge of Jerusalem, presents a very convenient opportunity to investigate the Anglo-Saxon *haredi* style. Har Nof is part of the municipality of Jerusalem, but it elects its own local council, which exercises autonomy in local affairs. About half the population in Har Nof is of Anglo-Saxon origin. The suburb is also home to local *haredim,* including *hasidim* of Vizhnitz and Gur (Vishnitz *hasidim* built their own enclave in the suburb).

The community is also home to Lithuanian *haredim* and even a few *hasidim* of Satmar. In addition, there are many religious-Zionists (national-religious Jews), easily identified by their knitted *kippot,* whose style of life is totally different from that of the *haredim.* Finally there is a small nucleus of non-religious residents, a group which is constantly decreasing in numbers as the *haredi* character of the neighborhood becomes more pronounced.

The largest Anglo-Saxon synagogue in the community belongs to the Boston *hasidim.* This is a very interesting group, part of the Lelov branch of hasidism. In 1903 the Lelover *Rebbi,* Rabbi David Biderman, summoned one of his close students, Rabbi Pinhas David Horowitz, and ordered him to emigrate from Eastern Europe to the United States and serve as a rabbi there. This was a rather extraordinary order at that time, since the United States was considered to be spiritually alien territory where one could easily lose one's Jewish identity. Rabbi Horowitz, so the story goes, sought to avoid obeying his *rebbi*'s instructions, but he finally complied. Horowitz settled in Boston (hence the title Bostoner *Rebbi*) and established his own hasidic group. His followers are those known as Boston *hasidim.* He dreamt of moving to the Land of Israel with his followers and even bought a large tract of land near Nebi Samuel in Jerusalem as a first step in the realization of his ambition. The stock-market crash of 1929 and the subsequent depression in the United States put an end to these plans. Horowitz died in the United States; but his son, Levi Yitzchak, the present head of the Boston *hasidim,* inherited his father's position as well as his dream of establishing a stonghold of Boston *hasidim* in Israel. In the early 1970s he investigated the feasibility of purchasing homes in the planned Har Nof suburb. Today, his followers, numbering a few hundred families, represent the nucleus of the local Anglo-Saxons. The Bostoner *Rebbi* spends half his time in Jerusalem and half in Boston. When he is in the United States one of his sons serves as the leader of his group in Har Nof.

The Boston synagogue is hardly typical of hasidic synagogues. Boston *hasidim* pray together with Lithuanians, Sefardim, and other Ashkenazim, with those who wear black *kippot* and those who wear knitted *kippot,* and with a few whose *kippot* are perched in a way that suggests they are unaccustomed to wearing any *kippa.* The tolerance and graciousness of the Boston *hasidim* have turned their synagogue into a local community center. Some 400 worshippers, most of whom are not Boston *hasidim,* pray there on Sabbaths.

The Bostoner *Rebbi* is unique among American *rebbis* for his openness and his ability to attract different types of Jews to various events which he sponsors. Nevertheless, Anglo-Saxon *haredim* do not consider the Boston style peculiar but rather paradigmatic of how Jews ought to behave to one another. For our purposes, the Boston group illustrates how Anglo-Saxon *haredim* relate to the non-religious, in contrast to the customary style of Israeli *haredim.* In fact, as we shall see, Anglo-saxon *haredim* other than Boston *hasidim* took the lead in some of the activities described here.

On Purim 1988, a number of Boston *hasidim* organized a unique activity. They sent their *mishloah manot* (gifts of food exchanged during the Purim holiday) to non-religious residents of Har Nof. The letter included in the gift package read as follows:

> To our dear neighbors, be joyous on Purim! The commandment of Purim embraces laws governing relations between man and his fellow-man—a meal with friends, gifts to the poor, the sending of food packages to one another. The joy and the gaiety encourage each man woman and child to draw near to one another. If one is shy—he can disguise himself. There are no excuses. If one is shy—he can send his gifts by a messenger! Whoever stretches out his hand [for assistance]—is to be given something! That is the power of Judaism. That being the case, we are sending you gifts, and we stretch out our hand for the beginning of ties, or their continuation—in your homes, in our homes, or in the synagogue. Happy Purim.

This was signed: "The Bostoner *Rebbi,* the Boston *hasidim,* the members of the Givat Pinhas synagogue, Har Nof." Rabbi Meir Horowitz, son of the Bostoner *Rebbi,* explains the idea behind sending the packages:

> The aim was to have the non-religious know that there are those who think about them. We want to speak to them, and not relate to them as people alongside of whom we just happen to live. We do not have enough ties with them, and the ties must be deepened.

Horowitz also commented on other programs in which Boston *hasidim* sought to develop relationships with non-religious without necessarily seeking to convert them to their point of view. His followers organized meetings with non-religious American Jewish youth visiting Israel under the auspices of the Jewish Agency. They hoped that this would draw the youth closer to Judaism.

Both religious-Zionists and non-religious Jews praise the attitude of the Boston *hasidim* with respect to Israel and Zionism. For example, at the end of 1987 a cornerstone for a public park in Har Nof was to have been dedicated. The event was scheduled to take place outdoors, but as the date drew closer the organizers were afraid that it might rain and ruin the ceremony. Aryeh Frankel, the national-religious representative on the local council, asked Rabbi Meir Horowitz to permit the event to take place in the Boston synagogue. A key figure at the ceremony was to have been the Mayor of Jerusalem, Teddy Kollek. Kollek was under severe attack from *haredim* because of his support for the opening of selective places of entertainment in Jerusalem on the Sabbath. Nevertheless, Horowitz did not hesitate. The entrance to the synagogue was decorated with national flags; some even flew from the roof of the synagogue. Both the non-religious and the national-religious were very moved by this gesture. The Israeli *haredim,* on the other hand, were upset and circulated leaflets in Har Nof attacking the Boston *hasidim.*

Another example of the special way in which the Boston *hasidim,* and by extension Anglo-Saxon *haredim* in general, relate to the non-religious is in the area of education. Until 1986, religious-Zionist, non-religious, and *haredi* youth all shared the same school building in Har Nof. The religious-Zionist and non-religious were registered in one school and *haredim* in a second school, called Sanhedrin, but all attended classes in the same building. Most of the Sanhedrin youth came from American *haredi* homes. The majority of Israeli *haredim* preferred to send their children to more extremist schools. At the end of the 1986 school year it became clear that one building could not house all of the students from both schools, and a struggle ensued over who would move to a second, less satisfactory, building. The second building had six classrooms with no divisions between them. The religious-Zionist and American *haredi* leaders agreed that three classes from each of the schools would be housed in the second building. However—at the insistence of Rabbi Eliezer Menahem Shach—the Israeli *haredim* who sent their children to Sanhedrin rejected the compromise. They were concerned over the absence of any partition between the classrooms of the two schools in the second building. This meant that religious-Zionist and even non-religious youth would mix with *haredi* pupils. The Israeli *haredim* preferred that six classes of *haredi* students should move to the new building and thereby preserve their isolation. Furthermore, at the insistence of *haredi* leaders outside the community, tall partitions were now erected in the old building to separate the classrooms of the *haredim* and the *non-haredim.* The Anglo-Saxon *haredim* were unhappy but deferred to the Israeli *haredim.*

The most interesting example of an attempt by Anglo-Saxon *haredim* to reach a compromise with the non-religious concerned a dispute over closing Har Nof's roads on Sabbath. At an early stage, the *haredi* residents of the suburb demanded that all roads be closed to vehicular traffic on Sabbaths and festivals. Their claim was that the overwhelming majority of Har Nof residents observed the Sabbath and therefore there was no reason to permit traffic on Sabbath. The non-religious strongly opposed this measure and the religious-Zionists sought some kind of compromise. The Anglo-Saxon *haredim* asserted an independent position and maintained their independence, although the compromise proposal which they favored was not adopted.

According to one religious-Zionist representative on the local council, Rabbi Meir Horowitz informed him that he personally was not disturbed by the non-religious' driving on the Sabbath. Horowitz proposed that side roads be closed but the main roads left open. Shimon Messer, a Boston *hasid,* claims that he and another representative of the Anglo-Saxon *haredim,* Rabbi Yeshaya Bakst, met with the representatives of the non-religious and agreed that areas where there were only religious people, which included about 60 percent of Har Nof, would be closed to traffic. Travel would be permitted in other areas. According to Messer, the religious-Zionists accepted this arrangement, but the Israeli *haredim,* with a majority on the local council, vetoed it.

Aryeh Frankel, another of the representatives of the religious-Zionists, has a different version. He claims that it was his group who initiated the compromise with the non-religious and that to their surprise some of the Israeli *haredim* in addition to the Anglo-Saxon *haredim* were prepared to accept it. However, the head of the local Israeli *haredim,* Meir Gershon, foiled the plan.

Shlomo Reuven, a representative of the non-religious in the suburb, is least ready to acknowledge the independence of the Anglo-Saxon *haredim,* and yet his very criticism of them accords recognition to their own orientation. He agrees that the American *haredim* were less prone than the Israeli *haredim* to impose religious demands, although, he adds, there are extremists among them as well. The difference, he maintains, is that they are more adept at the political game, and are better able to speak to the non-religious than are other *haredim.* Thus, for example, in the negotiations on closing the roads, they presented themselves as very moderate and willing to compromise but warned that the Israeli *haredim* would not agree to such a move.

The differences between the Anglo-Saxon and Israeli *haredim* of Har Nof resulted in an experiment unique within the Israeli *haredi* world—the effort to establish an independent Anglo-Saxon *haredi* list to contest a local election. Shimon Messer, one of the leaders in this effort, tells how the new list was established:

> We did not find another party which suited us. Neither the religious-Zionists nor the *haredim* represent us. We decided that it was worthwhile to attempt to found a new list. We went to the Bostoner *Rebbi* and proposed the idea. Why to him specifically? Because his synagogue is the largest in the neighborhood, and all the different elements are present there. The *Rebbi* gave us his blessing. The Boston *hasidim* did not support us financially, but only morally.

Despite the fact that the list was an Anglo-Saxon list and not exclusively one of Boston *hasidim,* it became known locally as the Boston list. The elections took place in January 1987. Three other lists contested the election. One was composed of non–Anglo-Saxon *haredim,* a second list was composed of religious-Zionists, and a third of non-religious candidates.

The Anglo-Saxon list called itself *L'ma'an Har Nof*—"For Har Nof"—and presented 13 candidates for election. It was headed by Rabbi Dr. Yeshaya Bakst, a dentist who was also a rabbi and *mohel* (one who is able to circumcise a child in accordance with Jewish ritual). The list included a lawyer, accountants, businessmen, an internist, a pediatrician, a journalist, an administrator and teacher at Yeshivat Ohr Somayach, and the head of the new controversial yeshivah, Maaravah. All were Anglo-Saxon immigrants, eleven from the United States. All candidates on the list were gainfully employed, mostly engaged in occupations pointing to a way of life different from that which was customary among Israeli *haredim.* The list's platform stated that:

> The silent majority of tolerant people of all groups and camps finds expression in *L'ma'an Har Nof.* A vote for this list for the council will bring improved conditions for all.

The list projected its candidates in the following way:

> There are among us professionals from various countries, with religious backgrounds which differ from one another, who have united into a single camp in order to earn the trust of the Har Nof residents and the Jerusalem municipality.

The platform also spoke of what needed to be done in Har Nof—new parks, classrooms, synagogues, improving road safety and cleanliness. In other words, most of the publicity was devoted to matters affecting the total community and very little was said about religious affairs. In comparison, the local *haredi* list devoted the lion's share of its platform to religious matters and religious services.

The election campaign of the Anglo-Saxon list was addressed to all the residents. It emphasized quality-of-life issues more than any other topic. It stressed that its members were not politicians, and that they were only running for office to improve local conditions. One election leaflet proclaimed:

> You too are called to join the group of those who hate politicians. We too belong to this group. We are angry at the atmosphere of strife which is prevalent in the neighborhood and which gives the place a bad name. We hate politics. All of us, therefore, have united in order to establish a list of serious candidates for the local council, representatives who are concerned with the life of the community and who will be concerned and act for the residents of Har Nof. We have experience in community and professional services. In other words, we know what it means to keep trying, to cooperate with others, and to implement a program. If this is the language that you too understand, the language of implementation and of cooperation, join us *L'ma'an Har Nof*.

The campaign material does not reflect the *haredi* character of the sponsors or the religious orientations of the candidates. Nevertheless, pre-election agreements were made with the local *haredi* list rather than with the religious-Zionist or non-religious list—a matter of some significance in the subsequent election analysis. The agreement involved pooling the surplus votes of the two lists (such agreements are commonplace in Israeli politics, where elections take place on a system of proportional representation). An agreement of this kind increases the chances that another council member will be elected from one of the two lists. The local *haredim* also agreed not to run their own candidate for council chairman, a position filled by separate ballot, but to support Rabbi Yeshaya Bakst, the Anglo-Saxon candidate. These agreements were exploited by the religious-Zionists to buttress their claim that the Anglo-Saxon list was really a *haredi* list in disguise and that a vote for the American *haredim* meant strengthening all *haredim* in Har Nof. Rav Shach, in turn, urged all *haredim* to support the *haredi* list. According to one observer, he was particularly adamant in this regard.

The Anglo-Saxons were very disappointed by the election returns. They had been confident of winning a sizable number of seats, in view of their estimate that roughly half the Har Nof residents were Anglo-Saxon *haredi* immigrants. Of the 2,417 registered voters, 1,969 actually voted. The local *haredi* list won seven seats, an absolute majority of the 13-member council. The religious-Zionists won three seats, the non-religious one, and the Anglo-Saxon list only two seats. Rabbi Yeshaya Bakst, with support from both Anglo-Saxons and local *haredim,* received 67 percent of the votes and was elected council chairman.

The leaders of the Anglo-Saxon list offer an interesting explanation for their defeat. One might have expected them to attribute their dismal showing to the fact that they paid insufficient attention to the religious sensitivities of their potential voters. But they offered the opposite explanation. They attributed their defeat to the agreement on surplus votes with the local *haredim,* claiming that this left the local residents with the mistaken impression that there was no real difference between the two lists. Consequently those with *haredi* inclinations preferred the local *haredi* list, and the religious-Zionists refused to support them. It remains to be seen if the Anglo-Saxon *haredim* will contest future elections and if so how they will conduct themselves in future campaigns.

The claim of the leaders is, as we observed, interesting in itself. But there is some reason to doubt whether the analysis is accurate and whether the Anglo-Saxons do intend to distance themselves from the local *haredim* in the future. Since the election, the Anglo-Saxon council members have cooperated rather closely with the representatives of the local *haredi* list. Shlomo Reuven, the representative of the non-religious on the council, says that, although the Anglo-Saxon representatives are more moderate, they follow the lead of the local *haredim.* Divisions over council issues tend to separate the non-religious and religious-Zionist representatives on one side and representatives of the two *haredi* lists on the other. According to Reuven:

> Their problem is that they don't have power. Whenever the members of the *Ahi* (local *haredi*) list come to them with the written *halakhah* (i.e. Jewish law), they say: "We cannot oppose the *halakhah.*" Thus, in practice, the extremist Israeli *haredim* are the ones who set the tone.

The point which Reuven raises is central to the behavior of the Anglo-Saxon *haredim* in general. Their opinions are different from those of the Israeli *haredim.* They *do* want better relations with the non-religious. Their life-style *is* one which enables them to act as a bridge between the *haredim* and the non-religious in Israel, but they lack the self-confidence and perhaps the courage to oppose the views of the local *haredim.* This is also the most credible explanation for the failure of so many Anglo-Saxons in Har Nof to vote for their own list. Little as they like the idea, the Anglo-Saxons defer to Israeli *haredim,* especially when the Israelis carry the blessing of a Torah sage. They themselves are aware of this process despite their own discomfort. Shimon Messer says:

> In my opinion, the group of *haredi* extremists totals no more than about thirty or forty families. By extremists I mean those who are liable to throw stones at someone non-religious traveling on the Sabbath, etc. But there is a dynamic which draws others after them. Let us say that two of them go down to Rabbi Shach and manage to obtain a letter condemning those who travel on the Sabbath—the entire Yeshivah world will go along with them, and then these thirty or forty families can influence fifty percent of the suburb.

Rabbi Yirmiyahu Abramov also hints at this dynamic. He stresses his abhorrence for the physically violent struggle between the *haredim* and the non-religious. He says that demonstrations and the throwing of stones are not his way, and that he prefers to concentrate on education and information. But he also admits that, if the Torah sages tell him to demonstrate, he will do so. If the Torah sages order him to change his opinions regarding the struggle for the character of the society, he will defer to them.

This self-effacement was expressed in the struggle over the schools in Har Nof. As a result of the order from Rav Shach, the Anglo-Saxons withdrew from the compromise they had negotiated with the religious-Zionists over the transfer to the new school building. Significantly, they maintained an independent position on the issue of closing roads on Sabbath, probably because no highly respected rabbinical figure from outside the community intervened on this matter.

The story of the Anglo-Saxon community in Israel may be one of missed opportunities to create better understanding between *haredim* and non-religious. One hears these same opinions from some of the American *haredim* themselves, who express their own disillusionment with a process which requires them to defer to the Israeli *haredim.*

Is there any hope that as the Anglo-Saxons become better adjusted to life in Israel their self-confidence will improve and they will become more aggressive in affirming their own positions? It is highly unlikely that this will occur. As the Anglo-Saxon *haredi* becomes more settled in the country, he undergoes a process of "haredization." The majority of the Anglo-Saxon children study in the official *haredi* educational network, do not take supplementary academic courses as their parents did in America, do not serve in the army, and are thus socialized to a *haredi* world-view. The Knesset member Avraham Verdiger seems to have been correct in his assessment, and the American *haredim* tend to agree with him. Anglo-Saxon *haredim* have influenced *haredim* only in secondary matters. In fact, all they have really done is strengthened certain patterns of consumption or life-styles associated with relative affluence—patterns that were discernible among a minority of Israeli *haredim* even before the recent influx of Anglo-Saxons; but their influence on substantive matters seems to be rather slight.

Nevertheless, Yeshivat Maaravah continues to function despite the prohibition of Rav Shach. Anglo-Saxon *haredim* did maintain an independent position on the issue of vehicular travel on the Sabbath. They did organize a list of their own with a message that was very different from the customary message of Israeli *haredim.* And their leaders do wonder about the tactical wisdom of their political alliance with Israeli *haredim.* For those concerned with fostering greater understanding and cooperation between *haredim* and non-religious in Israel, the activity of the Anglo-Saxon *haredim* remains a beacon of hope.

Amnon Levi

2

The *Haredi* Press and Secular Society

Terminology

In this chapter the term "secular" is used instead of the term "non-religious." Secular is a more accurate translation of the term *hiloni,* which is how the *haredi* press refers to the non-religious. The term "secular" is a pejorative in the *haredi* world, and that pejorative applies to all those who are not religious. Furthermore, the *haredi* world does not generally distinguish the non-religious "traditional" from the non-religious "secular" Jew and, as we shall see, its image of the non-religious Jew more closely resembles the secular than the traditional one.

Introduction

A study of relations between *haredi* and secular society leads inevitably to a survey of the *haredi* press. *Haredi* attitudes toward secular society cannot be understood without some knowledge of its communications media. This chapter examines the image of secular society in the *haredi* press. Who are its heroes and who are its enemies and how dangerous is the threat of secular society to the *haredi* way of life?

It is especially appropriate to examine the *haredi* image of secular society and secular Jews through the *haredi* press, because almost every sub-group of *haredim* has its own publication. The *haredi* world views its press as the communists did. To adapt Lenin—a publication is not simply a source of information, or even an ideological paper, but an instrument in the battle in which each *haredi* group is engaged.

The two *haredi* dailies serve the two largest groups. In a formal sense, *Hamodia* is the organ of Agudat Israel, the predominantly Ashkenazi *haredi* political party. In fact *Hamodia* is controlled by the Ger *hasidim,* the dominant bloc within Agudat Israel. The second daily, *Yated Neeman,* is the communication medium of Rabbi Eliezer Shach, the most important personality of Lithuanian *haredim* and spiritual leader of most Sephardic *haredim* and the Sephardic *haredi* party, Shas. (He is sometimes referred to as the patron of Shas, to distinguish his role from that of the committee of Sephardic rabbis led by former chief rabbi Ovadiah Yosef, who are the official spiritual mentors of the party.)

Other haredi publications include *Hamahaneh Haharedi,* the weekly of the Belz *hasidim; Haedah,* founded by the *Edah Haredit* in Jerusalem (a central organization of the *haredi* community); *Hahomah,* identified with one of the factions of the most extreme of all *haredi* groups, Neturei Karta; *Kfar Habad,* the organ of Habad (Lubavitcher) *hasidim; Az Nidberu,* the paper of Vishnitz *hasidim;* and so on—each group with its own periodical.

In addition to these papers, a new type of periodical has appeared in the last few years—the commercial *haredi* papers *Yom Hashishi* and *Erev Shabbat.* They constitute a revolution in *haredi* journalism and reflect a different approach to secular society, an approach we will examine below.

The *haredi* press, by the way, is not the only network which circulates information about and to the *haredi* public. A second, albeit informal, mechanism of communication is the wall posters in *haredi* neighborhoods, something without parallel in the non-*haredi* world. Since the most extreme among the *haredim* read no newspapers, or perhaps read a paper like *Haedah* which doesn't carry news stories, there is a need for a medium to convey "hot" news. A "hot" item might consist of the demise of an important rabbi, but it might also be an attack on or a defamation of an ideological enemy. The walls of Meah Shearim (the major *haredi* neighborhood in Jerusalem) stand, so the late Satmar *rebbe,* Rabbi Yoel Teitelbaum, is reputed to have said, because of the multitude of posters which hold them up.

A highly developed network of rumors constitutes a second informal medium of communication. The fact that we are talking about a small closed society, where everyone knows everyone else, encourages the flourishing of rumors and wall posters. This essay, however, deals only with the formal methods of communication, that is, the *haredi* press.

The Nature of the Haredi Press

The distinguishing feature of the *haredi* press is that in many respects its pages reflect its image of what life ought to be, not what life really is. If *haredi* norms demand that reality be changed, this is reflected in the press, sometimes in a rather coarse manner. For example, except for a special women's corner, there are no reports on women in the *haredi* press, and there are no articles on entertainment, hit songs and singers, etc. It goes without saying that there will be no mention of female singers. *Hamodia*'s parliamentary reporter, Zvi Rosen, once prepared a column in which he included a question that had been raised by M.K. Rabbi Yaacov Yosef of Shas. The Shas representative demanded to know why the army had wasted so much money in a search for the popular singer Ofra Haza, whose plane had crashed somewhere in Israel. Rosen left out Haza's name, however, knowing that the name of a female singer would not pass the paper's internal censorship. He merely reported that M.K. Yosef had raised a question concerning the waste of public money in the search for a female singer whose plane had crashed. The paper's editors, however, then removed even the designation "female singer" and substituted "a family of singers." This despite the fact that the remainder of the story now made no sense. It referred to "the family of singers" who were one of six passengers in the plane.

In some respects, the *haredi* press may be understood as an outlet for press releases rather than a medium which conveys information. It doesn't report a situation so much as announces what this or that rabbi, the patron of the particular paper, thinks about reality. Another way of saying this is that a *haredi* paper is a collection of ideological statements and polemics; interpretations of the world through the needle's eye of a particular group.

Those who control the paper utilize it for a variety of purposes. It is an instrument for educating children by means of appropriate stories and adults through articles written in accordance with the proper ideological line. It serves the consumer by telling him, for example, which kashrut supervision is acceptable and which is not; and it is also a weapon in the battle with the *haredi* group's enemies and a forum in which threats of excommunication are aired. Indeed it sometimes seems to the outsider that the *haredi* paper is an instrument for everything except the objective presentation of reality.

In order to present the world as it should be, a score of topics are taboo—sex, crime, sport, leisure go virtually unmentioned in all the *haredi* papers. Someone whose reading is limited to the *haredi* press alone would have never read of AIDS. Of all topics, sex is subject to the most stringent taboos. The biblical phrase "and your camp shall be pure" is the *haredi* ideal. If there is no alternative the press will use the euphemism "distant from ugliness and resembling it." *Hamodia* has a spiritual counselor apppointed by the former *rebbe* of Ger who oversees the morality of the paper. His official function is to serve as copy-editor, but he is also the moral censor of the papers. At *Yated Neeman* the work is done by a committee of rabbis who insure that nothing appears that is contrary to the ideology of Rav Shach.

Those who confine their reading to *Hamodia* or *Yated Neeman* or *Hamahaneh Haharedi* or *Kfar Habad* or *Haedah* or *Hahomah* don't know that there is an event called the Israeli Festival, don't know what movies are currently showing, never heard of the Olympics. What objection do they find to something like sport? One answer may be culled from the following item which appeared in *Yated Neeman:*

> The *haredi* press doesn't cover sporting activities at all, and if there is anyone who didn't understand this until now, then in the light of the decision of the Association of Journalists the reasons will become clear. [The reference is to a decision of the Association of Journalists to deny coverage to a Jerusalem soccer club for one month because of violence against the newspaper reporter who covered this team.] Competitive sport is no longer a means to physical health but is, today, a means to corrupt the soul. This new "idol-worship" focuses on sport "gods" of various kinds and turns spectators into aggressors. (September 29, 1987)

Anyone who confines his reading to the *haredi* press will know nothing of rape or crime, but he will believe that the land is filled with great rabbis, halakhic geniuses and spiritual guides for the present generation. Tales about them fill the pages of the press, stories of their wonders are to be found at every corner. Whoever reads *Hamodia,* the more worldly *haredim* joke, might think the world is all pink. They themselves read the secular press, having learned that the world is dominated by other colors.

A good opportunity to examine the credo of a *haredi* journalist is to be found in a reply by the editor of *Hamodia,* Moshe Akiva Druck, to the Minster of Education, in March 1986, when the latter asked all newspaper editors to exercise greater restraint in what their papers published. Druck answered that the *haredi* press needed no such admonition, since its editors were conscious not only of the right of the public to know but of their right not to know. This, wrote Druck, is a matter of pride to the editors of the *haredi* press. He once said to me in an interview:

> We deny the right of the public to know. This has become the motto of the secular press, and it's not right. We will not offer information beyond a point inimicable to our principles. All this talk about the right of the public to know is foolishness. The information in the hands of the public doesn't provide it with a basis to make judgments anyway.

Since the actual "news" is a secondary matter, most of the news stories in *Hamodia* and *Yated Neeman* are reprinted from the wire services. The papers themselves employ very few reporters. The core of the paper consists of the articles, analyses, and interpretations all framed in accordance with the *haredi* world-view.

But rules also mean ways of getting around the rules. In both *haredi* dailies, on the left hand side of the inside front page, is a column of lighter journalism. In *Hamodia* it is called "From Day to Day," and in *Yated Neeman* "On the Agenda." Here forbidden matters are reported on through various ruses. For example, almost the entire country follows the fortunes of Israeli soccer teams when they play foreign ones, especially the Soviet Union. So, in the course of an attack on all international sport as an example of "declining Greek culture," the results of a contest between Israel and the Soviet Union will be reported. Or a column might devote a paragraph to an attack on the Eurovision song contest as "unJewish" and in the course of the attack mention that Israel had just won the contest. This system has made these columns exceedingly popular. They are often the first item to which the *haredi* reader turns when he opens his paper.

The *haredi* press has also a style of its own. It cultivates a private language with its readers. For example, quotation-marks are extensively used to indicate that the writer's intentions are ironic. *Haredi* leaders bitterly contested the decision by the government to introduce daylight-saving time, because of the inconvenience it caused to those who worship in a synagogue each morning. *Hamodia* wonders how "the Minister of Energy arrived at the sum of five million dollars that in his imagination he believes will be 'saved'" and the reader knows that nothing will be saved. When *Hamodia* attacks the secular press it refers to their journalists as having "clean minds" and the reader understands immediately that its meaning is that they have "dirty minds." Secular education will be referred to as "progressive education"—responsible for so many criminals sitting in the prisons. The use of quotation-marks and other devices peculiar to the *haredi* press is possible because the reader is part of a closed community with private jokes that everyone understands. Thus one can refer to a "clean mind" when signifying a dirty mind without fear of misunderstanding. At the same time this style reinforces the reader's sense that he is part of a closed community.

In recent years the *haredi* press has undergone revolutionary changes, adapting itself to the innovations introduced by two new weeklies, *Yom Hashishi* (Friday) and *Erev Shabbat* (Sabbath Eve). These are commercial papers that don't represent any one segment of the *haredi* public. On the contrary, they aspire to reach all religious Jews, including the national-religious population. They were established not to serve as ideological instruments but to make money. *Yom Hashishi* was founded by two editors, Israel Katzover and Yitzhak Nahshoni, who gained their experience in the secular media. Their paper was first called *Yom Hashishi* and then changed its name to *Erev Shabbat.* But in November 1987, in the wake of business disagreements with the owners, the two editors, along with the entire editorial board, resigned and reestablished *Yom Hashishi.* The *Hamodia* writer Zvi Rosen was appointed editor of *Erev Shabbat.*

This commercial *haredi* press created a new type of *haredi* paper. There were new graphics, many photographs, simpler, less florid language, and an effort to imitate the investigatory style of the secular press. *Yom Hashishi* employed women as writers. (*Hamodia* also employs a woman writer, for topics outside its women's section, but her initials rather than her full name are used for her byline, so readers are not aware of her sex.) The new *haredi* press devotes considerable space to news stories, with much less emphasis on interpretative articles. This press, as we shall see below, is highly critical of secular society; but, paradoxically, it also contributes to the secularization of the *haredi* press.

Who is Secular? Who Is Haredi? The Haredi Press's Version

Let us begin with a matter of terminology. How does the *haredi* press refer to a secular Jew? The first distinction that we find in the *haredi* press is between "Israelis" and "Jews." The *haredim* are Jews; secular people are Israelis. For example, *Yated Neeman* published an article which referred to the cries of pleasure which broke out among the spectators in the courtroom when John Ivan Demjanjuk was sentenced to death for crimes committed at Treblinka. The secular press was critical of the expressions of pleasure with which the sentence was greeted. This, in turn, angered *Yated Neeman,* which wrote:

> *Among us Jews,* when it hurts—we cry out. When other Jews feel pain, when we remember our brothers who rotted in sorrow in their imprisonment, who died sanctifying God's name, we allow ourselves to cry . . . . We have followed the indifference of [secular] youth during the course of the trial we saw them nodding while the atrocities of Treblinka were unfolded, we saw them joking, whispering, and we recalled that on the soccer fields this youth is not indifferent. There they are wide awake . . . we have noted that the norms have changed here, that Jewish antisemitism is almost official policy today . . . *and these Israelis,* who are so indifferent to Jews, allow themselves to feel and express emotions only when matters affect Arabs. We cannot find the proper words to define the spontaneous explosion that erupted in the courtroom. But [our] joy in the fact that *Israelis* dared declare that they are part of the people who went to the gas chambers in the Diaspora may be a poor man's happiness, but it is nevertheless a joy. (May 8, 1988—emphasis added).

What did the reader learn from this article? There are Jews and there are Israelis. Jews are sensitive to the fate of their people. Most Israelis—cold blooded sorts—only become emotional on the soccer field or, alternatively, when Arabs are hurt. But there are exceptions among Israelis. On some occasions some of them act like Jews.

Hamodia defines the term Israeli in more specific terms. In an article entitled "The Israeli Citizen" the paper compares the contemporary Israeli with the Jewish heretic of the past.

> Today, there is a new Israeli generation which defines itself as Israeli citizens but does not identify with the Jewish religion. The arguments are not between one Jew and another over how many commandments are to be observed or on belief in the creator of the world. There isn't even any argument with one who knows his creator and rejects Him. There are no longer any Jewish heretics. There is ignorance about Jewish identity. But these new Jews are without religion, only Israelism and citizenship. . . .(May 18, 1988).

On the eve of Israel's 1987 Independence Day, an article in *Yated Neeman* refers to the *haredim* as "sons of the light of Torah," contrasting them with "sons of the secular darkness." The writer describes how horrendous it is to live in the secular state called Israel, and concludes by saying that "we *haredim* pray and long for the end of the nightmare of exile among Jews," suggesting that life in the state of Israel is a life of exile.

Hamahaneh Haharedi, the publication of Belz *hasidim,* goes one step further and distinguishes between two nations. One writer compares how the secular people and the *haredim* celebrate the holiday of Shavuot, the holiday of the giving of the Torah:

> At the same time as about one hundred thousand lost souls wandered around the polluted bathtub called the Kinneret [Lake Tiberias], hundreds of thousands of Jews all over the country and all over the Jewish world sanctified the evening by study [reference to the tradition of studying sacred text throughout the night]. Thus two nations, foreign to one another and alienated from one another, are emerging, one not even understanding the language of the other. (May 25, 1988).

In another article *Hamahaneh Haharedi* refers to this other nation as "*goyim* [Gentiles] from the seed of Israel."

> We have here a minority of *goyim* who do everything they can to overcome the "embarrassment" of their Jewishness. And against them a large majority of Jews, some better and some worse. The common denominator of the Jews in this country, as distinct from the *goyim* of the seed of Israel, is that they cannot express themselves or control what happens in this state or within Israeli public opinion. (April 12, 1988).

Elsewhere the paper describes secular people as "infants captured by *goyim*" and says:

> If there is a concept of "infants captured by *goyim*" [such a concept exists in rabbinic literature to indicate Jews who are not held responsible for their transgressions since they don't know any better], then there is no one whom such a concept better fits than the masses of Jews who received a Gentile "state" education which finally transformed them into a *goy* like all *goyim.* The secular government of Israel will never be forgiven for this crime: it will be remembered forever in Jewish history. (May 25, 1988)

Hamodia adds the interesting conception that *haredi* society is a society in uniform. The secular Jew identifies the *haredi* as anyone wearing black clothing, and this requires anyone dressing in this manner to behave as a representative of the camp. Therefore, the paper goes on to add, the *haredi* public must exercise caution and eject those at its own margins, in order that it be better prepared to confront secularism. (June 7, 1988)

There is a different mode which the *haredi* press sometimes employs in describing secularists—the paternalistic mode. This is evident in the expression "infants captured by *goyim.*" In the reference above, from the Belz paper, this expression was located in a context of linguistic aggression. The Habad paper *Kfar Habad* emphasizes the paternalistic side, the effort to educate the secular Jew but also to bring him closer to Judaism. In most cases *Kfar Habad* avoids the term "secular" by substituting "one who is not yet religious." When "secular" appears, it is always in quotation-marks. In an editorial in May 1988 the paper described the children's parades that Habad organized on the holiday Lag B'omer. These parades are a matter of controversy within the *haredi* public: Rav Shach has prohibited them. *Kfar Habad,* perhaps in order to justify them, tells how important they are in drawing the secular closer:

> The participation of hundreds of thousands of "secular" children accompanied by their parents and teachers in the great parades in the cities of Israel—proves beyond everything else that the heart of Israel is awake, and the longing for Torah and authentic Judaism exists in the heart of the entire people, at all levels.

Here, we note, the reference is to one people, albeit of different levels. But there is still hope of returning the secular community to authentic Judaism. Elsewhere in the same article the secular are referred to as "assimilated returned to the bosom of the people."

The paternalistic attitude reflects the ambivalence of the *haredi* press to the secular public. On the one hand they are a foreign people, *goyim* from the seed of Israel, and on the other hand brothers whom one must dissuade from wandering down the evil path. There is a sense that behind the fury which the *haredi* press expresses against the secular community lie the wounds of love, and it is concern for the secular Jew, who is likened to a brother, that accounts for the harsh language which that press employs. Here, for example, is an article from *Yated Neeman* written in the form of a personal letter to a secular brother:

> I heard you, my brother, I heard your complaints, the accusations you leveled against us, the religious, the observant. . . . You said that we have rebelled against the light, isolating ourselves in closed ghettos . . . that we have developed a nation within a nation, that we have raised a generation which lives within the four cubits [of Jewish law] and never leaves them. Ah, my brother, what innocence there is in the accusation that we have welcomed this isolation, as though it was something desirable to begin with! But you are to blame! You are the one who enclosed us, who cast us to our alley-ways, who drove us out from among you. (May 9, 1988).

The writer goes on to explain that his secular brother has dirtied the streets with pictures of obscenities and abominations [an allusion to sexually suggestive ads], inflicting harm on the soul of the *haredi* and forcing him to isolate himself. Beyond the recriminations, the familial tone can be heard. This is not a conflict between Jews and *goyim* from the seed of Israel but between two brothers, and if the feud is a family affair, hope remains for its resolution.

But however anxious the *haredi* may be to heal the rift between family members, there can be no compromise with the secular way of life. This is always contrasted with that of the *haredim* to the detriment of the former. According to Zvi Rosen, writer for *Hamodia* and present editor of *Erev Shabbat:*

> The *haredi* press will always report on the secular world from a perspective of superiority, hostility and negation. The press will emphasize, for example, the difference between Sabbath observance by *haredim* and the manner in which the secular spend their Sabbath, noting the materialism of the secular. The secular public will always be

represented as rebelling against observance and commandments, as very materialistic, as a public which has lost all values and lives a life of licentiousness. Every article in *Hamodia* will carry a message to the reader—see where the secular decline reaches. *Hamodia* doesn't report on crime, but in its articles it will use crime in order to show where the path of secularism leads. It will report on abortion laws, and present the secular as people who do not value the sanctity of life and therefore kill. The *haredi* public views the secular with derision—how can they permit themselves, one generation after the Holocaust, not to sanctify life?

Attitudes toward the Secular State and Zionism

Even worse than secularism in general is the organized established secularism reflected in the State of Israel. The secularism of the State is worse than bad, it is thoroughly rotten. The *haredi* press delights in every defect in the State in order to prove that it is, in its very essence, an error. When a strike breaks out in the health sector, *haredi* papers without exception attack the secular state which abandons its sick. Only in a secular state, the *haredi* press protests, could such a thing happen. The slogan and scriptural proof which recurs in article after article is the phrase of patriarch Abraham to Abimelech—"there is surely no fear of God in this place, and they will kill me" (Genesis, XX:11). In other words, the fact that Israel is a secular state without fear of God accounts for all its misfortunes. This, according to *Hamahaneh Haharedi,* explains why the "corrupt and evil health network abandons the sick and the poor and crushes the elderly and the weak" (May 25, 1988). When judges were arrested on suspicion of accepting bribes, *Haedah* (issue no. 459) sees them as a symbol of secular corruption and writes:

> It is a primary lesson for us, that all those raised on the knees of heretical ideas are naturally inclined to every act of corruption and crime. "There is surely no fear of God in this place, and they will kill me," our first father said, and this truth of the Torah is eternal . . . particularly when we are talking of those who sit at the head of the kingdom of heresy. . . . Hence there is no room for surprise among the Torah faithful at recent events.

Zionism, even more than secularism, is perceived as the central enemy of *haredi* ideology. The press is filled with articles analyzing the negative aspects of Zionism. One headline in *Hamahaneh Haharedi* (April 20, 1988) read "Zionism = Secularism = Assimilationism = National Suicide." *Hahomah,* the periodical of Neturei Karta, asserts without reservation that Zionism is worse than Nazism. In an article in the Adar-Nisan (Spring) issue of 1987 it asks:

> Which is worse, Zionism or Nazism? Our rabbis taught that "one who leads a person to sin is worse than one who murders a person." The Nazis burned the bodies of the community of Israel and the Zionists burned the souls of the community of Israel, and one who leads another to sin is worse than one who murders.

If Zionism is a sin, the father of Zionism is an abominable criminal. In the wake of a biographical column in the secular daily *Davar* on Herzl, *Hamahaneh Haharedi* had the following to say about him:

> . . . some insane person who failed throughout his lifetime and "was privileged" to bear crazy uncircumcised descendants who converted and committed suicide. . . . This doesn't surprise us. A nation which abandoned its God, its faith, the traditions of its fathers, and the teachings of its rabbis, which distorts the words of its prophets and rebels against its laws, deserves no better than this insane mentally disturbed and incompetent leader. Paper can not bear to record the details of his perversions. (May 4, 1988)

Hamahaneh Haharedi, it may be argued, is a small unrepresentative paper. But when the afternoon daily *Maariv* attacked *Hamahaneh Haharedi* for publishing this diatribe, *Yated Neeman,* representing the Lithuanian branch of the *Haredim* and the Sephardic elements in that camp, rushed to its defense. Furthermore, *Yated Neeman* itself had some rather strong words to say about Herzl in April 1987, after Israel's president, Haim Herzog, visited Basle. Herzog was photographed on a balcony where Herzl in his day had been photographed. *Yated Neeman* wrote as follows:

> Criminologists have observed the surprising phenomenon of the criminal returning to the scene of the crime despite his knowledge that the police are awaiting him there. Uncontrollable urges impel him to do so. Sometimes it happens that the product of a crime returns to the scene of the crime. This too has no logical explanation. That is how we understand the historic photograph [of Herzog at Basle]. In the

> photograph of Herzl taken ninety years ago we see an assimilationist who turned into a nationalist Jew; in the present picture of Haim Herzog we see a religious Jew [Herzog is the son of a former chief rabbi of Israel] who turned into a nationalist secularist. . . .

Another way in which *haredi* society demonstrates its contempt for the State of Israel and the distinctions between itself and secular society is by reversing names of well-known institutions of the State or avoiding language which would add status to these institutions. For example, *Hamahaneh Haharedi* will not use the initials IDF (Israel Defense Forces), but substitutes the initials FSI (Forces of the State of Israel) or will simply use the term "Israeli army." *Hamodia* is careful not to use the term *mishkan* in referring to the president's home or to the Knesset building. In biblical usage *mishkan* means sanctuary, but in modern Hebrew it refers to a building such as the president's mansion *(mishkan Hanasi)* or the Knesset building *(mishkan Haknesset). Yated Neeman* will never report that a secular court *pasak* (ruled) on anything, since only a religious court can rule. Thus the paper will report that a secular court "decided" or "decreed" something; and when the Israeli wire service carries a report on an Israeli court decision and uses the term *p'sak* (ruling), the paper will rewrite the word to conform to its style.

The Major Secular Enemies

While secularism and Zionism are arch-enemies of the *haredim,* there are categories of Zionists and secularists for whom a special animus is reserved. Enemy number one of the *haredi* press is without doubt the secular press. One finds, almost every day, references to the secular press, to secular journalists and to their norms of behavior. *Haredim* perceive themselves as persecuted by the secular press, who stigmatize them, generalize unfairly about them, deride and humiliate them. *Yated Neeman* published an article titled "Where Is It Worse?" asserting that the persecution of Jews in Yemen is less onerous than the persecution of *haredim* in Israel.

> Devouring religious Jews is one of the favorite hobbies of the average secularist, perhaps from hatred toward the religion of his forefathers which pursues him and gives him no peace, and perhaps for other reasons. No one has examined how far things have gone, no one has

> counted the number of articles dripping poison written in the style of the Nazi [paper] *Der Shturmer* that are published during one month alone in the general press. What haven't they written about the religious Jew, that he is a "leech" a "jellyfish," that a dog is better than him, and all other kinds of Arab curses? (May 23, 1988)

Under these circumstances, the paper goes on, it isn't clear why Jews of Yemen complain that the Yemenites call them "cursed Jews." After all, that is mild compared to what the secular press labels *haredim* in Israel. "They don't know how good things are for them there in Yemen, with its hostility and hatred, where the Jew has not yet been vilified the way he has been vilified here in the land of Israel."

Hamodia reports how the secular press, enemy number one of the *haredim,* cooperates with the police, another antagonist, to convict them of a crime which, *Hamodia* attests, is never committed—burning the Israeli flag on Lag B'omer [a holiday in which children customarily light bonfires].

> After the police announce that the "flag of the state has been desecrated," all the journalists—the group who set the anti-*haredi* tone—inform their editors. The more professional and sophisticated among them pull out archival pictures from their drawers in which *[haredi]* children and infants are shown rolling garbage-cans in a public square. The picture is known from previous incidents, but what does the liberal editor care when a journalist brings a photograph "fresh from this evening?" Under the picture, without any pangs of conscience, he [the editor]writes that it was photographed on Lag B'omer at a time when tens of flags (not shown in the picture. . .) were burned in *haredi* neighborhoods. (May 9, 1988)

The paper goes on to call this an "anti-*haredi* intifada."

It isn't surprising, according to the *haredi* press, that the general press is so hostile. This stems from its very conception of journalism. According to *Yated Neeman*:

> "Freedom of the Press" is an expression that fits the journalists, and in the name of this expression everything is permitted, and everything is excused. There is no secret, no modesty, no truth, no fairness, etc. etc. In short—licentiousness. "The right of the public to know," another expression, [is] the product of the desire of the journalist to give maximum publicity to a maximum number of topics with a maximum of

> detail, to examine in intimate detail the private life of individuals. . . (June 21, 1988)

Another enemy is the judicial system. The *haredi* public does not accept the legitimacy of the secular judicial system in Israel and therefore welcomes any sign of defect in its functioning. Critical articles appear in the *haredi* press with every revelation of a mistake in that system. We already noted that *Yated Neeman* will not use the term *p'sak* [ruling] to refer to decisions of a secular court. *Haedah* even denied the right of the secular courts to try Demjanjuk.

The *haredi* press also reserves a special measure of hostility for Israel's political left, with particular animus directed toward Knesset member Shulamit Aloni and her party, Ratz (the Movement for Citizens' Rights). The concept "political left" is extended on occasion to include the Labor party. *Yated Neeman* once printed a picture of the then Prime Minister Shimon Peres with his head attached to the body of a vulture (*Peres* in Hebrew means vulture). The caption under the picture asked, "What non-kosher [impure] bird appears in this picture?" But it is the left-wing Zionist parties, Ratz in particular, that earn the greatest measure of hostility. Here is an example from *Hamodia:*

> The decline of the Knesset as a result of the passage of evil laws continues without abating. Knesset member Shulamit Aloni obtained a majority for what is called "mercy killing." This is an indication of the degenerate state of the Knesset and what we may expect in the future from "elected representatives" such as Shulamit Aloni. "There is surely no fear of God in this place, and they will kill me," the Torah said, and reality proves how true this is. When the topic is the survival of Jews against Arabs, that same Knesset member is transformed into the defender of "humanism." That's because it is on behalf of the Arabs. But in this case, with what ease [she] is ready to introduce a law that would in fact give doctors the legal right to decide on terminating the life of sick people, which is nothing more than an indirect opening for murder!

When Peace Now organized a demonstration to take place in Samaria in the wake of the intifada, *Hamodia* noted that the demonstration was deliberately scheduled for Shabbat, since this is what the "Ratz leftists" wanted. Local Arabs welcomed the demonstrators and *Hamodia* concluded by observing that "two of a kind found each other." (June 10, 1988)

The Left in the eyes of the *haredi* press is associated with the universities, intellectuals, and academics—enemies almost by definition. All of them are only a short step away from betraying the homeland. The enthusiasm of the *haredi* press in seeking out potential traitors seems inconsistent to the outsider. After all, the *haredim* themselves vigorously oppose Zionism and adopt, at best, an attitude of neutrality toward the State. But, inconsistent or not, this is how it is. In *haredi* society one even finds the strange combination of anti-Zionism with strong nationalist feelings. Even the distinction between hawks and doves loses much of its meaning. One can find *haredim* who are unabashed admirers of Arik Sharon or Menachem Begin but favor the return of all the territories because one is forbidden to antagonize the non-Jews.

The *haredi* press gives ample expression to its disgust at what it sees as the potential treachery of the Left, of university graduates, of the academy in general. When the editors of a radical left-wing paper were arrested on charges of membership in an illegal terrorist organization, *Hamodia* came up with the following headline to an article on the topic: "How do Graduates of Hebrew Universities Reach the Point Where They Do Things Likely to Result in Trials for Acts of Treachery?" The article noted that:

> We aren't dealing with those at the margins of the State of Israel's society, not with street urchins, not with slow learners—we are dealing with the graduates of Hebrew universities, with the best of the youth, with those who possess a conscious ideology, with the relatives of the social and national elite. "There is surely . . . and they will kill me!" That which we feared has happened! The wave of treachery must be stopped immediately. (May 18, 1988)

Another enemy of the *haredi* press is religious-Zionism in all its manifestations. This includes the National Religious Party, the political representative of religious-Zionism; but also the chief rabbinate, the rabbinical expression of religious-Zionism. When the chief rabbinate reinforces the decision of the government of Israel to require Soviet Jews to come directly to Israel without allowing them the opportunity to drop out along the way, *Yated Neeman* editorializes as follows:

> The chief rabbinate has demonstrated once again that "statist" considerations take precedence over halakhic, Torah, or Jewish ones. The

> good of the state—or, as they express it in their distorted and misleading definition, "the command to settle the Land of Israel"—takes priority over the welfare of Jews rotting under the oppression of a cruel and hostile government. *That* is another step that illustrates the distorted scale of values which the rabbinate of the State has developed and which found expression in the past in their "ruling" according to which keeping Judea and Samaria [the West Bank] are preferable to saving lives. They who glorify the phrase "love of Israel" have proven this time that what they really mean is love of the state of Israel and not love of the people of Israel. (June 21, 1988)

Other objects of hostility vary according to circumstances. The rule is that the *haredi* press is hostile to the secular state in all its expressions. The instruments of government—police, army, courts, government offices, etc.—automatically become objects of criticism. Every mishap in the government provides the opportunity to attack Zionism in general and not only those responsible for the mishap. A strike, a revelation of corruption or theft, a sensational declaration in some government institution, is attributed to the nature of Zionism and the State and never as an independent event.

A Typology of the Press and its Attitudes to Secular Society

Not all *haredi* papers react in the same manner to non-*haredi* society. There are two general typologies of the *haredi* press: On the one hand, that distinguishing ideological papers, generally older, from the newer commercial press; on the other, the general *haredi* press versus the specialized one. As a rule the specialized press—periodicals which represent one hasidic group or one sub-group of *haredim*—is more extreme and more sharply critical of secular society than the two general *haredi* papers, *Hamodia* and *Yated Neeman.* A scale of the *haredi* papers in terms of their enmity toward secular society would look as follows.

In first place would be *Hahomah,* the periodical of Neturei Karta, and *Haedah,* published by the *Edah Haredit.* These two papers have no reluctance in comparing the secular Zionist state to a Nazi state. Next comes *Hamahaneh Haharedi* of the Belz *hasidim*. It is difficult to understand why this paper is so hostile. Perhaps this is the residue of the former affiliation of the Belz *hasidim* with the *Edah Haredit* (they resigned a few years ago). A better explanation, according to one *haredi* journalist, is that since Belz *hasidim* are so involved in the life of the State, because they come and go in secular society, they feel obliged to balance this relationship with a press that is sharply critical of any secularism. This explanation finds support in the fact that Yisrael Eichler, a journalist whose attacks on secularism and the secular state are among the most extreme, has many associations with secular Jews, had a weekly radio program, and has appeared in many secular forums as the representative of Belz *hasidim*.

Next in line in its hostility to the secular is *Yated Neeman*. This paper thrives on all sorts of controversy and is often critical of religious and even *haredi* groups such as Habad. But it does reserve its sharpest barbs for the secular public. *Hamodia* is far more moderate. There, over the course of many years, a blueprint for criticizing secular society has developed. *Hamodia* would never call Herzl a criminal or insane, and they would not defend an article in another *haredi* paper that did so. On the other hand, *Hamodia* devotes more space to attacking the secular public than does *Yated Neeman*. This may stem from the fact that, since *Hamodia* never criticizes groups within *haredi* society, it has a lot more space in which to criticize secular society.

The most moderate of all in its criticism of secular society is *Kfar Habad*. This paper is the exception to the rule that the specialized *haredi* press is more critical than the general one. The absence of overt hostility is, of course, part of Habad's ideology. *Kfar Habad* presents itself as the mentor of the secularists, as one who would show them the way to the proper life. It is never harsh in its criticism.

The approach of the commercial press, whether of the more extreme *Yom Hashishi* or the more moderate *Erev Shabbat*, is quite different. In a nutshell, they have adopted the form and style of the secular press—graphics, advertisements, and pictures—in order to attack secularism itself. Yitzhak Nahshoni, one of the editors of *Yom Hashishi*, explained this in an interview:

> Until our paper was established the *haredi* press, under the best of circumstances, was defensive in its posture toward secular society. It responded only when the *halakhah* or the political interests of the religious were attacked. Its practice was to ignore all other secular attacks, as though they were not worthy of response. We came to the conclusion that we had an instrument with which it was possible not only to defend but also to attack. We decided that if the Chief Educa-

> tional Officer of the army, Brigadier General Nehemia Dagan, attacks yeshivah students [Dagan had called on the government to draft them], I'll hit him under the belt where it hurts him the most. I'll make my attack painful, but I will express myself more moderately than other *haredi* papers. I won't say he's crazy or a fool.

Yom Hashishi has become the instrument of an unprecedented series of attacks on secular society. The attacks were direct and personal on everyone considered an enemy. When Brigadier General Dagan criticized yeshivah students for refusing to serve in the army, *Hamodia* and *Yated Neeman* responded with lengthy polemical articles. *Erev Shabbat* responded with a front-page news story, apparently without foundation, charging that Dagan said what he did in order to obtain a senior post in the Jewish Agency. Whereas the *haredi* press constantly criticizes the secular press in general terms, *Erev Shabbat* has a weekly column in which it levels its fire at specific items in the secular press which *haredim* might find of special interest. It is sensitive to the difference between the secular papers, it knows the names of secular journalists, it pays special attention to those it feels are especially anti-religious and challenges them. It gives out grades, disparaging some and praising others. In an August 1987 issue, *Erev Shabbat* devoted an entire article to the secular press. It offered a general description of secular journalists in very negative terms and then turned to a specific discussion of papers and journalists. One paper was labled "cheap, yellow, nihilist" and one journalist "a frustrated writer whose future is behind her." A prominent figure in the electronic media was described as "the friend of a drunk [another journalist] who died this week," etc. This kind of personal style was foreign to the older *haredi* press. Indeed, among *haredim,* the paper is referred to disparagingly.

Paradoxically, this new form of *haredi* paper is actually an imitation of the secular press. This is a commercial press that has adopted many of secular society's norms and in some respects provides a window on the secular world for *haredim.* When *Yom Hashishi* was established in 1983, the notion was to create a paper that would circulate among all segments of *haredim* and be available to anyone who wished to advertise commercial products among them. Today, *Yom Hashishi* is distributed by the secular publisher Amos Shocken, with whom the editors have an agreement on advertising as well as distribution. In the wake of this breakthrough older *haredi* papers followed suit.

Until a few years ago the only announcements in the *haredi* papers were family announcements or those sponsored by some group. The new *haredi* papers helped bring secular companies to the attention of *haredim* through advertisement. According to Nahshoni:

> We came and said that the secular public has something to sell the religious public, and there is no reason why they shouldn't do so. If Fiat wants to sell something to the religious public—at one time it didn't know how to do it. The openness which we made possible had further consequences. Today many factories have a special line for *haredim,* with the approval of *haredi* rabbis, and arrangements suitable for the needs of *haredim.* Lately there was even a special fair for the *haredi* public in B'nai B'rak. Who ever thought of such an idea in the past? When did a [furniture] company like Rim ever think of manufacturing separate beds for the religious public? And how did it suddenly happen that Tadiran decided to produce a new refrigerator for Sabbath observers? We are tied to these developments. We didn't create them but we helped in their development. Producers who advertised with us had their hand on the pulse of the *haredi* public and kept them in mind when they planned production. They began to think of ways to make their product more attractive to *haredim.*

But strangely enough, it is not only in matters of style (e.g. graphics and advertisements) that the gap has been narrowed between the *haredi* and secular press, but in content as well. For example, secular personalities were now interviewed in *haredi* papers. When Shimon Peres was prime minister, *Erev Shabbat* interviewed him. Peres was pleased that he was afforded the opportunity to reach the *haredi* public, and *Erev Shabbat* earned the prestige of having interviewed him. In addition they had the opportunity to question him about troubling religious issues and provide the *haredi* reader with a direct answer—without the intercession of *haredi* parties. Raphael Eitan, the former army chief-of-staff and now a Knesset member, was interviewed on the topic of education. *Erev Shabbat*'s goal in this case was clear. If even Raphael Eitan praised religious education, the matter was an achievement of no small means to the *haredim,* an achievement that *Erev Shabbat* was happy to be able to announce. Yet these interviews surely also provide a measure of legitimacy for the secular personalities who were interviewed and for the world which they represent. Furthermore, the very interest of the *haredi* reader in Eitan's opinions suggests how tenuous the self-imposed isolation of many *haredim* really is. And so, strangely enough, this new press that is so critical and aggressive and in many respects nastiest toward secular society has nevertheless narrowed the secular–religious gap.

The *haredi* press itself has had difficulty accepting the new weeklies. The new press was the subject of some sharp attacks and earned the label "the new stumbling press." Here is what *Yated Neeman* writes:

> We have two types of papers on the *haredi* street. One deals with regular up-to-date information, interpretative articles in the spirit of Torah and the expression of Torah ideas on contemporary issues. By contrast, a new form of press has arisen and a new spirit fills it. Imported directly from outer space, it is not a real partisan in the conflicts it reports, it has no sense of responsibility or pain for every problem that arises . . . the goal, the touchstone is one thing; in the language of the street it's called—scoop! Everything is measured by the criteria of sensationalism, and by that alone. . . .

Rav Shach, in turn, has prohibited the reading of *Erev Shabbat* and was quoted as saying that he cries when he hears that proper Jews carry *Erev Shabbat* under one arm and their phylacteries under another. But the fact is that this press is flourishing. In addition, according to Nahshoni, despite the aggressive attitudes of his paper toward the secular population, it would ultimately provide a bridge to them. "A public that is not anti-religious and comes across a paper like ours can learn much about the religious public from reading it," he says.

Meanwhile the rest of the *haredi* press, despite its criticism of the new press, has adopted its offensive posture. Since its first appearance, the commercial press has had a strong influence on the ideological press, especially on *Hamodia* and *Yated Neeman*. Here, for example, is an article from *Yated Neeman* (June 8, 1988):

> The *haredi* public, including its lay leaders, does not know how to attack. Not even to attack in order to prepare its next defense. The *haredi* public and its lay leaders only knows how to defend and defend.

Other papers have also adopted the language of war in their description of secular society. In general, the *haredi* press has become increasingly aggressive and hostile toward secular society.

The Secular Press—How Does It Describe Haredim?

As a secular journalist who has followed *haredi* society over a considerable period of time I was surprised by this militancy, by the amount of hatred and the criticism which I found in the *haredi* press. Articles such as the one on Herzl in *Hamahaneh Haharedi* or the one directed to the Jews of Yemen in *Yated Neeman* surprised and, I confess, irritated me quite a bit. I was annoyed by the exaggerated description, the extremism, the aggression in the description of secular society. I was provoked by the *haredi* press's assumption that moral behavior is never to be found in secular society: an assumption expressed in the phrase "there is surely no fear of God in this place, and they will kill me." The commercial *haredi* press was especially provoking, and on occasion it aroused in me a sense of derision. This question, however, is not the topic of this chapter. But in order to understand the attitude of the *haredi* press toward the secular, in order to understand their employment of the language of war, defense, attack, one must at least understand the direction of thinking among the secular press toward *haredi* society.

A reader who reviews articles on *haredi* society in the secular press is immediately struck by the fact that it too describes relations between the two societies in the language of war. The secular press uses the same phrases, sometimes with even sharper tones. War, terror, battle are the terms that recur, especially from the coercive rule of the anti-Zionist *haredim*.

Gideon Samet of *Haaretz* on August 9, 1987 under the caption "The Blacks Attack Again" warns that the secular will abandon Jerusalem if the *haredim* continue their terror. *Al Hamishmar* writes on August 27, 1987 that "the *haredim* of Meah Shearim are stockpiling violent weapons."

Ran Kislev wrote a series of articles in *Haaretz* on the spread of *haredi* orientations. On January 1, 1988 he describes the flow of funds to Yeshiva students and notes that this money strengthens the black yeshivot that are a "fifth column" within the network of religious education. An article by Yoel Marcus in *Haaretz* (September 22, 1987) apppears under the heading "There is Nothing to Talk About—Discussions with *Haredi* Extremists Will March the Jewish People, Step by Step Back to the Dark Ages." Gabriel Strassman in *Maariv* (July 26, 1987) describes the war between the *haredim* and the archeologists under the heading "Petrified Fanaticism."

Darkness, blacks, fanatics, fifth column, terror, war, enemy. And there are even harsher expressions. No paper is free of this, no journalist can swear that he has had no part in this group defamation. To the credit of the secular journalists it can be said that they do not, for the most part, attack the *haredi* for his faith or his way of life as the *haredi* press does to the secularists. Nevertheless, the secular press has surely sinned against the *haredi* public in its gross generalizations. The secular press attributes violence, militancy, extremism to all *haredim* whereas it is clear that the absolute majority are not like this.

As one who writes about *haredim* in a secular paper I am aware of the responses of the readers to articles dealing with them. The secular public is very hostile to *haredi* society and welcomes reading hostile descriptions of *haredim*. On the other hand, the extremists among the *haredim* are happy to transmit this language of conflict to the secular reporter, because they also view the relationship between the two societies as one of war.

There are no nuances in battle. No distinctions between groups of *haredim,* between moderates and extremists. They are all black, the secularist will tell himself, thereby providing an excuse to hate them all. I recall the time I wrote an article about the different styles of clothing characteristic of different *haredi* groups. The differences in jacket length, hat style, of stockings, are very pronounced. Many secularists with whom I spoke refused to acknowledge that there were differences in the clothing style of the different *haredi* groups. As far as they were concerned, all *haredim* wore black and distinctions between them were pointless. They refused to face the fact that real people of different sorts were found beneath the clothing. The *haredim,* on the other hand, were always convinced I was mocking them. I sought to portray them as a community of people with their own style of life, customs, and traditions, which extend to such matters as fashion, the role of women, and the ideal of beauty, independently of their religious beliefs. The *haredim* themselves objected to such portrayals, which they perceived as negative and irrelevant.

The secular press has certainly had a role in the creation of the negative image of the *haredim*. Perhaps this is inherent in the nature of newspaper writing. It highlights extremes. In this respect we secular journalists are in the same boat as the *haredi* journalists—with the one important difference, already mentioned, that the secular press does not present *haredi* life as inherently immoral.

On the other hand, it is wrong to believe that the press—*haredi,* secular, or both—is entirely responsible for the tension and aggressiveness that characterize the relationships between the two publics. It is too simple to blame the press for everything. In fact, journalists on both sides are expressing a real sense of fury and a deep hostility that is rooted in both societies. The press may feed the fire but it didn't light it. Both *haredi* and secular press represent warning signs that point to tension, ignorance, and a large measure of hostility between the *haredim* and secular society.

Samuel C. Heilman

3

Religious Jewry in the Secular Press

Aftermath of the 1988 Elections

Introduction

IN EVALUATING the Israeli press's treatment of religion and politics and of *dati** Jews in the aftermath of the 1988 elections, one needs to recognize some of the assumptions upon which a free press in a democratic society operates and to perceive the design or structure of contemporary newspapers. I begin with some organizing assumptions: the written press, besides being an organ of information, is also a business; in a free society, it sells news on the open market. In order to remain in business, to keep people buying its newspapers, the press must above all else provide its public with information that they find important, interesting, perhaps even entertaining, and useful. One might even suggest that the press must—at least tacitly—cultivate and confirm its readers' sense of what is important and interesting. This is what is meant when we speak of a paper's reflecting its readers' interests. In practice, this often results in particular papers developing specific audiences whom they generally address.

If the editors are correct in their interpretations of their public's

*The Hebrew words *dati* and *haredi* may be translated in a variety of ways. Their meaning in the context of this paper is best captured in the English equivalents "orthodox" and "ultra-orthodox."

interests and if they are successful in cultivating readers and gathering the information that public wants or needs, they stay in business. If not, their papers gradually lose readers and in turn advertisers and ultimately cease publication. Even a subsidized newspaper, for example an organ of a political party, is ultimately dependent upon its member-readers' support and interest.

General circulation newspapers operate on the same assumption except that, because they seek to attract a mass audience, they must provide information that will be perceived to be of interest and importance to the largest possible segment of the population. Normally, therefore, they focus on events and information that touch the most people in the society.

A second assumption concerns the definition of news. News—particularly if it is to stimulate people to buy and read a newspaper—must have an immediacy to it. The material and events it covers must be seen to have altered reality as it was known beforehand. It must be perceived as new. Nothing, as the well-known aphorism goes, is as stale as yesterday's newspaper, for it describes a reality with which everyone is presumably already familiar.

This leads to the third assumption: news is that which is not altogether in line with expectations. What follows precisely from expectations and is known naturally is not news. In the classic definition, the fact that a dog has bitten a man does not make the news or sell newspapers, since dogs are at any given time likely to be biting people, and it is natural for people to know that. It is, however, news when a man bites a dog, since that event is beyond normal expectations. Thus papers by definition tend to emphasize the unexpected. They write more about men biting dogs than the reverse.

Accordingly, because the unexpected and immediate makes news, and in order to sell lots of newspapers to lots of people, editors often end up describing a reality that seems constantly startling and filled with crisis and the unforeseen. Reading the paper, one might forget that dogs bite men more often than men bite dogs.

In its quest for readers, the free press often is forced to distort reality. This, of course, is obvious to anyone who reads a news report of an event in which he has played a part: there is always something in the report that frames or defines the reality differently from the direct experience of it.

The design and structure of contemporary newspapers is to some extent a corrective to the inherently distorting character of the news. Generally, this structure consists of the division of the newspapers into parts. One part of the paper—the first section and most prominently the front page—is generally presented as containing relatively unmodified facts: the so-called news. These items are presented with datelines, beneath headlines which are meant at once to capture readers' attention and identify the story that follows. Here the facts are supposed to dominate and the only editorial intervention occurs in selecting the stories to cover and choosing the headlines and the placement of articles in the paper. To be sure, the decision to call something news is crucial, for it defines reality. To say that on such and such a date in such and such a place a particular event is worth reporting is to say that that event constitutes an important—perhaps even the paramount—reality in that place at that time. Moreover, headlines—both in their size and in their placement—also implicitly editorialize, as by size, placement, and content they characterize the relative importance and the construction of the reality the articles report.

Beyond the news section are the editorial and features segments of the paper. Here, opinion and open interpretation of the events reported in the news, as well as more expansive treatments of events, dominate the pages. Presumably, this section is meant to make the news more fully comprehensible and to put it into context. Editorials and columns as well as feature stories suggest that knowing the bare facts alone is insufficient for the informed reader. Of course, the presence of editorials and columnists also indirectly serves to reaffirm the reader's assumption that opinions and editorializing are absent from the news pages. In fact that is not the case since, as already suggested, editorial decisions on coverage and headlining do reflect interpretation and world-view.

To give the impression of a free press, newspapers often provide columnists of varying points of view and also allow for readers' letters. But here too, the ultimate decisions on which opinions are published and letters printed remain with the editors of a particular paper. The universe of discourse is ultimately limited.

The (Secular) Israeli Press

These assumptions and this structure play an important role in our understanding of the treatment of *dati* Jews in Israeli general-circulation newspapers. Included in this brief survey of the press are the newspapers *Ha'aretz, Yediot Aharonot,* and *Ma'ariv,* the three largest general-circulation dailies; *Davar,* a daily paper associated with the General Federation of Labor (the Histadrut), but aiming at a mass readership; and *The Jerusalem Post,* the largest English-language daily. Finally, I shall also consider two of the local weekly papers—Jerusalem's *Kol Ha'Ir* and *Jerusalem*—which, while focusing primarily on community concerns, like the local weeklies in Tel Aviv and Haifa, give relatively greater coverage to *dati* Jews because they are a more visible element of the local Jerusalem scene.

Beneath all the reports and editorials in these newspapers—including *Kol Ha'Ir* and *Jerusalem*—lies the realization that *most* of the readers of the papers are *not dati. Datiim,* after all, are a minority in Israel. Moreover, in Israeli society, so-called religious Jewry has developed its own press. The religious-Zionist *datiim,* those who have chosen to enter the mainstreams of Israeli national life, commonly read the general press, but they nevertheless have their own newspapers and journals which more specifically address issues that affect their own interests and world-view. The number of *haredim* reading the general press is far smaller; indeed some who do so are reluctant to be seen reading it in public. The general-circulation press is generally considered off-limits to *haredim,* and there have been violent attacks against dealers who try to sell these papers in *haredi* neighborhoods. *Haredim* rely in great measure on their own papers to give them the information they want and need. (Hence, it is not surprising that *haredim* and even religious-Zionists distinguish between the general-circulation press, which they label "secular," and the "religious" press. This means that the secular press can generally disregard the religious readers in their mass audience. Or, to be more precise, they can afford not to be interested in attracting such readers and may therefore be insensitive to their interests and feelings. This is particularly true for *haredim.*

Several consequences follow from all this. First, the general-circulation secular newspapers, writing for the mass audience which is largely non-*dati,* only devote space to the *dati* community when what it does seems to affect the lives of the general population, i.e. their readers. Thus, as a second consequence, what is news about the *dati* world is essentially what is unexpected and therefore interesting to the general (i.e. non-*dati*) public. This essentially limits the coverage of *dati* life to matters that have external meaning, to what is comprehensible to the non-*dati;* what is significant *inside* the *dati* community is commonly not treated by the secular press.

Thirdly, when the secular press does cover the *dati* world, it commonly paints the outlines of that world with a broad brush, because a more detailed sketch would be beyond both its readers' interest and their cultural competence. It rarely attempts to provide a nuanced picture of life in the *dati* world—except, as in the aftermath of the elections, when some of the nuances are themselves of interest and therefore news because they play a part in party politics and coalition-building.

Finally, because of the press's inherent interest in the new, it is often forced to focus on events which seem to be novel or suddenly changing. This often gives the general reader the impression that matters in the *dati* world are changing in a dramatic fashion. Indeed, the secular press may over-emphasize the pace of change. Dramatic changes always capture attention, but at the same time they create an impression that may potentially engender anxiety in the non-*dati* reader.

This press thus doubly distorts the reality of *dati* life. First, like all press reporting, it distorts by emphasizing the dramatic, changing, and unexpected. But second, because it covers the *dati* world from a distance and for a readership that in a sense chooses to remain at that distance, the general press further distorts the reality by describing events in ways that primarily make sense and are of interest to a mass (non-*dati*) audience. It slants the news in their direction.

What is true in the news pages is even more so in the editorials, columns, and features which seek to put the facts into place.

The 1988 Elections and the Datiim

As noted, the secular press will cover events in the *dati* world of interest to the general public. The aftermath of the 1988 elections for the Knesset brought about a plethora of such coverage, both in the news and in the editorial and features segments. The elections resulted in increased *dati* representation in the Knesset, an outcome which many Israelis for a variety of reasons—not the least of which being that the pollsters did not adequately survey the *haredi* population in advance of the balloting—found unexpected. The total of eighteen Knesset seats won by *dati* parties, a significant expansion over their showing in the previous election, was news, especially because in the system of Israeli coalition politics these seats appeared to many analysts to be the ones which would tip the political balance and decide whether Labor or Likud would form the next government. Suddenly, the *datiim*—who often remain at the fringes of general concern—were touching the general public in unexpected ways; and the general-circulation press had to pay attention. They had to cover not only the immediate results of the balloting but also the social significance of the vote as well as the political demands being made by the religious parties as their price for participation in the coalition. The editorialists and columnists had to explain to the readers just who these *dati* Jews were, often in greater detail than they had had to in a long time, and what the significance of their victory and demands was.

This turn of events provides a convenient and useful opportunity to examine the way in which the general-circulation press treats the *datiim.* To be sure, the politically charged atmosphere existing in the aftermath of a hotly contested election, particularly in a system built around coalition politics, certainly must have an effect on the press coverage and editorials, skewing them in the direction of stressing power and contention. There might therefore be some risks of overgeneralizing these elements as an important component in the relationship. Nevertheless, one might also suggest that it is precisely in such an atmosphere that feelings and attitudes are laid bare most vividly and boldly, and therefore that this is exactly the time to look at the coverage. That is, power politics strips away the veneer and gets us to basic attitudes.

Headlines

Perhaps a good place to begin a survey is to consider the message embedded in the headlines which dealt with the *datiim.* Recall that headlines at once characterize the story below them and emphasize certain elements of it. Thus, a collection of headlines can serve to reveal something of the way in which the press characterizes the entire subject of the *datiim.* Consider some examples.

From *Ha'aretz*

NOVEMBER 3, 1988

—Shamir decides not to bow to *dati* extortion even if the negotiations continue.

—Jews of Southern California worry about the enhanced strength of the *dati/haredi* camp.

—Non-*datiim* in the U.S.A. apprehensive over concessions to the *datiim* which will split the nation.

—The enhanced strength of the *haredi* bloc and the failure of Meimad may create a situation that will bring about the alienation of the secular left. [Meimad was the party of moderate and left-of-center *datiim.*]

NOVEMBER 4, 1988

—On the consequences that will follow for education in Israel if it is run by the *dati/haredi* camp: Parents have reason to be anxious in the face of the possibility of the narrowing of our children's horizons.
—The leadership of five American-Jewish organizations: "Accepting the conditions of the *datiim* will cause great damage to our relations and to the relations between Israel and America."

From *Davar:*

NOVEMBER 2, 1988

—"These are the final days of the exile," the hasidim in Brooklyn celebrate.

From *Ma'ariv:*

NOVEMBER 3, 1988

—Mea Shearim celebrates: "You didn't want the 'kosher law'—now you'll get the supervision of our courts."

"You didn't want yeshivas, soon we will buy the buildings on Mount Scopus." [Reference to the Hebrew University.]
—Baba Baruch [an ostensible miracle worker, a revered religious figure for a section of Moroccan Jews]: "I don't want a political post—not even the premiership."
—On the Ben Yehuda Street mall in Jerusalem there is anxiety: "The State is becoming *haredi.*"

"Now we are transforming democracy and a minority will rule over the majority."
—After the *haredi* revolution.
—B'nai B'rak: "We have ceased being a black bloc; now we are equals."

NOVEMBER 14, 1988

—Professor Urbach: "A *dati* society may encourage violence."

NOVEMBER 20, 1988

—A rabbi from B'nai B'rak flees Israel after a company he owns becomes caught up in debts.

NOVEMBER 23, 1988

A yeshiva student suspected of torching a store selling secular newspapers admits: "I use drugs."

From *Yediot Aharonot:*

NOVEMBER 3, 1988

—THE *haredi* revolution: Expect a high price.

—Rabbi Peretz [leader of the religious party Shas Torah Guardians, now the third largest party in the Knesset]: "There will be no 'haredization' of the State."

—The divisions among the *datiim* led to the *haredi* gains.

These headlines, only a very small but in many ways a representative sample of those dealing with the *datiim,* reveal a great deal. First, in most cases they refer to a situation in which the *datiim* seem to be encroaching into the world and lives of the non-*datiim.* The latter, the audience to which the papers are reporting the news, are presented with a sense that the *datiim* are about to affect their existence: they will demand concessions, control education, transform American-Israeli relations and democracy, buy universities, bring about violence. In short, there is a revolution. The image of the *dati* is of an adversary—an image that is made even sharper in the columns and editorial pages which speak of "us" against "them." (See, for example, *Ha'aretz,* November 7, 1988). Moreover, this adversary, often ignored at other times, and whose numbers are small relative to the population at large, is characterized as suddenly having won a great and dramatic victory. The victory and its repercussions are news. They sell newspapers.

Consider some of the charged words and phrases that fill these headlines and characterize the events and their possible impact: extortion, a split in the nation, bring about alienation, narrowing of our children's horizons, damage to internal Jewish and Israel–American relations, transforming democracy, a minority will rule over the majority, revolution, we are not black but equals, encourage violence, haredization of the State, splits. These words and phrases create an impression of an onslaught against the values and way of life of the readers. They imply, as indeed the editorials and feature articles will make far more explicit, a fundamental conflict and opposition between the religious on the one hand and the non-religious on the other.

Moreover, the headlines can even communicate impressions which the stories—the fine print—alter. Thus, the *Davar* headline implies the exile is over and Brooklyn hasidim will soon flood Israel, while the story makes clear that this is only the exclamation of an overly excited hasid. Or, the *Ma'ariv* headline suggests the possibility that the *haredim* are about to buy the Hebrew University and turn it into a yeshiva or force the general population to submit to the kashrut supervision of their courts, while the story makes clear that these are opinions flowing from the unbridled enthusiasm of some anonymous or obscure individual. Similarly, in a story reporting on a *haredi* who was caught with a cache of stolen tear-gas canisters, the Jerusalem local, *Kol Ha'Ir,* notes that "authorities reject the possibility that these materials were accumulated in order to aid the *haredim* in their wars against the secular." But of course to raise this possibility—even if to deny it—in a news report is at once to recall that there is indeed a "war" between the two groups and that the possibility of violence exists.

Quoting someone's opinion, particularly if the person quoted is a major public figure, also becomes news. The headline which consists of a particular dramatic publicly expressed opinion thus circumvents the objections to editorializing or presenting opinions as news. Thus, as cited above, the assertion by Professor Ephraim Urbach (himself a major public figure and an identifiably *dati* Jew) that violence may be an outcome of a *dati* society now becomes a news item. Similarly, the opinions of some American Jewish leaders that the religious parties' demands will cause damage to relations between Israel and America seem to be a fact when in reality they remain for now an opinion. Or, the headline in the November 14th *Jerusalem Post,* "Rabbi Sofer quits in disgust. Sages Council [the governing body of one of the *haredi* parties] 'more like market than like rabbinical gathering'," manages to promote a point of view that the paper's editors consider newsworthy. It allows the paper to subtly indict the Council of Sages under the banner of news.

The headlines can even suggest the prospect of events by indirection. Saying something will *not* occur can, paradoxically, sometimes make it seem more imminent. Thus, *Ma'ariv* reports that the Moroccan holy man, Baba Baruch Abuhatzeira, does *not* want to be prime minister or that Rabbi Peretz does *not* expect the haredization of the state. But these statements plainly raise a possibility in the reader's mind. Why deny these aims, the reader reasons, unless they are conceivable?

In a sense the immediate reactions to the election results seem to have freed the press to express anxieties, fears, and frustrations that at other times linger just below the surface of general public consciousness. Moreover, the "man-bites-dog" nature of journalistic reportage enhances the sense of a dramatic reordering of the normal relationship between the *dati* minority (and the even smaller *haredi* minority) and the public at large. Hence, the effect of the headlines and the stories that follow them is to give the public a feeling that the world they know is turning over: the few will rule the many, horizons will be narrowed, the nation will be split.

Cartoons, although commonly on the editorial pages, can and often do graphically illustrate these underlying images. A cartoon by Moshik in *Davar* on November 15, 1988, is typical. It depicts Prime Minister Yitzhak Shamir receiving a driving lesson. Seated next to him is a *haredi* instructor. The car is stopped at a crosswalk on Coalition Street, while in front of it unbroken streams of presumably secular Israelis are crossing the road. In obvious anger, the *haredi* instructor is turning to Shamir, and screaming: "I said, 'Drive!'" The image of the *haredi* urging the government to run over the public is transparent. Another cartoon, appearing in *Ma'ariv* on November 6, shows a *haredi* seated on the shoulders of Yitzhak Shamir who is dressed as a policeman. The two are chasing a young girl wearing a tank top and shorts who is screaming: "Police, they want to rape me!"

The emphasis on the unexpected which is inherent in journalism is even more clearly apparent in headlines and stories in the community papers, *Kol Ha'Ir* and *Jerusalem*. These papers focus on news and feature articles which are meant to give locals a sense of what is going on in their city. Often this results in stories that provide descriptive, almost anthropological, accounts. But note what these papers choose to chronicle and report when it comes to the *datiim*.

During the period in question *Kol Ha'Ir* reported on the large sums of money available to *haredi* institutions of learning. That story was juxtaposed with one about a yeshiva in Mea Shearim that bought a building in which an aged couple resides and which now requires that couple to climb steep outdoor stairs to their apartment so that their coming and going will not disturb the yeshiva students. It published article after article which chronicled the activities of *haredi* lawbreakers. Thus on November 25, 1988,: "The *haredim* break in again to the Bank Leumi building in Ramot Weiss in violation of the court's injunction." On November 18, 1988, the paper reported the story of a Mea Shearim yeshiva student arrested for illegally importing tear gas. A November 25 story headlined "The dirt of Shas" was in fact a report on the illegal campaign posters that Shas Torah Guardians' supporters had pasted all over the city.

The paper featured a story on the drop-outs from the *dati* world, and published a picture of a young *haredi* apparently staring at a crude photo of an erect penis. It described the ways in which the *haredi* world is becoming undermined by technology and the impact of videos and blue movies which have made illicit entrance into the precincts of the religious.

As for *Jerusalem,* many of its stories echo those in *Kol Ha'Ir.* It too writes of a "violent weekend in Mea Shearim" or that "Many among the 'dead' voted in the polling places of Mea Shearim."

Stories such as these, which describe rabbis absconding with funds or fleeing from debts, yeshiva students using drugs or engaging in violence, "unmask" the *datiim* and deflate their claims of religiosity and implicit moral superiority. That is, the so-called "religious" turn out to be lawbreakers, scum, fractured by quarrels, and thus no better and perhaps even worse than the general population. The picture of the *dati* world that is painted in these papers is one of crime, violence, hypocrisy and schism. For those who might have expected otherwise, this is indeed news. And for those who may be vexed by the religious' assertion of their moral rectitude, it may even be welcome news.

Columns, Editorials, and Feature Articles

The news pages in the secular press present an implicitly unflattering picture of the *datiim,* but the columns, the editorials, and sometimes even the feature stories are far more explicit. Here the commentary and interpretations are often blunt and outspoken.

While it is difficult to categorize all such pieces, and some writing is actually a combination of various types, a review of the treatment of the "religious" sector suggests some general categories of such writing. I call the first type "characterization and analysis." These pieces give the reader a sense of how the writer understands the essential meaning and character—i.e. the nature, qualities, and constitution—of "religious" Jews.

In the aftermath of the elections characterizations and analyses were plentiful, for they expressed a desire to put the unexpected into some coherent framework. They told readers what had happened and with whom they now had to deal. Consider some examples.

Writing in *Ha'aretz* on November 7, 1988, Baruch Bracha characterizes the situation and the goal of the *haredi* parties as follows:

> The *haredi,* anti-Zionist parties are now taking advantage of their parliamentary strength in order to try to force the question of who will have the right to immigrate to the State of Israel, a state whose establishment they so opposed. And the religious-Zionist party co-operates with them . . . [and] dictates its Orthodox world-view to the secular majority in the state.

A similar attitude was taken in several editorials that appeared in *Ha'aretz* during November. On the second of the month, the paper proclaimed: " . . . there is yet another danger: the rise of the *haredi* non-Zionist parties. . . . [and] the extent of the conquest by the spiritual reactionaries." On the fourth, it editorialized that the "strengthening of the religious parties is an especially worrisome phenomenon."

Writing in *Davar* on November 4, 1988, Amir Oren suggested:

> The party which won this week in the Knesset elections is not new. This is "the party of God," or in Arabic "Hizballah."
>
> . . . Rule has passed from the Knesset to the Beit Ha'Knesset [synagogue], and Israel has been made into what Jerusalem has become during the last few years: a *haredi* and Arab state besieging the alienated and shrinking Hebrew majority.

In the same paper, Shimon Weiss asserts that "the great dividing line" between the *datiim* and all the rest of Israeli society "is not only political but cultural and a way of life."

Writing in *Ma'ariv* on November 14, 1988, Hanoch Bartov asserts:

> Every concept of democracy which represents modernity is transformed here [among the *haredim*] to mockery and scorn. [This is because the *haredim* all say:] "What the Council of Torah Sages decides we who fulfill their words shall carry out."

In *Yediot Aharonot* on November 7, 1988, under a heading that reads, "They are conquerors not extortionists," Levi Yitzhak Hayerushalmi writes:

> Those who possess a Torah consciousness have one aim: to establish and maintain the rule of religion in the State of Israel. There are two

> paths to this: the path of isolation or the path of integration. . . . They are militant and know well the ways of war. . . .

What all these characterizations, and the many others like them, share is the effort they make to paint *datiim* of all stripes as different from the mainstream and as seeking to overturn general society. As the *Jerusalem Post*'s editorial on November 7, 1988, puts it: "their aim is to remake Israeli society." Bracha, who draws no distinctions between the religious-Zionists and the *haredim* but sees all as one, characterizes them as striving to take over what is not really theirs. Weiss suggests that they are part of a different culture because they live a different sort of life. The implication is that in some way they are not really Israelis. Oren goes further (as also does Avishai Margalit in *Yediot Aharonot*) in that he equates them with the arch-enemy, the fanatic Hizballah, who besieges and thus attacks the true Israel, the way of life of the majority. This same device of coupling the *haredim* with the Arabs is used in, for example, a piece by Gidon Samet in *Ha'aretz,* in which he refers to the "*haredi* intifada." And in *Ma'ariv* Gabriel Strassman, in an article entitled "Anxiety about the *Haredim,*" suggests the "real threat against the Zionist idea is here in Israel, not in the U.N. or Uganda." Hayerushalmi repeats the image of war, while the title of his piece calls up the other practice commonly associated with the *datiim:* extortion. And Bartov suggest that the *datiim* mock and scorn the way of life his readers presumably hold dear. This is what B. Michael, writing in *Ha'aretz,* calls "the holy evil." But all these characterizations are predicated on the expectation that the readers will interpret the facts as do the columnists and editorialists, that they see matters as "worrisome" and dangerous.

There are also characterizations which are coupled with analysis of a sort. These aim to be even more persuasive because they provide a putative basis for the characterizations. To be sure, the analysis is often *ad hoc,* truncated, or even faulty; but what is important here is that it seems to support the characterization. Some examples follow.

In an article titled "Political Extortion," Ran Kislev writes in *Ha'aretz* on November 6, 1988:

> Until the Ninth Knesset, the division of two-thirds [of the vote for religious parties] for the National Religious Party and one-third for the two *haredi* lists was strictly preserved. The division in the last elections was reversed. [This is because] there are no significant differences between the religious outlook of the National Religious Party of Dr. Shaki [who headed the party's list] and the three *haredi* parties.

On November 10, 1988, writing in the same paper, Boaz Shapira explains that the strategy of the *haredi* parties, and in particular Agudat Yisrael, has always been "a maximum of religion for a minimum of people," and during those same years the goal of the National Religious Party, the more moderate *dati* party, was "a minimum of religion for a maximum of people." Now, he concludes, the strategy of both is "a maximum of religion for a maximum of people."

Showing how powerful and insidious the *haredim* are, Yitzhak Ben-Horin, writing in *Ma'ariv*'s weekend magazine, analyzes the economic punch of "the *haredi* fist" and how it will inexorably affect the economy of the country. Describing the operation of a *haredi* blacklist, the story paints the image of a wealthy religious community using economic muscle to get the rest of society to fall into line. Here, as throughout these analyses, the images of the religious are negative, but, because reasoning is offered, the characterizations may carry greater weight.

A second type of feature story or editorial focuses on implications. It is meant to arouse in the reader an understanding of what follows from the events, what forces have been unleashed. Implications are by definition subtle and indefinite, and I therefore distinguish them from predictions, which tend to be focused and specific. In implications, the writing tends to be more tentative, with the editorialists, columnists, or reporters implying possibilities—and of course planting these in the minds of their readers—without necessarily committing themselves to the absolute accuracy of their observations. Consider these examples.

Dan Margalit, in a November 6 *Ha'aretz* piece headed "The Shrimps are not in Danger," writes about the secularists' anxieties—about their fear that they

> will be forced to wear *tzitzit* or to wrap themselves in a *talit* and say "God willing" when it is necessary and when it is not and to give up the beach and the movies.

Two days earlier in the same paper, Gidon Samet wrote:

> the rise of the reactionary powers among the national-religious cannot, by its nature, occur except with the abasement of the basic rights of the secular population.

Likewise, he anticipates "a difficult struggle over the character of modern Israel." In a similar vein, in *Ha'aretz* on November 7, 1988, Avraham Tal writes of "the *haredi* attack which will threaten the free character of the state." And in an editorial on the eleventh, the paper singles out one of the parties, the Shas Torah Guardians, and says that its demands "cause a schism between Israel and the Diaspora." Similarly the *Jerusalem Post* editorializes, on November 3, that the religious parties "will vie for the lead in wrenching Israel away from its commitment to the Declaration of Independence and into an undertaking to *Halakha*," a process that will necessarily "push forward the process of Israel's theocratization."

These pieces and others like them do not acutally predict specific changes, rather they imply changing realities that the writers believe emerge from a rise in *dati* and *haredi* influence: people will have to maintain a more religious demeanor, the secular population may be required to give up certain freedoms and rights, and the society will be changed.

An even more subtle implication emerges from pieces which supposedly describe the reality and then allow the reader to draw his own conclusions. Thus, for example, Dvorah Getzler, writing in the *Jerusalem Post* and describing the singing of the Hatikvah at the Twelfth Knesset swearing-in, reports that the *haredim* have succeeded in getting the anthem sung by a skullcapped singer and a choir of male voices (without the forbidden voice of woman), but these successes are apparently insufficient. Describing the event, she notes that this year,

> As the crowd's singing of the anthem swelled through the chamber, the *haredim* were conspicuously silent, with Agudat Yisrael's Moshe Feldman covering his face with his large black hat and swaying as though in prayer. Shas's Minister Yitzhak Peretz made his way to the otherwise full cabinet table only after the anthem was sung.

This is a report filled with implication and innuendo which readers can hardly miss. The *haredim* want change even beyond what they have already wrought; they do not identify with those whose voices "swelled the chamber" with the words of Hatikvah.

Some columns and stories, however, go beyond implication and innuendo and openly and specifically predict what will happen. These pieces are didactic and often moralizing. They tell the readers:

here is what happened, but even more importantly here is exactly what is yet to occur. In this way they have the power not only to manage impressions but to foster expectations.

In the aftermath of the elections, predictions were embedded in many a newspaper's second section. Among the many themes that were repeated in a good number of the predictions, two stand out. One was the matter of the religious population time bomb: the *datiim* were having more children than the non-*datiim* and thus they would ultimately outnumber them. In some cases comparisons were drawn with the other antagonistic group that is often also described as representing a population time bomb: the Arabs. The parallel was by no means accidental. It reaffirmed the similarity of the two groups that some fear will overrun the Israeli general public.

The second theme inherent in the predictions was what in numerous columns was called "haredization" and sometimes "khomeinization." These predictions warned of an inescapable process which would ultimately transform Israeli society into a theocratic one ruled by rabbis and the strict dictates of Jewish law. As Gidon Samet, writing about the *datiim* and *haredim* in the November 4 *Ha'aretz,* put it, "what they do not gain now . . . they will try to get later." Or, in the words of Tovah Tzimuki, writing in *Davar* on November 11:

> In the coalition negotiations the religious are trying to gain only amendments to the law. But in the future they will demand more. They will want the rule of the *halakha* [Jewish law] in its fullest sense.

In *Davar* on November 10, Yitzhak Meridor predicts:

> The revolution in education [to be brought about by the religious, who seemed at the time poised to take over the education ministry] will not be swift. They will cut here in science and art and there they will expand the hours for studies in Judaica and the love of Israel.

The writer further predicts that such programs at present part of the school curriculum as education in democracy, tolerance, and coexistence with Arabs will be suspended or eliminated. Instead "the haredization of education will grow stronger, and the process of bringing in yeshiva teachers, 'the black teachers,' to the public religious schools will speed up." The result, says Meridor, will be that students will "learn less English, less chemistry, and less mathematics."

Hanoch Bartov, couching his prognostications in questions, asks rhetorically if in the end the rabbis will also be deciding on matters of peace and war as well as other matters of national consequence.

In *Ma'ariv* on November 8, David Kurzweill predicts:

> we may look forward to extortion in the direction of religious legislation that will cause hatred among brothers and the detachment of people from religion in Israel in the most extreme form possible.

Ephraim Sidon, in a cynical piece in the November 6 *Ma'ariv,* suggests that "the state will move backwards, Zionism will contemplate with wonder how non-Zionist parties [i.e. the *haredim*] will run state matters." Another column meanwhile argues that in the future we shall be distributing tithes of major proportions to the *dati* students of whichever rabbis hold governmental power.

These, of course, are predictions that paint a picture of a society completely dominated by the dark forces of tyranny, by black teachers and rabbis, by anti-intellectuals and extortionists, by those who want to remove the light of science and learning and replace it with religious coercion. Such predictions are enough to strike fear or at least resentment in the heart of any general reader.

To be sure, there is another sort of prediction: to the effect that the *datiim* and *haredim* will be undone. These predictions suggest that they have overreached themselves and will unleash a backlash of resentment against them; or, in other cases—most prominently in the more ethnographic accounts in *Kol Ha'Ir*—they predict that the *haredi* world will be split by its own internal conflicts or by the forces of the outside world which will enter, insidiously, and undermine their isolation and way of life. Of course, coming as they do in the general-circulation press, these predictions are not intended as warnings for the religious as much as they are meant as words of hope and promise for the general reader who may be feeling overwhelmed. These predictions say, in short: "Fear not; we the majority shall win in the end."

Another type of column or feature story is written in the form of a background piece. It is meant to provide readers with a kind of journalistic interpretation of the factors which account for the current realities. Generally, background pieces take the form of popular history, sociology, anthropology, or psychology. But, unlike the academic versions of these disciplines, journalistic background pieces may inject a far more sharply focused—even demagogic—

point of view into their writing. This kind of writing generally makes its way into the magazine inserts but it may also be the substance of an extended column. Here the writer shows that he is really an expert on the matters in question because he knows what are the real antecedents of the phenomenon. Of course, these background pieces are really interpretations, for they choose to highlight certain factors while glossing over others. These choices thus often serve (sometimes inadvertently) to slant the coverage. Consider some examples:

Adar Avishar, writing in the November 16 *Ma'ariv,* quotes a source that suggests that:

> the religious parties try to calm the public telling them they will not undermine their rights, but what the public does not know is that the impositions and threats began long before the results of the elections were known.

An editorial in the November 24 *Ha'aretz* observes that "for years the National Religious Party and the *haredi* parties have been carrying on a culture war in Israel."

In a long interview with Moshe Horowitz, who is writing a book on Rabbi Eliezer Schach, the leader of the Lithuanian *haredim, Kol Ha'Ir* columnist Shachar Ilan quotes the view that "the Lithuanian opinion is that when a yeshiva boy in the Ponovetz yeshiva learns [Torah] better, he saves from conversion a Jewish student in Paris who is about to assimilate." Elsewhere in the article Ilan points out that Rabbi Schach's son has a Ph.D. in philosophy, adding with tongue in cheek, "may it not happen to us." This is background framed in irony, which serves to at once provide information and to nourish particular images which are less than flattering. Similarly, Aviva Lurie writes about *haredi* faith-healers who turn out to be charlatans.

Supplying insights into the various streams of the *dati* world, Levi Yitzhak Hayerushalmi in *Ma'ariv*'s November 25 weekend supplement notes, "the secular Jews—even in a thousand years—will not know or learn how to hate the *haredim* as the members of the *haredi* camps hate one another." To support his assertion, he proceeds to tell the story of a broken marriage agreement that resulted from two families following the dictates of opposing rabbis. He quotes a variety of *haredi* sources, adding: "the internal dispute—as many believe—may halt the process of those who are returning to the faith." This, he goes on to explain, is of great significance, since

> The returnees to the faith, who in their first steps were accepted with some suspicion, represent today an important prize. They have brought about a change in *haredi* Judaism. They have familiarized *haredim* with the outside world without their having to enter into that world.

This knowledge of the non-*dati* world that the *haredim* have, a knowledge that Hayerushalmi presents as part of sociological background, can be unsettling for the non-*dati* reader who already has been aroused by the victory of the religious parties and its impact on his way of life. Indeed, as if to make certain that these readers will not miss the point, Hayerushalmi goes further and adds:

> "We enjoy an advantage today over the secular Jews," an outstanding *haredi* personality said to me. "The secular Jews perhaps know something about us, but they don't perceive us. . . . They see us [from only one side] as strangers, peculiar, different, eccentric, idle, retarded, something from another world. But we perceive *them* today in their totality: not [only] from the newspapers and not from gossip. The returnees to the faith have brought us much knowledge. To many among us there are strong ties with the secular Jews. We visit them, come to them, appear in their circles and their institutions. . . .

Hayerushalmi concludes with the stark piece of background information that now drops like a bomb on his readers: in 1948 there were about fifty yeshivas—today there are over six hundred, with more than 40,000 students, increasing by about 1300 to 1500 students per year. The background information is chilling: THEY are growing.

The final type of column or feature is best categorized as a recommendation which, at its extreme, borders on anguish. In the aftermath of the 1988 elections newspaper columnists made a variety of recommendations. Not all of them slanted the reader's view of the *dati* world. But some did. Many expressed a conviction that the *dati,* or more particularly the *haredi,* way of life and world-view must be counteracted. Sometimes the case was made in an essentially dispassionate tone. At other times the stand taken was more vigorous, as for example in the November 7 *Ha'aretz.* Here Natan Donvitz describes among other things what he believes will (or should) be the Israeli soldiers' reaction to the *dati* in the elections:

> We shall not serve in the occupied territories as long as the representatives of the thousands of *haredi* yeshiva draft-dodgers serve in the government. We do not serve the black powers.

Finally, beyond vigorous stands are columns which I can only call "cries from the heart." These are more impassioned than the most emotional recommendations. They are written roars that express—sometimes in tones verging on hysteria—feelings that seem to come from deep inside the writer and seek to touch something deep inside the reader. These are pieces which are highly emotive. An editorial in the *Jerusalem Post,* headlined "the Threat is Real," which laments the desire of several of the *dati* members of the new Knesset to press for clemency for the convicted Jewish murderers of Arabs, has something of this quality of a *cri du cœur*.

However, perhaps no single column better exemplifies this than one by Amnon Denker in the November 4, 1988, issue of *Davar*. He writes in the first flush after the elections, when the orthodox and ultra-orthodox parties were still celebrating their unexpected victories, when the general public was shocked, and when anxieties were freshest. Although it is really people who probably share Denker's views who will read these words, his piece directly addresses the *haredim* (who, as already noted, were unlikely to read his column):

> . . . But you do not leave me alone, for you are in the government and have power. All right, then what is left for me to do, in order to protect my soul so as not to be harmed by you, is to be your antagonist and enemy. To ban and to curse. I want no dialogue with you for I have nothing to say to you. I want no part of you. For me, you are banished and outcasts. You are anti-school and anti-hospitals and anti-universities and anti-science, anti-literature, and anti-theater, anti all that is dear to me. From today on, I will not speak to you, I will only speak about you, and only evil. We must battle against you every day in every place. You are perhaps strong, but we are after all the majority and we shall be victorious, for this is the only state we have: while for you what does it matter from whence they send your identity cards which you counterfeit for voting purposes? I will protect my soul and the souls of my children from you, from your evil, primitive, mindlessly brainwashed spirit. I will speak and write against you in every place, because you are the greatest danger to my existence here.

This is a cry from the heart that draws the battle lines, fires up the readers, makes news, and sells newspapers. It is of course extreme. It evokes all the anxieties of the non-*datiim* and represents the worst fears that *haredim* harbor about their treatment in the secular press. And it is totally unforgettable reading.

Conclusion

While it is clear that the secular press views the *datiim* from the point of view of an outsider, and while it also is true that as an outsider it is often less than sympathetic to or understanding of the positive elements of these forms of Judaism, it would be a mistake to infer from all the evidence cited above that there is necessarily a malevolent motive behind this coverage. Rather, as I suggested at the outset, the general press writes for the majority. In Israel that majority is not particularly interested or prepared to read about why people choose to be *dati* in one way or another or what their religion means to them. These questions are too nuanced and parochial for the general press. Its readers want to know why the man bit the dog, they want to see the dramatic changes, and they want to be confirmed in their own way of life. All this means that, to learn something about the internal nature of Orthodox Judaism, one needs often to look at sources other than the daily newspaper. But that, of course, is old news.

Naomi Gutkind-Golan

4

The Heikhal Cinema Issue

A Symptom of Religious–Non-Religious Relations in the 1980s

THE BATTLE over the opening of the Heikhal movie theater on the Sabbath contained most of the elements that lie at the heart of the struggle between religious and non-religious Jews over the nature of Israeli society. Conflicts over the opening of other entertainment facilities on Shabbat took place during this same period. Examples include the "Shabatarbut," a series of semi-popular cultural events that take place on Saturday mornings in the Habima Theater in Tel Aviv, the "Pishpeshuk," a flea market situated along a major highway, the screening of films in Bet Agron (the office of the press services) in Jerusalem, the operating of a cable-car service to a look-out point in Haifa, and the use of the soccer stadium in Ramat Gan. But it was the opening of the Heikhal cinema in Petah Tikva which garnered front-page headlines and the lion's share of television coverage month after month. Part of the reason had to do with the public's perception that what was taking place in the small street outside the Heikhal cinema was a major confrontation about basic principles of religion and state. Part of the reason rested on the peculiarities of the media coverage, to which we shall return.

We will recount the details of the Heikhal saga in the first section of the essay. The next section analyzes the role of the fourth estate, which, like a Greek chorus, contributed elements of its own, stoked public passions, and never confined its reportage to a dry presentation of facts. The third section, based on interviews with sixteen prominent Petah Tikva personages, describes their view of the political, cultural, and social meaning of the conflict. In the final section I offer my own summary.

What Actually Happened

In the municipal elections of October 1983, Dov Tabori, candidate of the Labor Alignment, was elected mayor of Petah Tikva with a decisive majority. The religious public split its vote among four separate slates. Anecdotal evidence suggests that some even voted for Tabori in protest against the local branch of the National Religious Party (NRP), and its leader, Avraham Marmorstein. Tabori was supported by two local groups in addition to the Labor Alignment. They campaigned for him promising that he would "open up the city for us," a reference to the expectation that places of public entertainment and leisure would be opened on Shabbat.

Not only was Tabori elected mayor but his Labor Alignment slate won a sufficient number of seats on the municipal council to form a majority without requiring the help of the religious parties. At his inauguration he promised that "those residents of Petah Tikva who wish to see movies on Friday nights will not need to travel to Tel Aviv."

In response, Marmorstein announced that the National Religious Party would not join the majority coalition; and leading public figures of the Likud, the NRP, Agudat Israel, and Poalei Agudat Israel established a Committee for the Observance of the Sabbath which conducted most of the activity on behalf of what this essay refers to as the religious front or the religious public.

The response of the religious public did not faze the new mayor. In a letter to the management of the Heikhal cinema, he indicated that he would not oppose their showing movies on Friday nights even though this would be in violation of a municipal bylaw.

As the date of the first screening, February 24, 1984, approached, posters signed by the two chief rabbis of Petah Tikva, Rabbi Baruch Shimon Salomon and Rabbi Moshe Malka, called upon the public to join in a public demonstration against the desecration of the Sabbath in the city.

An estimated ten thousand local residents heeded the call. It was the largest demonstration ever held in the history of Petah Tikva and it united all the religious factions from religious-Zionist to *haredi*. Inside the theater the movie was shown without disturbance.

The following Friday and in the weeks that followed many hundreds and sometimes thousands of religious Jews in Petah Tikva and neighboring Bnei Brak established a new Sabbath ritual. After the Friday-night meal they would walk to the Heikhal cinema square to demonstrate against the screening of movies. They were confronted by a much smaller group of non-religious people, generally fewer than fifty, and the police endeavoring to keep the groups apart.

The demonstrations, however, had no effect, and the religious front extended its battle to new arenas. In March 1984, the chief rabbis of Petah Tikva burst into a municipal council session in order to protest the desecration of the Sabbath. Their followers and supporters engaged in altercations with municipal ushers. This had no apparent influence on anybody. The chief rabbis invited the Mayor to a discussion in order to convince him of their position. Bnei Akiva, the religious-Zionist youth movement, proposed a public discussion and debate. The representatives of the religious women in the city, led by the rabbis' wives and other activists, sent a special delegation to see the Mayor. None of these efforts met with success, and religious leaders now sought to pressure Tabori through their national political connections.

Avraham Shapira, a leader of Agudat Israel, and Shimon Peres, leader of the Labor Party, invited Tabori to meet with them. Peres was anxious to enlist Agudat Israel's support for the Labor Party by demonstrating that his party was not anti-religious and had the power to offer real assistance to religious parties. Whatever pressure he sought to bring to bear on Tabori was to no avail. Tabori announced that he was willing to resign if the head of his party, Shimon Peres, asked him to do so, but he would not retreat from his principles. Peres could hardly issue such a request in view of the fact that Tabori had turned into the darling of the media. Tabori, in turn, emphasized the ideological nature of his battle. In one lengthy interview he exclaimed:

> The struggle with the *haredim* will be remembered throughout the generations as a battle for the opening of the city, which was, as it

> were, besieged by the Sabbath. This is a struggle over democracy. The religious twenty percent wish to impose the Sabbath on the eighty percent who are non-religious.

Avraham Marmorstein's reaction, "in Petah Tikva forty percent of the people are religious, and not twenty percent," hardly changed the general perception of Tabori as the champion of individual rights. The demonstrations in Petah Tikva won international as well as major national coverage, especially when pictures began appearing of policemen in physical confrontation with *haredim,* identifiable by their distinctive dress.

Professor Ze'ev Low, a prominent religious scientist and member of the government committee to limit employment exemptions on the Sabbath, now proposed that the religious front change its tactics. Since operating the cinema, he argued, was against local municipal bylaws, the appropriate instrument for the religious front was the courts. A complaint was lodged, and the Mayor responded by convening the municipal council to amend the city's bylaws. The amended bylaw empowered the mayor to permit the opening of a commercial enterprise or place of entertainment on the Sabbath if he found that it was in the public interest to do so.

Israeli law requires that municipal bylaws be approved by the Minister of the Interior. The amendment was therefore forwarded to the Minister of the Interior, Dr. Joseph Burg, who was also the leader of the National Religious Party. Burg refused to approve it.

Meanwhile, a hearing was held before Judge Shelley Timan on the request of the religious front that the court issue a cease-and-desist order against the Heikhal cinema. The city's rabbis and the members of its religious council claimed that: *(a)* the operation of the cinema on the Sabbath violated municipal bylaws and the laws regarding rest on Sabbaths and festivals of the State of Israel; *(b)* the amendment to the municipal bylaw had not been approved by the Ministry of the Interior; and *(c)* Rabbi Moshe Malka, the chief Sephardic rabbi of Petah Tikva, lived in the vicinity of the cinema, and the screening of films on Friday nights disturbed his rest.

During this period related developments attracted further attention to the controversy. Rabbi Yaakov Shlomo Friedman, a ninety-year-old resident, the rabbi of the Berlin community immediately after the Holocaust and the recipient of an Honored Citizen award from the city of Petah Tikva, returned his certificate of honorary citizenship in protest against the opening of the Heikhal on the Sabbath; five false bomb threats against the municipal building and the Heikhal cinema were received; Moetzet Gedolei HaTorah—the supreme rabbinic authority of the Agudat Israel movement—called for a mass prayer meeting in "Sabbath Square" in Jerusalem, and Tabori stated:

> Why do they accuse me of being the first to violate the Sabbath in Petah Tikva, when during the time of Pinhas Shtampfer, the first mayor, who was a religious man, the cafés were open on the Sabbath, and I myself danced in them on Friday nights when I was young? . . .

But it was the isolated and probably inevitable occasions of violence in the course of the weekly demonstrations that captured most of the public attention. The first such incident occurred when Police Superintendent Barda, in command of the police on duty at the demonstrations, arrested the Ashkenazi chief rabbi, Baruch Salomon, along with a number of *haredi* students on charges of causing a disturbance. At that time Minister of the Interior Burg was also serving as Minister of Police, and he ordered the immediate release of the rabbi and the students. Superintendent Barda resigned in protest.

The photograph of Rabbi Salomon wearing a *tallit* (prayer shawl) as he left the police station was published in Israel under the caption, "This is the man whose arrest threatens an entire government" (Agudat Israel had threatened to resign from the government unless the rabbi was released). Salomon was carried off on the shoulders of his supporters, who sang: "Long live our master and rabbi!"

The accumulating tensions concerned Labor Party leaders, who were preparing for the forthcoming national elections in November 1984 and were especially anxious to resolve their differences with the religious parties. The Labor Party leader, Motta Gur, reminded his colleagues that the Rabin government had fallen less than ten years earlier over a Sabbath issue. Tabori, under pressure from his party colleagues, offered a compromise to the city's rabbis: tickets to the Friday-evening performances would only be sold prior to the onset of the Sabbath and not after the Sabbath began. Israel's chief rabbis favored the compromise, but the Petah Tikva rabbis rejected it, influenced no doubt by a telephone-call from the *Rebbe* of Gur who insisted that they stand firm.

The success scored by the cinema persuaded owners of various other businesses to try their luck. Moshe Eliyahu, the owner of the Gan Eden café, opened his doors on the Sabbath, and when Rabbi

Salomon walked in and protested, he said: "I have debts, and it's a pity to lose the receipts of the seventh day." The rabbi promised help. The next day, Moshe Eliyahu appeared at the offices of the rabbinate and asked for $30,000 to cover his debts. He had no bank guarantees and his request was rejected. The following week, his café was again opened. Rabbi Salomon and his disciples arrived to protest, bottles flew, the police were summoned, and the media had a field day.

The national character of the Petah Tikva conflict was further highlighted by the guests whom each side invited to participate in the Friday-night demonstration. Each week, one of the chief rabbis of an Israeli city or the head of an advanced yeshivah would arrive to express his support publicly for the demonstrators. The non-religious circles invited guest stars on their behalf, including Penina Rosenbloom, something of an Israeli sex symbol, a heroine of Tel Aviv night life.

In April 1984 the advocates of Sabbath openings planned a mass protest of their own on the Sabbath with the participation of Israeli singing star Shalom Hanoch. Hanoch announced that "only a Supreme Power will prevent me from appearing." The 1,300 tickets printed for the event were sold within a week. But Shalom Hanoch then excused himself from appearing with the statement that he had "no desire to mix into a political struggle." Perhaps he was subject to the same pressures as those of which Dov Tabori complained. The Mayor told the media that his house had been swamped by telephone messages threatening his life.

Another incident at the time which earned media publicity was the exchange of correspondence between the Mayor and Professor Shmuel Kantrowitz. Kantrowitz, a religious academic who lived in Petah Tikva, was angry at what he considered an excessively high water bill. In a letter to Tabori about the bill, he added sarcastically: "I hope the Mayor will spare some time from his war against our holy Sabbath in order to increase the efficiency of municipal services to the public." The Mayor responded with a hope that "when after 120 years you lie in hell, you will remember that courtesy precedes Torah."

The press, radio, and television all quoted the exchange of letters. In excusing himself Tabori explained that he was the victim of a character-assassination campaign. His letter-box was full of abusive mail. Cars with loudspeakers drove past his house screaming, "Hitler, Himmler, you belong in an insane asylum." It was hard for him to preserve his equanimity. Tabori also threatened to organize a retaliatory campaign against the chief rabbis, including threats, harassment, and intimidation. He never carried out his threats.

In addition to staging the Friday-night demonstrations, the religious front invited distinguished rabbinical figures to deliver lectures on the steps of the Petah Tikva municipal building during the week. The police arrested a number of rabbis in attendance, claiming that they were disturbing public peace. All the rabbinic courts and religious councils in the State then went on strike for a full day in protest against the arrest.

The need to arrive at an understanding with the police became acute. The heads of the religious public held conciliation talks with Commander Gabi Amir, head of the Central Command of the police. The Commander now declared that no more than five hundred people would be permitted to demonstrate and only at times agreed to in advance by the police. He later reduced the number from five hundred to fifty, claiming that the protests were exhausting the police and forcing them to violate the Sabbath.

In May 1984, Petah Tikva continued to attract international attention. The film *Yentl* was to have been shown at the Heikhal cinema but was withdrawn by order of Barbra Streisand, who was visiting Israel at the time.

The religious public again renewed its legal struggle. Three lawyers representing its interests asked the Supreme Court of Israel to issue an injunction closing the Heikhal cinema. Judges S. Levin and S. Netanyahu rejected the request, but ordered that Tabori show cause within twenty days as to why he had not exercised his authority to stop the screening of movies on Shabbat in violation of municipal bylaws. The Mayor could, for example, have sent municipal supervisors to impose fines on the cinema. Avraham Ber, counsel for the Mayor, responded that municipal inspectors would indeed impose fines on the Heikhal cinema. The religious public saw this promise as the first victory in its struggle. Ber then announced that "the city supervisory department does not want to work on the Sabbath," and Tabori added, "does the religious public want me to force the supervisors to desecrate the Sabbath and to issue summonses on the Sabbath in order to close businesses on the Sabbath?"

The stormy protests resumed. Superintendent Barda, who had withdrawn his resignation, categorized them as illegal, and ordered the police to disperse the protesters by force. Following the establishment of a new national government after the 1984 Knesset elections, the Labor Party representative Haim Bar-Lev assumed responsibilities as Minister of Police and the police adopted a tougher stance toward the demonstrators. A number of protesters were dragged onto police vehicles, while those around them screamed, "it is forbidden to travel on the Sabbath."

The demonstrators, in turn, broke agreements reached with the police about the location of the demonstrations and the times of assembly. Instances of the pursuit of religious demonstrators by the police multiplied as inevitably some of the demonstrators, elderly rabbis among them, fell or were pushed to the ground. The religious front was disturbed by the dangerous turn of events and announced their wish to avoid "confrontation with the Israeli police." The police, however, claimed that when demonstrators shouted "Nazis" at them, this was a form of intolerable abuse.

Temporary calm was restored by the decision of the Heikhal management, responding to demands of the Mayor, to refurbish the theater. The Golan-Globus company, which had entered into partnership with the cinema, closed it for over a year, to reopen in April 1986.

In March 1986, large advertisements called upon the public to view the refurbished Heikhal cinema, the pride of movie theaters in Israel. New screens, upholstered chairs, and some of the most modern projection equipment in the world had been installed at a cost of two million dollars. In response, dozens of rabbis and activists met in Rabbi Salomon's home for a "war council."

On April 2, 1986, the Heikhal reopened in the presence of Knesset members, mayors, members of the film industry, and directors. All the tickets for the première performance were sold out. In the square outside the Heikhal religious Jews demonstrated, and opposite them stood two left-wing Knesset members, Yair Tzaban and Yossi Sarid, with a handful of supporters.

The police were anxious to prevent a recurrence of Friday-night demonstrations which required them to mobilize dozens of policemen on extra duty. Consequently, they refused to issue any demonstration permits. The religious front went to court. The police representatives claimed that the police simply did not have sufficient manpower to supply permanent policing each Friday night outside Heikhal. The court ruled that permits for mass demonstrations were to be issued for seven consecutive weeks. After that the police need only issue permits for symbolic demonstrations with fewer than fifty participants.

Within the religious community itself, the demonstrations had lost much of their popularity. Part of the reason may have been exhaustion on the part of the demonstrators, part of the reason may have had to do with the questionable legality of the demonstrations and the attendant violence, and part of the reason may have had to do with the questionable consequences of the demonstrations. The National Executive of Bnei Akiva forbad its members to participate in the demonstrations. Rabbi Moshe Malka, the chief Sephardic rabbi, ruled that demonstrations on the Sabbath were forbidden, because they led to more desecration of the Sabbath than observance. According to Rabbi Malka:

> The police mobilize patrol cars and walkie-talkies, television crews report, Jews turn on their television sets on the Sabbath to see what the demonstration was like. Who is responsible for all this, if not we ourselves, by supplying the raw material?

Most of the Sephardic rabbis in Israel and a number of Ashkenazic rabbis indicated their sympathy for Malka's position.

At this point a new group, "Academics for the Preservation of the Values of Judaism," composed of about fifty religious professors and scientists, was formed. The group felt that an information and persuasion campaign ought to be mounted and directed at the nonreligious public. The leaders of the group composed their own manifesto, in which they explained that the struggle over the Heikhal cinema was a struggle over the preservation of basic Jewish values in accordance with the law. The religious academics offered to elaborate or debate their position in front of any group who would invite them. But their announcement drew no response.

The views of Rabbi Malka and the religious academics were not shared by the entire religious public. Rabbi Baruch Salomon and his loyalists continued their demonstrations with reinforcements of *haredim* from neighboring Bnei Brak. The weekly visits from prominent rabbis and heads of yeshivot continued.

These demonstrations, which were unlicensed, drew sharp responses. At the end of June 1986, Rabbi Haim Walkin of Petah Tikva and Rabbi Baruch Salomon were both fined and given conditional prison terms for "illegal assembly." The local police force announced that its members were on the verge of revolting. They were not prepared to come to the cinema each Friday night. But the number of demonstrators declined from week to week until no more than fifty people could be expected to attend. The lawyers for the demonstrators sought to infuse new life into the struggle by arguing that Judge

Shelley Timan was disqualified from judging demonstrators brought before him on the ground that he was biased. Their appeal was rejected.

After three years of stubborn struggle, 78 demonstrations and two arrests, Rabbi Baruch Salomon resigned as chief rabbi of Petah Tikva, acknowledging that public support for his leadership of the campaign for the Sabbath had dwindled markedly. He later withdrew his resignation, but he was unable to renew the struggle against the Heikhal.

The Committee for the Observance of the Sabbath, which had incurred thousands of dollars' worth of debts, submitted a dozen court claims and appeals to the Supreme Court, financed hundreds of posters, printed receipt-books for a public fund-raising campaign, and hired lawyers, was no longer able to obtain services because rumors abounded that its treasury was empty.

The Sabbath demonstrations ceased at the end of 1987. The Heikhal cinema continued to function on the Sabbath. The threat by the religious public that this might lead to civil war proved groundless. Religious and non-religious citizens continued to remain friends, in spite of the lengthy and dramatic struggle. Only a handful of the most zealous continued to compose plans for a renewal of the struggle, with the hope that the Knesset elections at the end of 1988 would add new fuel and provide new resources for it.

The Fourth Estate Enters the Fray

The media played a critical role in the Heikhal conflict. Rarely has a dispute in one of the smaller cities been given such extensive coverage in the national press. The zeal of the local reporters, as one of the most avid among them, Bruriah Attar of *Yediot Aharonot,* admitted, was based not only on their evaluation of the national importance of the event, but also on what they perceived as their chances of getting bylines on the front pages. Those who were used to seeing their names near the bottom of the last page were intoxicated by the opportunity to see their names at the top of the first page. "This stimulated us to seek more and more juicy stories that would justify having them printed in a prominent place and would improve our status within the newspapers," said Attar.

By chance, when the Heikhal story first broke, the major newspapers in Israel had just assigned new reporters to the city, and these reporters saw the conflict as an opportunity to enhance their own careers. When there was no "action," they made it their job to generate excitement. For example, reporters asked the television crews to direct their floodlights at *haredim,* readily identifiable by their black dress. That infuriated the *haredim,* who raised their fists and shouted "Shabbes," the Yiddish equivalent of the Sabbath. This, in turn, became a newsworthy incident. According to Rabbi Baruch Salomon, the reporters not only fanned the flames, but distorted facts. They accused him of raising his hand against a policeman, something which he says he never did. This led him to break off all relations with the media, an act which may have compounded the injury to his cause. The sense of outrage which the religious leaders felt toward the media was fed by Bruriah Attar's report, following the first demonstration, that "many hundreds had participated." The religious public was convinced that the true number was closer to ten thousand. Asked why she had underestimated the number of demonstrators, Attar answered with feigned innocence, "doesn't 'hundreds' also include 'thousands'?" But she admitted that most journalists felt that the movie house should be open on the Sabbath, and this attitude was reflected in their reports.

Nevertheless, the religious demonstrators, Rabbi Salomon to the contrary, continued to seek media coverage. Attar explains that even those *haredim* who hid their faces when the television cameras were pointed at them, or who had never spoken to a strange woman in their lives, called her at home to tell her in advance exactly when and where the next demonstration would take place. When her paper printed that hundreds had participated in the demonstration, rather than the many thousands, they were all furious at her. "They called me a troublemaker and a hater of Israel, but when the next Friday rolled around they telephoned to tell me where they would demonstrate." Some of the religious demonstrators who never read the secular press were able to recite by heart every section that had been written about them in the papers, and knew the reporters by their names and nicknames.

Haim Tovihu, the reporter for the religious weekly *Erev Shabbat,* sensed a clearly anti-religious atmosphere among the reporters who tended to congregate in one corner where the demonstrations took place. The reporters came to the demonstration as if they had just received a briefing by the Mayor's spokesman, he observed. Another religious observer notes that even reporters who were not present on a particular Friday evening would have articles under their byline in the Sunday paper which included details about the demonstration clearly unfavorable to the religious position. "They simply fabricated stories," says this observer. But Bruriah Attar offered a different explanation. After spending weeks together in the square in front of the cinema on Friday evenings, a certain collegiality developed among the reporters, and a reporter who was unable to come because of health or other reasons would receive a report of the demonstration by phone from a colleague on a different newspaper, sometimes even from a competing one. This might not be quite in keeping with professional ethics, but these are the facts of life, she noted.

In order to persuade the media to present a more balanced picture, the organization of religious academics held a press conference in Beit Sokolow in Tel Aviv. According to Dr. Meier Shneider, the reporters were hostile from the very outset. Instead of asking questions they delivered their own speeches. They weren't interested in what the religious public had to say, they wanted to let us know what they thought, he claimed. And following this rather unpleasant confrontation the press conference got three lines in the next day's paper.

Micha Yinon, chairman of the Broadcasting Authority, is a religious Jew. Efforts to persuade him to exert a moderating influence on the television reports also failed. Those who approached him reported him as saying that the television editors supported the opening of the cinema on the Sabbath and would not provide the other side with any broadcasting time. There were also attempts at persuading the local reporters to moderate their stories. Some of them claimed that their reports were objective and that it was the editorial staffs who added bombastic and anti-religious headlines to the stories.

The cartoonists who dealt with the Heikhal controversy portrayed the demonstrators as *haredim* instead of acknowledging that many religious-Zionists also took part in the protest. Cartoons depicted the demonstrators as dressed in black, wearing traditional *haredi* garb, even though more than half of the demonstrators wore conventional suits, white shirts, and knitted *kipot,* identifying them as religious-Zionists.

Similarly, when new photographers sought photogenic scenes, they focused their lenses primarily on the white batons of the police, with a background of the black garb of *haredim.* On one occasion Rabbi Salomon tripped and fell, and a half-page photograph of the rabbi sprawled on the ground appeared on the front pages of the Israeli press.

The religious public also exploited such pictures. According to one of the news photographers present when Rabbi Salomon fell, a number of young *haredi* men came to his photo laboratory the next day and purchased prints of the event. These prints appeared the following week in *Time* and in the Jewish newspapers throughout the world as evidence of "police brutality."

The religious press generally treated the Heikhal story more soberly than the non-religious press. It is true that expressions such as "they are beheading the Sabbath" or "the police lie consistently to the media" appeared, but there was no concerted attempt, as there was by the non-religious press, to provoke the parties involved.

The most blatant example of this provocation appeared in *Maariv* in July 1986, under the headline "Watch out, Salomon." According to the reporter, the demonstrators

> . . . lost in the streets, lost in the courts, lost in the municipal council, and there are a number of unsavory hooligans in Rabbi Salomon's army who, should they fall into my hands or into those of another reporter covering the demonstrations, would be killed, and neither Rabbi Salomon nor God in Heaven would help them.

The only defense one can offer on behalf of the reporter is that he wrote this piece after fifty demonstrations and fifty Friday nights which he had been unable to spend with his family.

The Meaning of the Conflict

The battle over the Sabbath in Petah Tikva ended in victory for the non-religious. Some of the religious comfort themselves with the thought that "the flood was halted." "Had it not been for our struggle," says Rabbi Salomon, "the other movie houses and cafés would also have opened on the Sabbath."

There are, therefore, different assessments of the outcome of the conflict. It is not surprising that sharp differences of opinion also emerged over the meaning and significance of the struggle. Was the Heikhal controversy the expression of a *Kulturkampf* or was it, perhaps, something more prosaic?

The Heikhal Controversy as the Expression of a Kulturkampf

According to Rabbi Baruch Salomon, the struggle which he headed was not an isolated event but a link in a process in which more and more breaches of Sabbath observance in public and by public institutions have emerged. This process, he believes, is fueled by a growing ignorance of Judaism. According to Rabbi Salomon:

> A new generation arose in Israel that did not know Joseph [i.e. was ignorant of its roots], that did not know the taste of a proper Jewish Sabbath, whose educators did not explain to it the nature and importance of the day . . . The representatives of this youth were the ones who breathed down the neck of Dov Tabori, and complained that the city was "closed" on the Sabbath, was boring, and was diaspora-like. In the 1940s and 1950s the Labor and leftist activists at least remembered their youth. Avraham Herzfeld [a prominent labor figure] visited the Yeshiva of Rabbi Kahaneman [*haredi* yeshivah in Bnei Brak] and reminisced about his studies in the Mir Yeshiva. President Zalmạn Shazar [former president of Israel] would visit the Hebron Yeshiva on Kol Nidrei night to hear the stirring message of the Yeshiva head. The activists of the left, the right, and the religious camp shared a common cultural basis. This disappeared from public life when a new generation grew up which had no Jewish background. Today they are opposed to the Sabbath and tomorrow they will attempt to abolish marriage and divorce according to *halakhah*. The young generation is not willing to pay a price for living together with the religious public; a price which, as its parents understood, had to be paid. We need strong and wise Israeli leaders who understand that a *Kulturkampf* is liable, Heaven forbid, to lead to two nations in the State.

Rabbi Moshe Malka, the Sephardic chief rabbi of Petah Tikva, supports the view that the conflict over the Heikhal represented a stage in a *Kulturkampf,* adding another factor—the waning of what he considers to be Zionism. But note his very special definition of the term:

> The desecration of the Sabbath is putting out the fire of Zionism, which is barely glimmering. My Zionism was expressed in my fierce desire to move to the Land of Israel in order to honor the Sabbath and festivals and to fulfill the laws dependent on the Land [those religious laws which can only be fulfilled in the land of Israel]. If they prevent me from doing this, what business do I have being here? The only chance to change matters is by effective religious persuasion which will convince the non-religious population of the importance and sanctity of the Sabbath. If we can persuade the non-religious that we are interested in their welfare and not only ours in the battle for the Sabbath, they will believe us.

The conflict we are describing stems in part from mutual distrust, but more significantly from varied interpretations of the nature of Israeli society and the requisites of Jewish culture. Dov Tabori attributes the Petah Tikva conflict to the revolution which has taken place in recreational patterns, in leisure-time activities, and in the interpretation given to the term "culture":

> The idea of recreation has become central in the life of the non-religious Israeli family in the 1980s. Cafés, movie houses, and entertainment have become an integral part of the Sabbath. Tel Aviv, which is close by, with its scores of entertainment facilities open on the Sabbath, has created a new norm of leisure-time activity. I could not ignore these. . . . In the previous generation, there were few stimuli available—no radio, no video, no television. Had the religious public appreciated the cultural change which is taking place in the country and come to terms with it, there would have been communication rather than confrontation.

Tabori noted that such communication took place between, for example, Rabbi Maimon, Israel's first Minister of Religion, and his good friend and associate David Ben-Gurion. According to the Mayor:

> Rabbi Maimon, in order to obtain the *status quo* agreement which he fashioned with Ben-Gurion, agreed to compromises and concessions in the religious sphere. Today, after tens of talks which I held with rabbis and Hasidic leaders, I am convinced that the religious public is not willing to recognize the facts of life in the State, namely that this is a non-religious state, that the religious public is in retreat, that the temptations of the street culture and of entertainment are enormous, and that no demonstration, explanation, or political tactic will halt the process. On the contrary, I told Rabbi Salomon, "all the schools of Petah Tikva are open to you. Go and persuade our youth not to attend the cinema. After all, if there are no patrons, Heikhal will close on its own, and no one will complain about religious coercion."

Tabori felt that no amount of religious explanation would be able to change the cultural climate. He pointed out that the five-day work week which is likely to be introduced within a short time in Israel would enhance the importance of entertainment and increase pressure for opening establishments on the Sabbath. Tabori's hope is for the emergence of a new group of religious leaders able to shape a new *status quo.* If the religious public persists in its extremism, he feels, they will lose more and more ground in Israeli society.

Avraham Oren, a lawyer and the leader of a local group which organized to support Tabori in the municipal elections, offers a similar explanation. In the 1960s, he notes, Friday evenings were spent attending private parties in the homes of friends. In the 1970s entertainment patterns changed and people sought out the discothèques, live performances, and movies. Neighboring Tel Aviv became the center of Sabbath entertainment in Israel. The precedent this created, he says, taught us that one can enjoy a non-religious culture openly and on the Sabbath. The fact is that, in Tel Aviv, the religious public came to terms with it. They attended synagogue while the others went to the movie theaters, and there was no reason, Oren says, this couldn't be the same in Petah Tikva.

Pinhas Hagin, a representative of the left-wing Mapam party on the Petah Tikva municipal council, sees the Heikhal cinema not only as a place of entertainment, but as a symbol of cultural life in the city. It demonstrates, in his opinion, the determination of Petah Tikva residents not to forgo the theater, concerts, and lectures or visits to the museum on the Sabbath:

> The members of the older generation found a solution to their cultural demands by driving to Tel Aviv, and the youth were left to sit on the sidewalk railings. Where did the religious public want to send them? To the synagogues? That's not even adequate for the religious youth. They too need a cultural center for the hours after the prayer, and that is all the more true for the non-religious youth.

But if there is to be a *Kulturkampf,* Hagin would at least like to see it waged in a cultured fashion.

> I am opposed to sponsoring a musical event on Saturday morning opposite a synagogue. But I expect my religious neighbor to allow me to enjoy cultural activities in a closed hall in the city.

Dr. Meir Shneider, leader of the religious academics and a statistician by profession, also stresses the need to maintain moderation, but he has reservations about the possibility of bridging the gulf that separates the two sides. He reported on a meeting between the Mayor and leaders of the religious public. The religious delegation, he says, explained the significance of the Sabbath and how essential it is for the State itself to maintain its Jewish character. Tabori's response, according to Shneider, was that this was precisely the cause of the disagreement. "I want Petah Tikva to look like a western city and not like a Jewish one," Shneider quotes Tabori as saying.

"I got the impression that there was no one with whom to talk," Shneider concludes, "because we are talking about deep ideological differences. It is not the Heikhal cinema which lies in the balance, but all of Jewish culture and tradition, with all its components."

It was this recognition, he notes, that led him to the realization that demonstrations were not the correct path, and that there was a need for an educational campaign. "Education is a long-range process and is not furthered by demonstrations and posters."

Pinhas Hagin agrees with Shneider. He also sees education as the key to curbing the *Kulturkampf:*

> A boor and an ignoramus cannot be tolerant. In order to be tolerant, you must learn the Jewish heritage of which you must be tolerant. Earlier, efforts were made to provide youngsters with knowledge of Judaism through the "Jewish Consciousness" program in the elementary schools. It was artificial and it failed. Today there are those in the kibbutz movement, including the far left, who are searching for the right way, but unfortunately there are no similar attempts at coexistence in the *haredi* camp.

The Mayor, however, is skeptical. "It is not the school system which is to blame, but the nature of western culture," he observes.

Many of the parties to the conflict agree that the Heikhal controversy is a microcosm of the *Kulturkampf* in Israeli society, but they don't agree about who fired the first shot. According to Hagin, the radicalization of the religious camp explains the origins of the conflict.

> In the first generation of the State of Israel, religious-Zionism stressed the elements it had in common with the leftist movements in the country: settlement, kibbutz, defense. The Six-Day War marked a watershed. Immediately after it, the NRP began to move away from the left politically and from the non-religious camp religiously. At first the division was over the question of the Greater Land of Israel, and afterwards in the struggle over the Sabbath. Forty-eight years ago, there was a coffee-house open on the Sabbath in Petah Tikva and the religious did not attack those who entered it. But when the Gan Eden opened on the Sabbath, *haredim* smashed it up. That difference is the

whole story. When religious-Zionism became more extreme, it fell under the influence of the *haredim,* and that in turn aroused strong counter-reactions by the non-religious public.

Hagin is not alone in blaming the *Kulturkampf* on the growth of extremism among the religious-Zionists. But this explanation is generally shared by the older generation of non-religious leaders, a generation which views this extremism and the resultant conflict with great trepidation. Among younger non-religious leaders, a different tone is heard. Indeed, they take credit for initiating the changes they believe are necessary in Israeli society. According to Jackie Kramer, the former Petah Tikva spokesman of the centrist anti-clerical party Shinui:

> We became tired of the giving in to the coercion syndrome. We demanded as part of our political program in the municipal election campaign that the Heikhal and Oren cinemas and the Sharet Auditorium be opened on the Sabbath, that public transporation to the beaches be instituted, and that cafés be allowed to open. We told the moderate religious people in the city that if they disagreed, they would double and triple the Sabbath desecration. After all, young people would travel to Tel Aviv to see a movie. If they stayed in Petah Tikva, they would at least not drive. We were delighted to receive the full support of the media. Tabori too adopted our line and opened a fierce campaign, attacking the religious by using all types of strong epithets. The day before the première showing at the Heikhal cinema, I met with the commander of the Petah Tikva police and I told him, "if you the police react with a strong hand, if you break a few bones, the episode will end right there. If you act gently, you will not get out of this for months." I was correct. The religious public feels distressed at the culture which predominates in the country, but all its demonstrations will not prevent the inevitable.

Political Aspects

Describing the Heikhal controversy as part of a *Kulturkampf* provides only one explanation of what took place. The same people who described the controversy in these terms also offered an alternative suggestion—that the controversy stemmed from political ambitions. At least, some of them argued, the conflict could have been avoided if the parties to the controversy had been less concerned with furthering their own interests. This notion emerged, for example, in interviews with the two chief rabbis of Petah Tikva.

Rabbi Salomon characterized his conversations with Tabori as a dispute with "a politician who had to show a 'victory' to his voters," rather than a debate with "a man of spirit." Rabbi Malka believes that the entire issue developed solely because the religious public enabled Tabori to obtain a majority on the municipal council without it:

> It was a bad mistake of the religious activists, who did not join the municipal coalition. It is not important why. They were insulted and that was what they decided. What is important is that, by their error, they opened the way to the desecration of the Sabbath.

According to Dov Tabori, the Sabbath controversy broke out because of a lack of political understanding:

> It began because a religious activist was offended. He found himself in a situation which got out of control. He was dragged along by his own followers and they were unable to back down. Instead of leading the camp, he became its prisoner.

Avraham Marmorstein, the religious activist to whom Dov Tabori referred, responded as follows.

> The true problem stemmed from the fact that the coalition agreement that had been observed scrupulously for ten consecutive years was violated following the results of the 1983 elections. Tabori announced, as soon as he was elected mayor, that he no longer needed us, and that he would therefore no longer pay the price that he had in the past; and that he was going to open the Heikhal cinema on the Sabbath, as he had promised his voters. He also took the education portfolio from the NRP after it had been in its hands for forty consecutive years. On that day I decided that we would not join a coalition with such a person. And the chief rabbis of the city supported my initiative.

Jackie Kramer, who, as noted earlier, interpreted the struggle in terms of a culture war, also agreed that it had a political aspect:

> I am convinced that all those involved in this struggle had political motives. Even the rabbis. They too acted in order to enhance their reputations in rabbinical circles and among the religious population, and in order to garner funds and sympathy among Jewish communities throughout the world.

According to another politician in the Tabori camp, Tabori's advisers warned him just prior to the elections not to become involved in the cinema issue because that step was dangerous politically. He thought the opposite, and it appears that he was right. As a result of the struggle in Petah Tikva he became a national figure.

Paltiel Eisental, chairman of the local Religious Council, claims that the Heikhal controversy can only be understood in the context of the religious parties' decline at the national level. According to Eisental, this is a better explanation for the controversy than any cultural or social explanation:

> It was inconceivable, in the days when Mapai needed the twelve votes of the NRP [in the Knesset], for a mayor such as Tabori to do what was done in Petah Tikva. Within a day, Mapai would have liquidated the problem and called him to order. There have also been changes in the political emphases of the religious public. Tami [a Sephardic-religious party] concentrates on ethnic questions. Tehiya devotes all its energies to the struggle for the Greater Land of Israel. In the NRP, there was internal splintering and division, while on the left a generation of young leaders arose, not a single one of whom has the stature of Ben-Gurion. . . . Tabori arrived on the scene at a time when the ground was ready politically for the war over the Sabbath. The religious public did not realize this. It also did not see—until the last stages of the struggle—that it had no backing from the religious parties themselves. The religious parties stood on the sidelines, so even though the religious public responded *en masse* . . . it did not win.

The Legal Struggle

The courts were another arena in which the Petah Tikva struggle took place. There the religious public suffered one loss after another.

Public-opinion surveys indicate that the Israeli public regards the courts as the fairest of the branches of government and accords them far greater deference and respect than the legislature. It is troubling, therefore, to report the impressions of Shmuel Linzer, the attorney responsible for most of the litigation on behalf of the religious public in the Heikhal controversy. What he says may or may not be accurate, but it is a reflection of the fact that, to at least one segment of the religious public, the Israeli judicial system is perceived as "biased and unjust."

Linzer feels that even though Dov Tabori "openly trampled the bylaws that the municipality itself had passed," the court limited itself to pressing charges against the cinema. The Heikhal was in violation of the law for over 150 Saturdays, says Linzer, and during this time Tabori only issued two or three summonses. Yet the courts did nothing.

Other lawyers to whom he had spoken, Linzer continued,

> . . . agreed from their own experience that when one comes to an Israeli court with a case containing a religious element, it's no bed of roses. Most of the judges are not observant. Even the most lofty legal principles are open to interpretation. The result is that the legal path is not one which will enable the religious to make progress in enforcing laws of a religious nature. Trail blazing in the legal arena requires considerable resources and the retention of the best and most prominent of lawyers. The religious public in Petah Tikva did not act that way, and that was why it failed. Given the conditions as they were, this was a struggle that was doomed to failure.

Conclusion

The Sabbath wars descended on the Israel of the 1980s with both sides misunderstanding the meaning behind them and the balance of forces involved. The non-religious public panicked at what it regarded as the growth in the power of the religious sector and what it perceived as increased religious coercion. There were four reasons for this panic.

First, Israeli victories in the Six-Day War, the conquest of Judea and Samaria, and the reuniting of Jerusalem, generated an ecstatic, almost messianic fervor which attracted many youth, non-religious as well as religious, to organizations such as Gush Emunim. The establishment of religious settlements in the newly occupied land and fervent talk of "the Third Temple" exerted cumulative pressure on those groups who were unsympathetic to these developments.

Secondly, the growth in the number of *hozrim biteshuva* (Jews, primarily young people, who became Orthodox, a kind of "born-again Jew" phenomenon), which included kibbutz members, air-force pilots, and prominent entertainers, was widely reported in the press and instilled such fears that it generated a counter-movement to combat the tendency.

Thirdly, the weakened electoral power of the NRP, which shrank from 12 to 6 seats and then to 4 seats in successive Knesset elections, increased the power of the *haredi* Knesset members from Agudat Israel and Shas. The latter now set the tone in the Knesset, and their tone was extremist, without compromise or concessions; at least so it appeared.

Finally, the increased self-confidence of the religious population, the *haredi* public in particular, tempted it to seek new victories in imposing the observance of Jewish law in the public sector, attempts which it would never have considered earlier, when it had less confidence in its power and status. For example, the *haredi* public had always insisted that streets in its neighborhoods be closed on the Sabbath; but it now demanded that roads running alongside religious neighborhoods, such as the Ramot road in Jerusalem, be closed. When the authorities refused, it became "permissible" to engage in stormy demonstrations and throw stones at those driving on the Sabbath.

The religious public exploited its political ties and exerted political pressure to prevent the building of a soccer stadium in Jerusalem despite enormous popular demand for its construction. It embarked on a renewed struggle against the bus companies who operated buses before the conclusion of the Sabbath, although the bus companies had been doing this for many years. In its stuggle, the religious public utilized a classic technique of public pressure, street demonstrations—something of a national hobby in Israel.

In spite of this, most of the street demonstrations failed to achieve their objectives. This fact of life seems to have been lost on the religious leaders of Petah Tikva who sought to prevent the opening of the Heikhal. The powerful impression which the first mass demonstration outside the Heikhal cinema made further misled them. The fact is that the religious public was impressed by its own numbers. The demonstration resulted in a sense of exhilaration and euphoria. It may have served to please the religious public, who felt that they were doing something, and it undoubtedly flattered the egos of the leaders who were propelled into public prominence. But it is questionable if sober evaluations, even at a time when thousands of religious Jews were prepared to devote their Friday nights to attending the demonstrations, would have led to the conclusion that this was a likely path for success.

When the struggle intensified and assumed the form of a *Kulturkampf,* leading Israeli rabbis streamed to Petah Tikva, as did the Knesset members from Shinui and Ratz, two small anticlerical parties. But the most important point is that the vast majority of Petah

Tikva residents, the non-religious in particular, viewed the conflict from the sidelines. If this was a war of sorts, it hardly involved all of society. The majority remained at home Friday nights watching their television screens. The war was waged, ostensibly on their behalf, by a handful of political leaders whose only support at the national level came from the spokesmen of Ratz and Shinui. Journalists claim that they or their editors or both presented slanted versions of the conflict because this is what the public wanted to hear. That may be true for part of the public. But a survey of Petah Tikva residents conducted for purposes of this article indicated that over half the non-religious public in the city itself were indifferent to the opening of the Heikhal on the Sabbath.

Does this mean that there was no *Kulturkampf* and that the struggle over the Heikhal was simply a battle of political activists? Does this mean that leaders less stubborn than Dov Tabori on the one hand, and Rabbi Salomon and Avraham Marmorstein on the other, could have resolved the controversy quietly and peaceably? After all, a number of movie theaters in Tel Aviv are open on the Sabbath, and the religious public there never carried on the way it did in Petah Tikva.

The two explanations are not mutually exclusive. The struggle over the Heikhal cinema brought to a head the tension between religious and non-religious over the Jewish character of the State; it also provided the arena in which a new and ambitious mayor was able to demonstrate his courage and conviction, and in which the leader of a religious party, offended by the fact that the portfolio which he had held (education) was granted to someone else, tried to exact his revenge and demonstrate his strength.

And what of the consequences of the struggle? With the hindsight of less than a year since the struggle ended, we can see that it appears to have resulted in the partial alienation of the religious public from the political and judicial system in the State—though it is too early to say how serious this sentiment is. It is clear that the Petah Tikva controversy has undermined the self-confidence of the religious public, at least of many of its leaders. According to Shmuel Linzer, the power of the religious public is clearly in decline. This is evident, he feels, in elections, in the Knesset, and in the government. Its power in the media is virtually non-existent, and the Petah Tikva controversy demonstrates how little power it exerts in the streets and how little help it can expect from the courts.

On the other hand, the struggle does not seem to have made much difference to relations between the religious and non-religious in Petah Tikva and in the larger society. The recent demonstrations by the *haredim* in Jerusalem created hostility and resentment toward the religious public. The *haredim* emerged as a threatening, extremist, and fanatical group, possibly because of their resort to violence. A survey of Petah Tikva residents indicates that the demonstrations there did not poison the generally good relations between the religious and non-religious public. This may be a consequence of the fact that the demonstrations were, for the most part, restrained. If there was any bitter fall-out—it was to be found among some members of the religious public.

Naomi Gutkind-Golan

5

Mixed Communal Settlements

THIS ARTICLE is devoted to "mixed" communal settlements in Judea and Samaria. A mixed communal settlement is defined as a planned settlement of no more than several hundred people in which religious and non-religious Jews live in neighborly proximity and cooperate in running all public institutions. In order to ease the strains which such a mix entails, the communal settlement is likely to spell out in advance, in a written charter, the rules which will govern the use of such public facilities as roads, social centers, swimming pools, playgrounds, and synagogues.

In terms of numbers, we are speaking of a marginal phenomenon: of the 137 Jewish settlements in Judea, Samaria, and the Gaza Strip, only five are mixed communal settlements. These include Kfar Adumim with 90 families, Nokdim (22 families), Beit Horon (60 families), Ma'aleh Shomron (43 families and another 6 expected shortly), and Tekoah (80 families), for a total of about three hundred families. Another potential community, Alon, consists of a core group of families awaiting the signal to undertake actual settlement.

Those who choose to settle not only on the other side of the "green line," but in mixed religious-secular settlements, are a minority of a minority of the general Israeli Jewish population. It is reasonable to assume that this group shares a set of characteristics beyond a political ideology common to all settlers in Judea and Samaria.

What then are these characteristics, if indeed they exist, and what communal framework permits religious and secular to live together in harmony? What can the brief ten-year history of even the oldest of these communal settlements teach us about their problems and how they sought to resolve them? We hope to discover answers to these questions by looking especially carefully at one such settlement—Ma'aleh Shomron.

Ma'aleh Shomron, about an hour and a half's drive, by car, from Tel Aviv, was selected for a number of reasons. Its 43 families place it among neither the largest nor the smallest of the settlements. It is, however, one of the oldest settlements, which means we can draw upon its experience in answering some of the questions with which we have chosen to deal. Its distance from Tel Aviv means that settlers cannot regularly travel to the large city to escape the social problems which life in a mixed settlement might generate.

We supplemented our observations from Ma'aleh Shomron with interviews conducted in Kfar Adumim and Tekoah. These enabled us to estimate whether our findings in one community were generalizable to others.

The Distribution of the Religious and Non-Religious Population

According to Ma'aleh Shomron's general secretary, Yaacov Reich, of the 43 families in Ma'aleh Shomron, 15 are identified with the religious-Zionist (national-religious) movement, the movement of the knitted yarmulkes. The rest, he says, are secular. But the remaining secular families are distinguishable among themselves by their religious behavior. Roughly a fifth of them take part in Sabbath and holiday services in the Synagogue. Everyone, Reich says, fasts on Yom Kippur.

Ronit Bash, general secretary of Tekoah, maintains that about 60 percent of the families in that settlement are religious and the remainder secular. Kfar Adumin is said to be divided equally between religious and secular, with about half of the secular members attending synagogue on Sabbaths and holidays.

Pirhiah Damari, one of the founders of Ma'aleh Shomron, divides the settlement's members into three categories: religious, traditional, and secular.

> The religious are B'nai Akiva types. There isn't even one *haredi* among them. The traditional watch television on the Sabbath, but not before they say the blessing over wine. They also drive to the beach on the Sabbath, but only after they finish saying the Sabbath morning prayers. The secular settlers don't pray, and send their children to public secular schools in a nearby community. They choose to live in an area within the settlement where driving is permitted, in accordance with the charter on the Sabbath.

Nevertheless, as Damari observes, even the secular "are not militantly secular." They would never turn up the volume of their stereo sets on the Sabbath or conduct noisy parties in their yards, despite the fact that the charter permits everyone to do as he chooses on his own property. Nor, she adds, would they display bread during Passover or light cigarettes on the Sabbath.

Emanuel Warhaftig testifies to a similar phenomenon in Kfar Adumim:

> Our secular (settlers) don't work in their yards along the public road on the Sabbath, they don't operate their radios noisily, and they generally drive only on the side roads. Non-militant secular. The Acceptance Committee concerns itself with that and explains to families interested in joining about the nature of the settlement.

The religious mixture in the settlement, he points out, is extremely broad, running from "yeshiva students whose wives completely cover their hair to former kibbutznikim who had never met religious people before they joined the settlement."

Employment and Education

Most of the settlers in the mixed communal settlements (along with most of the settlers of Judea and Samaria) have at least a high-school education. At Ma'aleh Shomron there are two engineers, a lawyer, a psychologist, four social workers, several full-time army people, computer programmers, and many teachers. Most of the women work. Most of the population are salaried. Only two are self-employed.

Financially, the settlers define themselves as upper-middle-class. They travel abroad and have at least one car per family (a fourth of the families have a second car, provided by the husband's employer).

Almost all are building two- or three-story houses, after selling the three-or four-room apartments in which they lived before moving across the green line. Cheaper construction costs in Judea and Samaria enable most to double their housing space; but until construction is completed, they live in prefab structures half the size of their former city apartments.

The settlement's charter obligates all families to begin construction within one year of their arrival. Those who fail to do so are asked to leave. This regulation ensures that settlers are serious about establishing a permanent residence in the "territories" and not just exploiting the cheap housing that is available there before they move elsewhere to find a permanent place to live.

A Brief History

The three communal settlements discussed here have been in existence for from nine to eleven years. Two—Ma'aleh Shomron and Kfar Adumim—were founded by people who decided on mixed settlements from the beginning. This is an important point in understanding how these communities developed. Pirhiah Damari's husband, for example, was raised in a religious home but became nonreligious. Pirhiah herself is a graduate of a religious high school and a religious teachers' seminary. As she explains:

> We were not comfortable in the city. We didn't belong to the religious camp or to the secular camp. Something was missing. We were delighted when we saw the ad in the paper about the formation of a new nucleus for a mixed settlement. We came to the first meeting in the B'nai Brit auditorium in Tel Aviv and saw fifty families.
>
> At the first exploratory meeting we agreed that everyone could behave as he chose at home. At the next meeting opinion crystallized that on Sabbaths no one should drive within the settlement, but rather leave his car parked at the entrance.

The situation, she went on to explain, is like riding on a bus. If one passenger complains that it is too cold the other passengers will agree to close the windows even if they are suffocating from the heat. Similarly, she says:

> If it pains someone to see a car travelling on the Sabbath—you have consideration for him and don't travel.

> Afterwards, we debated what to do about education. It became clear that there was no need to argue a lot. It was agreed that the school would be mixed like the settlement. Morning prayers would be held but attendance wouldn't be compulsory. A child who doesn't want to take part simply brings a note from his parents.

Kfar Adumim was founded by a group of families who had founded Ma'aleh Adumim four years earlier. Ma'aleh Adumim had an urban character, that of a satellite neighborhood to Jerusalem. These families preferred a more small-town atmosphere. After a number of discussions, an ideological program crystallized around two principles: first, that settlement must take place in all parts of the Land of Israel in order to assert Jewish sovereignty throughout the land; and, secondly, a way must be found to bring the different parts of the Jewish people—religious and secular, Ashkenazim and Sephardim, immigrants and veterans, blue-collar and white-collar workers, adults and youth—together.

The group registered as a cooperative, but waived the right to strict selection of candidates for membership on condition that all those admitted observe the charter's rule forbidding driving on the Sabbath in public areas. In fact, after the founding of the settlement, it became clear that the charter was not enforced. The side roads were not yet paved, so people just drove up to the entrances to their homes; and religious settlers, who might have objected, chose to overlook what was taking place.

Before the founding nucleus actually moved to their present location they spent many lengthy evenings in planning the community's school. It was suggested that the school be religiously neutral—that is, that it not affiliate itself with either the state religious or the state non-religious school networks. Israeli law does provide for such schools, which it categorizes as "recognized" but not "registered."

The religious members, however, rejected this suggestion and insisted that the school be officially registered as part of the state religious network. After more intensive discussions, the secular members agreed to this demand on condition that the settlement charter specify that secular students are excused from prayers and from classes on Jewish law. Alternative classes were to be provided for them. This agreement paved the way for the establishment of the present school, which is now in it eighth year of operation.

Tekoah was established ten years ago by a nucleus of five families who had struggled for years to emigrate from the Soviet Union. Hanan Porat, one of the leaders of Gush Emunim, linked these families up with Rabbi Menachem Foreman, the rabbi of a nearby religious settlement. The immigrant founders wanted assistance from him in strengthening their national identity and learning more about Judaism. Some of the rabbi's friends, students of Yeshivat HaKotel in Jerusalem, followed him to Tekoah. Additional secular families trickled in from a variety of sources, many from other settlements on the West Bank. Many were "drop-outs" from religious settlements where they found they couldn't arrive at a *modus vivendi* with the religious majority. Then an organized group of college-educated immigrants from the United States appeared. The "Russians" were delighted. Their initial hope had been to establish a mixed settlement, and they had even developed a community model which, rather than blurring the differences between religious and secular, tried to encourage mutual consideration and tolerance. Despite this, there were disagreements about the nursery, and a mixed school was only established in the settlement's tenth year.

Mixed Communal Institutions

A religious/secular enterprise such as the mixed communal settlement is a new and vulnerable creation—altogether unconventional in Israeli society. Because of this, both the settlements in general and many of the institutions which they formed experienced difficult birth-pangs. The most sensitive issue dividing the religious from the non-religious is that of education, and we turn first of all to those institutions concerned with this.

The School

Pirhiah Damari, a former first-grade teacher in the mixed school of Ma'aleh Shomron, says:

> All of those who established the settlement wanted to set up a mixed school which would be part of the state religious network. The secular settlers also wanted their children to receive religious values. They approved a yarmulke budget. I bought yarmulkes for the class. Any child who forgot to bring a yarmulke from home received one from me for the duration of prayers. One student refused to wear a yarmulke; he did agree to wear a hat and I naturally consented. We did not insist that children wear *tsitsiot* [fringes to a garment which Jewish males are

> commanded to put on; they are generally worn under a shirt, but religiously zealous Ashkenazim wear them outside it], or that they wash their hands in the ritually prescribed manner before they ate.

Yair Gavish, one of the settlers responsible for cultural programs at Ma'aleh Shomron, is a secularist and a product of HaShomer HaTzair, the extreme left-wing youth group identified with Mapam. According to Gavish:

> Everyone agreed to morning prayers, so we required all the children to take part in them. With respect to the teachers—our condition was that none would say to the children that parents who drove on the Sabbath merited severe punishment at the hands of God, or that secularists were to be condemned. On the other hand, when our children came home with a demand that their mother light Sabbath candles—we did so. First we lit Sabbath candles and afterwards we turned on the television. The children accepted this as completely normal.

The mixed school in Ma'aleh Shomron was attended by a total of only 40 children. The parents were satisfied with the tolerant traditional nature of its education. The Ministry of Education, however, decided to close the school because it didn't meet minimal requirements. The government stopped paying teachers' salaries. The parents joined battle for the preservation of the school and took turns acting as teachers. But they lacked the endurance to continue making the sacrifices that this imposed upon them, and the school finally closed. The children of the religious families were bussed as a group to religious settlements in the area. The secular children were sent to state non-religious schools—which in the case of the high school meant bus-rides of over one hour. The traditionalists organized transportation to a Tali school. [Tali is a school system initiated by Conservative Jews in Israel. It is officially under the aegis of the state non-religious network but it offers augmented programs in Jewish subjects with a minimum imposition of religious observance and a pronounced tolerance for children from non-religious homes.] This effort, however, proved too strenuous and costly (there were charges for both transportation and school tuition), and the following year their children enrolled in standard state non-religious schools.

In Tekoah, problems which developed while setting up the religious public nursery prevented the construction of a joint elementary school. The non-religious settlers complained that the nursery-school teacher was too religious for their taste. They felt that her insistence that all the boys cover their heads with yarmulkes was unreasonable. The nursery teacher was eventually replaced by a new teacher, Rabbi Foreman's wife, a product of the religious Kibbutz Lavi. She refused to make an issue of the question of wearing yarmulkes, thus paving the way for the founding of the mixed elementary school which began functioning in 1988. How long it will last remains to be seen.

In the early years Tekoah's children learned in a neighboring state religious school to which everyone, religious and secular, came in yarmulkes. In the new mixed institution, in which only first- and second-grade classes are held, students are not required to pray: instead, the class discusses prayer. As one of the local sixth-grade girls notes: "The religious have a problem because it isn't enough for them to know about prayer—they have to pray." Her non-religious friend from the seventh grade responds: "But they don't have an alternative. They have to compromise."

The oldest of the mixed schools is found in Kfar Adumim. Not all of the secular parents there insist upon the right of their sons to go bare-headed or to study in alternative classes when subjects such as Jewish law are being taught. Some of them are anxious to expose their children to basic Jewish concepts even when offered in a "religious" environment.

The most serious of the settlement's educational dilemmas, one which aroused the entire community, was whether or not to accept outside children in the settlement's educational institutions (the daycare center, the nursery, the elementary school through eighth grade, and an *ulpanah* for older girls). The religious public argued vigorously that by accepting "masses" of children from secular homes the school would be transformed, *de facto,* into a secular institution. They argued that outsiders who were secular were not the same as the secular members of the settlement. The secular members of Kfar Adumim, the religious felt, by virtue of their membership in the community had agreed to a style of life and had undertaken certain obligations which enabled religious and non-religious to live together in harmony. This would not be true of outsiders. The issue was resolved by a communal referendum. It was agreed that only secular children who lived in mixed settlements like Kfar Adumim would be accepted.

This decision reinforces our impression that the members of the mixed settlements are conscious of the difference between "their" secular and religious sets, on the one hand, who are quite capable of friendly communal living, and "outside" secular and religious communities who are not.

In Ma'aleh Shomron tensions were also generated around educational issues, and these played a part in the departure of some members. The parents of the child who insisted on wearing a hat instead of a yarmulke left to join a secular settlement. Some of the religious founders left in anger because the community was unwilling to fund religious enrichment classes in the afternoons. They were also disturbed by their lack of success in establishing a branch of the religious-Zionist B'nai Akiva youth movement. Today most of the youth of Ma'aleh Shomron belong to Betar, a youth movement associated with Herut (the Likud), but there is a renewed attempt to establish a B'nai Akiva group.

The Rabbi

There is no rabbi in Ma'aleh Shomron. The religious residents bring their halakhic questions to the district rabbi. "If we could have been assured in advance that we could get a man as open and tolerant as Rabbi Foreman of Tekoah, we would have requested a rabbi," says one settler. "But how could we know something like this in advance?"

Rabbi Menachem Foreman, a native of Kfar Hasidim, a graduate of Merkaz HaRav, and married to a woman raised on a religious kibbutz, is imbued with the world-view of Rabbi Kook. In his words:

> One must emphasize the content and not the external shell: not attack externals but nurture the inner flow. Understand, for example, that children are not obligated to observe the commandments, although, for educational reasons, it is appropriate to accustom them to do so. But in certain situations it is more educational not to press such issues as covering the head, donning *tsitsiot,* engaging in prayer, etc. By pressuring one may achieve the opposite results—hostility and opposition.

When he was invited to Tekoah, Foreman knew that some of the couples there had not undergone a religious wedding ceremony, and there were even some whose Communist education had made them anti-religious. Despite this he came. He believes that he was invited to come because of the secular settlers' desire to identify more closely with Jewish nationalism. He senses an overriding need for the Jewish people of our generation to build bridges between the camps, and this is what brought him to Tekoah. He even persuaded several of his friends to join him. In his opinion there are more rabbis like him—trained in Israel, "Kooknikim," (i.e. followers of Rav Kook), who understand what he understands and are willing to lead mixed communities. But he is the only one Ma'aleh Shomron knows about, and its settlers are unwilling to "take the risk" of employing another rabbi. On the other hand, Foreman observed, "they built a ritual bath there and I'm told that it is in regular use."

Synagogue

Regular services are held in Ma'aleh Shomron only on the Sabbath. The minimal requirement for a prayer service of ten adult males (a *minyan*) cannot be organized during the week. The style of prayer—Sephardi, Ashkenazi, or Yemini—depends on the individual who happens to be leading the congregation. The public's tolerance for the variety of traditions is a matter of necessity. Unless all prayed together they couldn't even manage to find the minimum of ten males to constitute a *minyan* on the Sabbath.

Prayers in Kfar Adumim are less exotic. The settlers chose to pray according to what is called the land-of-Israel liturgy, first formulated for the Israeli army. Secular members attend the synagogue on holidays. It was suggested that their participation in the prayers, even if it isn't regular, strengthens the ties between the religious and non-religious.

The Recreation Center, Swimming-Pool, and Basketball Court

The children of Ma'aleh Shomron play undisturbed in the community's basketball court on the Sabbath. Religious members observe that Jewish law does not prohibit playing games such as basketball on the Sabbath. According to the secularist Yair Gavish, many things once thought impossible can be done.

> It's even possible to find a technical solution for horse-racing on Friday night without offending the religious. For example, the lights will be turned on and off with an automatic timer and tickets will be sold on Friday.

Gavish is also the assistant to the chairman of cultural programming in Ma'aleh Shomron and helps operate the recreation center.

The settlement's charter provides that dances, performances by entertainers, and other such activities will take place in the recreation center only after the end of the Sabbath:

> Once, we wanted to have a party on Friday night. What did we do? We set up a Sabbath clock. We also wanted to serve hot drinks, so we bought an electric coffee-urn which could be operated or disconnected automatically by a timer.

Ma'aleh Shomron's swimming-pool is not yet operational, and some disagreement still exists over rules to govern its use. According to a religious member, the pool will be open on the Sabbath but no tickets will be sold on that day. She was asked about non-members who drive up to the entrance of the pool. "We can't prevent their driving," she replied. The question of separate swimming hours for men and women was never raised.

In Tekoah there was a debate over which public institution should be constructed first, the synagogue or the swimming-pool. It was clear that there would not be sufficient money for both projects, and all sides agreed that the construction of a synagogue had priority.

The Governing Bodies

Ma'aleh Shomron has a five-man board of directors, all secular. The present secretary, a paid functionary hired from outside the community, happens to be religious. The previous one was not. The post, especially in a communal settlement in the process of construction, wears one down. This explains the previous secretary's stepping down after two years. Vacancies are open to applicants from outside the settlement and they have been chosen without regard to their religious propensities.

Tekoah's general secretary, Ronit Bash, is a woman. She first arrived in the settlement in the course of doing her national service (an alternative which some religious-Zionist girls choose instead of the regular army duty which most rabbis prohibit). She married, and remained in Tekoah, a religious woman serving as general secretary of a predominantly secular settlement—a phenomenon that represents quite a break with all sorts of Israeli norms, those of the religious sector in particular.

Ma'aleh Shomron, Tekoah, and Kfar Adumim are legally registered as cooperative organizations, which means they have a great deal of autonomy. But in order to join the settlement a potential member needs the approval of the Jewish Agency. Only then is the member invited to appear before the settlement's own acceptance committee. According to a former member of Ma'aleh Shomron's acceptance committee:

> The Committee is a vital institution in a mixed settlement. For example, a religious dentist presented his candidacy to us. We wanted him very much, but when he met with us I told him that the women here wear shorts in the summer and walk about with bare shoulders. We also have a family that drives on the Sabbath along the side roads within the settlement. He decided that under these circumstances he wouldn't fit in. We were pleased that these matters were clarified in advance instead of creating tension later.

Crises and Departures

The members of Ma'aleh Shomron use the case of the dentist to strengthen their claim that all the crises that the community has undergone in the nine years of its existence resulted from social, not religious causes. The settlement, say the members, never attracted religious extremists. Those who left, according to one informant, were simply unsuited for communal life—people who didn't fit in with their neighbors because they lacked the right "chemistry." However, it was easier for them to attribute their departure to religious reasons—for example, the fact that a neighbor lit charcoal in his yard on the Sabbath to prepare a barbecue—than to admit that they just didn't fit in socially. A religious informant noted:

> One of the unsuitable families operated an electric saw both during the rest hours of the mid-week and also on the Sabbath. They were inconsiderate of others rather than anti-religious. In contrast, we had other neighbors, a couple of heavy smokers, who lived right next door to us in the cramped trailer camp before we moved to the new houses. In the four and a half years we were there I never once saw them with cigarettes in their mouths on the Sabbath. I knew they smoked at home, but they never did so to my face.

Despite these and similar observations, there is evidence that some settlers left Ma'aleh Shomron for religious reasons. Two families left Ma'aleh Shomron a year ago because they themselves had moved to the right religiously. Their wives began covering their heads with scarves, and one of the husbands became a scribe (one who handwrites sacred texts in a religiously prescribed manner). They claimed they weren't prepared to link their future to a place without a rabbi. The settlement's major social crises did not originate from religious tension, but carried religious overtones.

Pirhiah Damari testifies:

> Two key members of our group, both religious, both members of the Board, fell out because of a disagreement over construction and plots of land. In the first year of settlement we all lived under crowded conditions in the prefabricated housing. The time finally came to parcel out plots of land by lottery and build our homes. At this point an argument broke out between the two men and then extended to their wives. One of them claimed that I, while teaching a class in which her son was enrolled, had discriminated against him and shown favoritism to the other woman's son. It's difficult to "sit on the fence" when two members of the Board fight in a small community. Ma'aleh Shomron was split down the middle. With tensions rising, religious issues suddenly arose. Non-religious members who had, heretofore, refrained from driving on the Sabbath now began doing so. I commented to them that this wasn't neighborly. One stopped; the second shrugged me off and drove on. In the end one of the disputants left, together with his friends, and the tension subsided.

The sequence of events suggests that when social tensions, having nothing to do with religion, arose, the compromises which had been made over religious issues were also shaken. Some members no longer felt bound by accommodations to which they had initially agreed for the sake of communal harmony. If this analysis is correct, it indicates the fragile nature of the compromises worked out around religious issues even by the population-groups who make up mixed settlements.

Ma'aleh Shomron's second crisis was associated with construction. A core of new religious families joined the settlement, and the Board demanded that each family deposit an advance as a guarantee of its intention to build a house. The settlement feared that the newcomers might be content with living in the prefabs for a few years and then move elsewhere. These transients would occupy the temporary housing and prevent the absorption of other newcomers who were intent upon making their permanent home in Samaria. But the new families refused to deposit the money. The dispute eventually reached the High Court of Justice. The outcome of the litigation was that twelve families left Ma'aleh Shomron. Some returned to the city, others moved to other settlements. Among those who left were four families who claimed that they weren't ready to invest in a home in Ma'aleh Shomron because the settlement wasn't religious enough for them. The group also included a *hozer bitshuvah,* a religious penitent, who fought with everyone.

The distribution of housing-lots and the beginning of construction forced the residents to arrive at a final decision on whether driving would or would not be permitted on the Sabbath. There was a great deal of controversy over this question. It was finally decided that the settlement would be divided into two neighborhoods, one in which driving on the Sabbath would be permitted and one in which it would be forbidden. At the entrance to the "religious" neighborhood signs announced "driving on the Sabbath or holidays forbidden on this road."

Everyone assumed that the observant would chose to live in the "religious" neighborhood and the secular settlers in the other. But it didn't always work out that way. A religious family might find a site or view in the "non-religious" sector especially attractive and build a home there anyway, without worrying how they would feel if a car drove by on the Sabbath. The opposite situation also arose; for example, although plots were initially assigned by lottery with the expectation that exchanges would then take place between religious and non-religious members, some secular families who won their lots in the "religious" section chose to build there because they liked the site. In retrospect it is apparent that those families who could not adjust easily to the conditions of a mixed settlement, those who tended to be intolerant and impatient with those unlike themselves in religious matters, left, and it was those who were better able to cope with these differences in ways of life who remained.

The Secret of Living Together: How Does It Work?

Yonatan Chernovil, religious, owner of a foundry and metal work shop, describes himself as a type of person who believes in human beings:

> If someone tells me he observes *Kashrut*—I eat at his house without fear. One is commanded to believe the word of Jews.

Chernovil, a resident of Tekoah, also declared himself to be "a type that doesn't get angry fast." He cites the following example:

> Several secular families lit a campfire near our home on one of the Jewish holidays and made a big racket. Despite the fact that I prefer quiet, I didn't say a thing to them. The same thing happens when my neighbor on the other side of the wall turns on his television on the Sabbath. I'm certain that he doesn't do so in order to annoy me—God forbid—but rather because his home is his castle.

Chernovil finds it very helpful that all are Zionists like himself and share his world-view. "What is Zionism?" he is asked. "To live in Tekoah and not in Brooklyn—this is the test of Zionism," he responds. Another Tekoah resident explains the secret of neighborly living like this: both he and his secular neighbors agree that the *haredim* who throw stones at those who drive on the Sabbath are engaged in wrongful activity.

Yaffa Rosenhak, a former Jerusalemite, comes from a secular but politically mixed family. One parent is a committed left-winger, the other a committed right-winger. She inquired at the offices of Amanah (the settlement organization of Gush Emunim) where she could find a settlement in the Jerusalem area that was not a religious ghetto. When she was told about Tekoah, she came prepared to compromise her own way of life in order to accommodate her religious neighbors. For example, she watches television on the Sabbath in her bedroom rather than the living room. If an observant neighbor should come in, she explains, she wouldn't want to give offence by letting him or her see the set turned on.

Yair Gavish also came from a secular home and was raised, as he noted, in the Hashomer Hatzair youth movement. But because his religious grandmother lived in his parents' home the food was prepared in accordance with dietary laws. In his youth movement, he noted, they taught him that religion was the opiate of the people; but he was convinced, by conversations with his grandmother at home, that religion is a beautiful tradition with heart-warming rituals, and a bridge of history. His wife was also raised in a secular home, but her father studied in a yeshiva in Europe before he "went bad," became a Zionist, and immigrated to Israel. From a political and social perspective, these two are close to Mapam. They are the left-wingers of Ma'aleh Shomron. "But we are the kind of people who think for ouselves and don't let others do our thinking," they add.

Yair Gavish has another explanation for his tolerance toward his religious neighbors, for whose sake he parks his car on the Sabbath a five-minute walk from his home:

> In Nahal [an army division composed of youth movement members who serve as one unit], the best group aside from ourselves were from B'nai Akiva. I remember Yaacov Hazan [a veteran leader of Mapam] saying that the left wing's biggest mistake was in not educating its youth about its Jewish roots or teaching about the tradition. That made an impression on me. My wife and I have come to the conclusion that we can't live with extremists from either side. But with fellow Zionists, even if they live in accordance with a religious style—I'll get along willingly. I once caught a neighbor driving on the Sabbath and I reminded him that we agreed in the charter not to drive. "You must honor that," I told him. On the other hand I fought to include a provision in the charter under which someone who owns a workshop and wants to work there on the Sabbath can do so. It's all right with me for a restaurant or pool to be open on the Sabbath with the condition that people buy tickets on Friday. When the school was in existence, I agreed to have my children pray. What's wrong with letting them see the prayer-book to which my grandfather was so attached all his life? I also make an effort to buy wafers and cookies with *kashrut* certification so that all the neighbors and the neighbors' children can eat freely in our home. Once, religious friends of ours came from Alon Shvut for an entire day. We bought prepared kosher food, throw-away plates, and plastic cutlery. The kind of religious who yell "Shabbus Shabbus" or call me a "carrion eater" get me boiling mad, but if someone accepts me, I accept him and meet him half way.

It is customary to celebrate bar-mitzvahs and circumcisions in Ma'aleh Shomron's recreation center. The *kashrut* problem is solved by buying prepared food or by asking women who observe *kashrut* to bake cakes. They accept this "burden" willingly.

Sometimes a number of families will organize a communal barbecue in someone's yard. Then everyone buys kosher meat and uses throw-away utensils. Friendships are not determined or destroyed because of religious or ethnic differences. When religious members are invited to the home of secular friends who, for whatever reason, don't make the effort to prepare food in accordance with their requirements, they will eat nuts of various kinds, fruit (fresh and dried), and packaged wafers rather than home-made cakes.

Friendship among young people is a more sensitive issue. A secular boy and religious girl in Ma'aleh Shomron were seen with arms around one another without exciting special comment. The young people agreed among themselves to limit parties and dances to Saturday nights (i.e. to avoid Friday nights), so that the religious youth could attend as well. The friendly relations are facilitated by the fact that there are no sharp differences in clothing and hair-style between the religious and secular—no boys with earrings or "punk" hair-styles, or, on the other hand, any who wear their *tsitsiot* hanging out. All the girls eschew extreme minis or bare backs. Differences between religious and non-religious dress codes are limited to the fact that religious girls wear only skirts and short-sleeved blouses in the summer whereas non-religious girls may wear pants or sleeveless blouses.

Orit and her husband Shlomo of Ma'aleh Shomron were raised in religious homes and are the products of state religious schools. Shlomo attended a high-school yeshiva as well. They do not consider themselves observant. They observe *kashrut* but also drive on the Sabbath. They summarize the manner in which they raise their children religiously and their feelings about relations between religious and non-religious Jews as follows:

> We drive on the Sabbath to swim in the sea, but we leave the children at home. They go to a state religious school and we didn't want them arriving at school on Sunday morning sun-burnt or tanned. We explained to them that for their own good, socially, they have to forgo the beach on Saturday, and they understood. Once our oldest son wanted to organize a dance party on Friday night. We persuaded him to postpone it to Saturday night, and in the end he was happy that he did so because the religious girls that he liked could come. This son knows that, despite the fact that we drive on the Sabbath, we observe *kashrut* strictly. Once he slept over at the house of a friend who eats non-kosher food. In the morning, he ate only cold uncooked food. Complicated? Problematic? So what? We have a religious brother who doesn't eat at our house just because we drive on the Sabbath. On the other hand we have very good friends in whose home we don't eat, because we know they don't observe *kashrut* strictly. Our secret is not to check anyone's *tsitsiot*. If someone claims to be religious, we don't trail around after him to see if he prays three times a day. Our secular members are considerate types. Our religious members are types who can live with everyone, and that's the whole story.

A weekly children's magazine, *Otiot* (no. 41–42, September 1988), published the following exchange among children from Tekoah which is especially instructive. A fourth-grade girl recalls:

> A couple of weeks ago on the Sabbath I went to the house of a secular friend. She was sitting there drawing. Later she even turned on a light. When I told Mommy we agreed that I'll stop going to her on the Sabbath and that's that. We're still good friends but on the Sabbath I'll stay home.

And a seventh-grader says:

> I don't turn on the radio or television when Shulamit [a friend] comes to see me, but I don't have to begin observing commandments in order for Shulamit to be my friend.

A ninth-grader notes:

> It's all a question of age. Most of the kids in the lower grades are religious and in order to be part of the gang you have to show some interest in religious observance. But in my class, ninth grade, we are the majority, so some of the religious kids become a bit "flighty"; they're "going bad."

The seventh-grader responds to this:

> I don't think this is the result of the influence of non-religious kids. The "flighty" ones are generally from less religious homes.

In response to the question whether religious or non-religious children make the greater compromise, a non-religious girl states that the secular do. "But," she goes on to say, "I think it's justified. A religious person can't surrender part of his religion."

A religious girl contradicts her and makes the following observation:

> We religious also compromise. We continue to be friends with those who turn on lights on the Sabbath.

But the non-religious girl is adamant:

> The secular people compromise more. I pray and wear a skirt in school. I don't see this as a big deal or a problem, but it's definitely a compromise.

Another religious girl observes that "as a matter of principle my mother lets me eat at secular friends', and only on Passover am I forbidden to eat outside."

A religious boy tells how his friends from outside the settlement saw him going around with secular boys and didn't understand how he could be friends with them. A religious girl reports that her friends from a religious settlement also can't understand how she has girlfriends in her own settlement who wear shorts.

Yossi Foreman, the rabbi's son, a student at a religiously extreme school sponsored by Merkaz HaRav Yeshiva, summarized the discussion:

> I learned from the secular people the importance of freedom . . . to do things because you want to and not because you have to. Now I look on things in a more sophisticated way than my religious friends [in my school]. They accept religion as an obligation—I as a matter of free will.

Mixed Marriage in a Mixed Settlement

A severe test of tolerance in the mixed communal settlement will come if religious and non-religious youngsters choose to marry one another. Will parents tolerate, even welcome, such a marriage, or will they view it as a sign of their failure to inculcate in their own youngsters their particular values? Although we don't know the answer to this question, we do have evidence that the mixed settlements not only absorb but provide a particularly sympathetic environment for mixed couples.

In the Blau and Eliahu families of Ma'aleh Shomron the women are religious, but the husbands are totally non-observant, driving and turning lights on and off on the Sabbath. In the Damari family, the wife saw to it that two sinks were installed in their kitchen, one for meat and on for dairy products, and the daughter attends an extremely religious girls' high school; but the husband, though he attended religious schools through high school, is now totally non-observant, as are their two sons. The males are careful not to mix meat and dairy dishes, and will warm food on the Sabbath only in a specially prescribed way without using the gas stove. The husband blesses the wine on Friday evening before he turns on the television or goes out for a Sabbath drive.

Orna, from Tekoah, is a secular young woman married to a religious man.

> We met on a tour to Thailand and have been together since. In the beginning we tried to be absorbed into my kibbutz, but that didn't go

> well. My husband couldn't adjust to a secular life, and the [kibbutz] administration wouldn't agree to provide him with kosher food or to cancel his Sabbath job assignments. We moved to Tel Aviv, but that wasn't for us. We tried to join a religious settlement in Judea, but I immediately felt like an outsider. The women neighbors interrogated me from the first day about whether my food was kosher and how I kashered it. They gave me *kashrut* tests. I fled from there. Finally, to our great good fortune, we found Tekoah. Here no one pressures. Everyone is respected, and the level of an individual's *kashrut* or religiosity is not important. So we stayed here.

Malka, of Ma'aleh Shomron, an artist and painter, wears long pants in the winter and shorts in the summer. She is a graduate of state religious schools and grew up in a moderate religious home in which *kashrut* and Shabbat were observed but married women did not cover their hair or men wear their *tsitsiot* outside their shirts. Her husband, David, in a knitted yarmulke, is a graduate of a yeshiva in Hungary. He would be delighted if his wife were more religiously extreme, as so many young religious-Zionist women are—covering her hair and lengthening her sleeves. "But," he says:

> If it doesn't go, then it doesn't go. I'm not going to endanger household peace over questions of dress and life style. That is why we left Petah Tikvah. Malka wanted a mixed settlement in which it would be possible to live a religious-Zionist life-style of the old time—without being *haredi* or extreme, with patience and willingness to compromise, and I followed her lead.

One of this couple's daughters is married, covers her hair, and lives next door to her parents. Their son attended a yeshiva high school and became non-observant.

Mixed couples are to be found in Kfar Adumim as well. In fact, a leader of Gush Emunim commented in an interview that in many of the mixed settlements the religious differences between husbands and wives are striking.

There are also many families in Ma'aleh Shomron who are ethnically mixed. These include couples of Libyan–Polish, Bulgarian–Yemenite, Yemenite–North-African, Dutch–Sephardi, Ashkenazi–Iraqi, Moroccan–Rumanian, and Swiss–Sabra origin. Indeed, ethnic mixture characterizes roughly half the families living there.

Summary and Conclusions

A common denominator seems to emerge from all the many families interviewed for the purposes of this chapter. All have experienced some period in their personal biographies which required them to develop tolerance for others, initially at the family and later at the communal level. In some cases these are couples from different ethnic backgrounds who had to be receptive to one another's customs, food, and culture if they were to live together. No less striking were the many couples who had to learn to live together at different levels of religiosity. In the course of my interviews I encountered couples representing a whole gamut of religious backgrounds, current religious propensities or both. There is a much greater variety of mixtures than just that of an observant and a non-observant partner. It also includes a penitent and a non-religious partner, a wife who is moderately religious and her religiously extreme husband, a religious partner and one from a very observant background who is now non-religious. These couples all had to struggle with the effort to learn how to accommodate one another. They are not the only kind of couples in the mixed settlements. There are those where both the partners are secular, or both partners religious and both from the same ethnic backgrounds. These homogeneous couples view mixed settlements as a solution to the social polarization which is tearing Israel apart internally. They chose to live in a mixed settlement for ideological reasons and not as an environment which is particularly hospitable to their own condition—but those who chose to do so for ideological reasons are a minority.

Do the mixed settlements represent a harbinger of the future? Are they likely to grow in number, and will their success encourage other religious and non-religious Jews to live together in mixed communities?

The answer seems all too clear. Even in Judea and Samaria, only a small minority choose to live in such settlements. The vast majority prefer to isolate themselves in groups which share not only a political ideology similar to their own, but also a similar life-style.

It is interesting that the official religious establishment (the state religious educational system) agreed to provide backing for mixed religious schools with moderate traditional atmospheres. The enthusiasm expressed by the leaders of Gush Emunim and a number of rabbis associated with it for mixed settlements also merits observation. But the silent majority of settlers in Judea and Samaria have "voted with their feet" in the opposite direction.

Ephraim Tabory

6

Living in a Mixed Neighborhood

WHEREAS SHARED religious symbols unite Israeli Jews on one level, controversy over the role of religion generates conflict on another level. Virtually all Israeli Jews affirm that Israel is and must remain a Jewish state, but they have very different notions about what this means in terms of relations between religion and state. This, in turn, can affect the relationship of Jews to one another. The issue of imposing or eliminating religiously based laws on the national and municipal levels is the subject of agitation and the cause of animosity which can carry over to the interpersonal level. El Al employees protesting political demands that the national airline cease operating on Shabbat sought to prevent *haredim* from entering the airport: the result was a fist-fight. Religious Jews have thrown stones at cars traveling on Shabbat. Police have had to separate demonstrators protesting on behalf of and against the opening of movie theaters on Shabbat. Nevertheless, the vast majority of religious and nonreligious Jews live together peacefully. By focusing on one religiously mixed neighborhood in Tel Aviv, this study seeks to analyze one way in which religious conflict has been contained.

The community studied, Sira (a pseudonym), is located in the northern part of Tel Aviv. The study of Sira is based on systematic observations conducted by the author and on informal interviews and discussions with a cross-section of all Sira residents. In addition, formal interviews were conducted with members of 79 religious families in Sira and with a random sample of 177 secular persons.

Residents who defined themselves as religiously "traditional" were not formally interviewed.

All of the 2,800 families in Sira are middle- or upper-class Jews. About five percent of the families identify themselves as religious, fifty percent say they are secular, and 45 percent say they are religiously traditional. All of the families live in condominiums, and there is generally no religious clustering within buildings. Religious residents are spread throughout the neighborhood. Over 75 percent of all neighborhood residents own cars (as opposed to a national car-ownership rate of twenty percent), and almost all have some university education. Sira is considered to be a prestigious neighborhood and it is in the highest municipal tax bracket. Over ninety percent of the residents have a western, Ashkenazic background.

This basic similarity in social and ethnic traits is important, because any conflict between divergent groups is more intense when the differences between the groups cover a whole set of traits and characteristics. Numerous studies of social conflict confirm that differences between groups of people are more severe if they have little in common. People who have much in common in one sphere will try to overlook differences in another sphere. The conflict between Jews and Arabs in Israel, on the other hand, is aggravated by the fact that the two groups differ in many major attributes, including religion, ethnicity, language, and social status; in addition, they live apart. The basic social and economic homogeneity of Sira residents serves to limit the intensity of the conflict that might arise over issues of religious observance.

The broad consensus within Israeli society affirming that Israel must be a Jewish state serves to provide a bond between religious and non-religious Jews. Great efforts are made to ensure a *Jewish* socialization experience in the public school system, even though religious students attend separate schools. The syllabus includes a substantial amount of material related to Jewish religion, customs, and history. There is a strong intertwining of Jewish and Israeli symbolism in the media as well. Radio programs, for example, begin each morning with the prayer *Shma Yisrael,* and daily broadcasts terminate with quotations from religious texts. The result of the socialization experience for religious and for non-religious Jews in Israel is that Jewish identity develops as a salient and central feature of one's self. This is very important, because the potential conflict between religious and non-religious Jews in Israel may be less affected by the number of people who are nominally religious or non-religious than by the extent to which they share attitudes about the Jewish tradition and Jewish values.

But whereas Judaism provides a basis for shared values between the religious and non-religious, it is also a source of conflict. This is because, in the eyes of religious Jews, Judaism is—to borrow a term Erving Goffman uses in his book *Asylums*—a "total institution" that is "greedy." Orthodox Judaism is an all-encompassing religion that prescribes and proscribes patterns of living for public as well as private life. According to the Orthodox, this pattern of life is incumbent upon the non-religious as well as the religious Jew. In Israel this leads to demands for legislation on issues that are usually considered beyond the domain of government intervention in western democratic societies. Examples include laws that forbid the sale of pork, restrict the display of unleavened bread on Passover, limit Shabbat bus service, or proscribe certain types of marriages that no other western society would envisage proscribing. Many non-religious people feel that such laws infringe on their civil rights, leaving them the victims of religious coercion. On the other hand, religious Jews feel that many non-religious Jews are not sensitive to their religious needs, or to the true significance of Israel's being a Jewish state. The question is how these individuals manage the tension that stems from different perceptions of the appropriate role of religion in Israeli society.

Residential Patterns for Ensuring Harmony

There appear to be two residential patterns that might minimize conflict between religious and non-religious Jews in Israel. One is for religious Jews to live in completely segregated neighborhoods. There they have almost no social interaction with non-religious Jews. Their children attend separate religious schools and belong to separate religious youth movements. Vehicular traffic may be restricted on Shabbat, and they encounter no other form of "desecration." They do not, for example, see or hear anyone playing radios or a musical instrument or watching television. For some, this segregation extends to their place of employment. There are banks and other institutions in Israel that employ only religious persons. Many ultra-Orthodox men and most religious women do not serve in the army, the one institution that Israel's founders refused to segregate along religious lines.

Such a pattern permits religious residents to continue their social practices in an environment that does not threaten to undermine religious control. Religious norms govern the lives of the segregated community without their interfering with the lives of non-religious Jews. Interpersonal conflict is limited because there are no intergroup relations on a primary level. Thus, for example, streets can be closed to traffic because no one living in the segregated community wants to drive anyway. Conflict over religious legislation may ensue at the political level, but it has less effect on interpersonal relations when the two groups hardly meet and when they retain autonomy over the conduct of their private lives.

Sira demonstrates a second pattern. The religious residents of Sira perceive themselves as modern Jews who prefer to live in religiously mixed neighborhoods. They try to minimize the differences between themselves and others. The dress of the religious and non-religious residents, for example, is basically identical, except for the *kipa* (skullcap) worn by the men, and the generally more modest dress of the women. But the men eschew black jackets and white shirts during the week and the conspicuously large *kipot* and beards that characterize *haredi* Jews. Married women do not always cover their hair in public as prescribed by Jewish law. Religious life is confined to one's private life inside the home, Shabbat being the one day in which greater public display is made of one's religiosity. This compartmentalization is both a cause of the religious Jews' decision to live in a basically non-religious neighborhood like Sira, and an effect of living in such an area. (Several women, for example, decided to stop covering their hair after they lived in Sira for a while.)

The religious residents are acutely sensitive to their non-religious neighbors. They testify that they cannot make the kind of religious demands that would appear reasonable in a religious or mostly religious neighborhood, the very type of neighborhood in which they choose not to live. Hence residential proximity might be said to promote understanding. And paradoxically the limited interaction between the two groups is a factor in reducing the potential conflict to manageable levels.

Religious Issues in Sira

A) Public Transportation on Shabbat

While bus service on Shabbat is officially prohibited in Tel Aviv until nightfall, the bus company actually resumes service late in the afternoon. It is inconceivable that this would happen in a religious neighborhood. In Sira, on the other hand, the bus stops directly in front of the synagogue. Congregants mingle outside before afternoon services and ignore bus arrivals and departures, even when they are forced to step onto the sidewalk so that they will not interfere with the vehicle's right of way.

No effort was ever made by the religious residents to have the Shabbat ban on bus transportation enforced in the neighborhood. One of the congregants, a politician in a religious party, once suggested moving the bus stop away from the synagogue. However, no serious pressure was exerted because the convenience of having the bus stop there during the week outweighed the Shabbat traffic issue.

B) The Health Club

Construction of a "country" club, planned for over fifteen years, finally began in 1988. The club will be open on Shabbat. The prevalent attitude among the religious leaders in the community is that any effort to curtail its Shabbat activities would fail, and that it was therefore futile even to try. None of the religious residents in the neighborhood expressed concern about the club's Shabbat activities. Several religious families have enrolled as club members.

C) Reform Movement Activities

A Reform synagogue just outside Sira is scheduled for completion in 1990. In order to introduce itself to the community, the Reform movement announced that it would conduct classes and other activities in a rented apartment in Sira. Handbills were placed in all Sira mailboxes. There was no reaction to this initiative on the part of the religious residents of Sira. The local meeting hall of Na'amat (a major women's organization) agreed to rent its facilities to the Reform group; the rabbi made preliminary inquiries about the possibility of pressuring Na'amat to withdraw its offer. In the end he decided to wait and see what the general community response to the Reform initiative might be. The absence of demonstrations or organized actions against the Reform effort was conspicuous, considering the charge advanced by the majority of Orthodox leaders in Israel that Reform Judaism must be denied entry to Israel because it is destructive of Jewish life.

D) The Operation of the Movie Theater on Shabbat

Sira has a 900-seat theater that was built in the early 1970s. In line with other movie theaters, Sira's was closed on the Sabbath. In the past, religious political parties argued that showing movies constitutes an unacceptable public desecration of Shabbat, and they were instrumental in preventing screenings on Friday nights. This situation changed in the 1980s. A growing number of Tel Aviv theaters opened on Friday evening. In Petah Tikva, the mayor supported public entertainment on the Sabbath, arguing that this provided neighborhood youth with a superior alternative to hanging out along sidewalk railings. The Sira theater commenced Friday-night screenings in 1985.

The rabbi of the community was now confronted with a public desecration of the Sabbath within a hundred yards of his own home. Demonstrations about Shabbat movies were also taking place at this time in central Tel Aviv and were scheduled to resume in Petah Tikva. Could Sira be an exception? At a Friday-night prayer service in the early summer of 1985 the rabbi announced that a demonstration would take place later that evening in front of the theater, and he called upon all the congregants to take part.

The demonstration was attended by about forty of the 250 men who had been present at the evening service. There was some singing of Shabbat songs and dancing, and the demonstrators then returned to their homes. There was no attempt to force entry to the theater and disturb the screening, or to prevent customers from entering the theater, as was done in Petah Tikva. The demonstration appeared to be a perfunctory matter, a ritual that one had to go through in order to fulfill one's religio-political obligations. Some respondents hinted strongly that the demonstration was encouraged by municipal officials who were sensitive to the demands of the neighborhood rabbi to close the movie house but felt that they could only act if some form of public pressure were exerted.

A public circular distributed to neighborhood residents called for a second Friday-night demonstration. The announcement was paid for by the synagogue but it carried no name of any sponsor. It called for the support of all Sira residents and offered the following reasons for opposing the Friday-evening movies:

> — we care about preserving the quality of life in our community;
> — we care that we can enjoy a quiet life in our community;
> — we care that on at least one day in the week—the Shabbat—we will not have noise, smoke, the crowding of the hundreds of cars from outside that come to the movie theater and honk their horns and take up our parking-places . . .

The religious issue is virtually absent. No mention was made of Saturday as the religiously prescribed day of rest. Part of the rationale may have been to obtain wide community support for the closing of the theater. But there is reason to believe that those who initiated the circular were determined not to let the movie theater issue disturb their harmonious relationships with the non-religious.

As a result of this "pressure," the municipality sought a temporary court injunction instructing the operator of the theater immediately to suspend operations for thirty days until a permanent court decision would be rendered.

In retrospect it is clear that an injunction restraining the movie operator from opening on Friday nights would have been sufficient to deal with the issue. There was no justification for closing the theater for thirty consecutive days. One explanation for what happened is that a standard form was used by the municipality in requesting the injunction (like those used in closing food establishments found to be insanitary), and that the absence of a need to close the movie theater during the week was overlooked. An alternative possibility, suggested by some of the participants in the events, is that the Mayor wanted to placate the local rabbi by seeming to act, while actually forcing the theater-owner to take steps that would lead to the opening of the theater on Friday nights. It is clear that other movie theaters in Tel Aviv opened on Friday nights with the authorization and permission of the Mayor, who was interested in providing Friday-night entertainment for his constituents. The rationale for the thirty-day injunction, according to this argument, is that the movie operator might not have taken the trouble to fight an order merely enjoining Friday-night screenings. However, he would be economically forced to appeal a restraining order that would heavily cut into his daily livelihood. In fact, he did appeal the temporary order, and the injunction was declared illegal and therefore void.

The ball was thus in the religious residents' court. One of these asked those persons living in the immediate vicinity of the movie house to sign a petition against Friday-night screenings. A non-religious resident was recruited to act on their behalf and initiate a civil-court proceeding against the movie house. The charge was that the noise stemming from the operation of the movie theater on Friday nights infringed on the peace and quiet of the neighborhood residents, and that it was in violation of municipal bylaws. The infringement of Shabbat *per se* was not mentioned at all. There were two reasons for this. The plaintiffs felt that the religious argument would not hold up in court, but even more important was their fear of turning the case into a religious issue that would strain relations between religious and non-religious Jews. No general meeting of the religious residents was called to discuss the issue or to solicit opinions about it. The reason may well have been that such a meeting might have demonstrated that the religious residents did not really care if the movie house was or was not open on Friday nights. Many reported that the issue was not a personal concern of theirs. They and others reported a reluctance to impinge on the rights of the non-religious. This was even true of those who testified that opening the movie theater was contrary to their conception of Israel as a Jewish state.

The local rabbi absented himself from the civil-court proceedings in order to play down its significance as a religious issue. Nevertheless, the defense argued that the real issue was not the noise, but rather the rabbi's desire to close the movie theater on Shabbat. The judge rejected the plea to close the theater, arguing that the municipal bylaw ordering the closing of cinemas on Friday nights was illegal since it was selectively applied to some Tel Aviv theaters and not to others. The judge also held that the disturbance to the community was minimal, since the main noise, caused by vehicular traffic, was limited to the fifteen-minute periods immediately prior to and following the screening.

The movie operator was ordered to pay the legal fees of the plaintiff, despite the latter's having lost the case. An appeal against the verdict was rejected by the court, and this time the appellants were required to pay the movie operator $4000 in legal fees. An attempt was made to raise this sum from the synagogue congregants. Only thirteen persons agreed to contribute, and the amount collected from them accounted for less than one-fourth of the money needed. Eventually two public religious institutions (supported by state funds) agreed to cover the costs.

This case demonstrates how little the religious residents cared about the public screening of movies on Shabbat. They were not enthusiastic about demonstrating on Friday nights, and if weekly demonstrations had been called for they would have failed miserably. A typical comment of the religious residents in the neighborhood demonstrates that the supra-religious issue of the public nature of Shabbat in the Jewish state was reduced to an interpersonal level.

> We have a real problem (with regard to the operation of the movie and also the bus line on Saturday) with what these things mean for the nature of Shabbat in Israel. But how can I tell my neighbor not to go to a movie because I don't want to go to a movie? He doesn't tell me what to do or not to do because of his personal beliefs. He doesn't bother me and I don't bother him. We have a live-and-let-live relationship based on mutual respect and tolerance. If I start telling him what to do, it will destroy our whole relationship.

The rabbi felt that he had to do something because the event was taking place in his neighborhood. He tried to exert some influence behind the scenes by calling on the municipal officials who he felt could help, and by personally petitioning the owner of the theater who had rented the facilities to the operator. He apparently understood, however, that he would lose the battle.

E) Saturday Sales in Private Homes

Stores and manufacturers have instituted a system of direct sales on Saturdays from the homes of cooperating individuals. These sales are announced by flyers delivered to the homes of all neighborhood residents and posted in the lobbies of the condominiums. This practice is so taken for granted by the religious residents, and it is "selectively ignored" with such effect, that in the interviews most religious residents did not even mention it as an example of Shabbat violation in Sira.

F) Tolerance for Non-religious Jews in the Synagogue

One might argue that the previous issues do not affect the religious residents personally, and that this is what accounts for their tolerance. This does not apply to the issue of synagogue behavior.

The synagogue in Sira has had bar-mitzvah celebrations almost weekly for several years. The celebrants are usually not members of the synagogue. They and their guests are one-time visitors. Non-religious residents of Sira and of adjacent communities choose to celebrate their bar-mitzvah in the Sira synagogue because it is conveniently located, charges a relatively low fee, or both. The synagogue, for its part, agrees to host these celebrations because of the feeling of its officers that persons who want to mark their bar-mitzvah should be entitled to do so even if they are not religious and not members of the synagogue. They have deliberately kept the fees to a minimum in order not to discourage bar-mitzvah celebrations on financial grounds. Their fear is that some parents, despite their relative affluence, would rather forgo the synagogue celebration than pay a large fee for a ceremony that they themselves do not really care about.

The problem with these celebrations is that the non-religious families are generally unfamiliar with proper synagogue behavior. Some will drive their cars up to the synagogue entrance and park them in the vacant bus stop. There have been cases of family members trying to take pictures (which is forbidden on Shabbat) during services. Female guests do not always dress modestly. Even the dress of the males indicates that they are non-religious and alien to the synagogue. The bar-mitzvah boys, who generally wear loud attire that is not usually found in an Orthodox synagogue, often remove their *kipa* while still standing on the synagogue steps.

Despite the inconvenience and unpleasantness caused by these bar-mitzvah celebrations to the regular worshipers, the synagogue has never refused to host them. No woman has ever been asked to leave because of improper dress. No sanctions were taken against people who tried to take pictures in the synagogue. It is a custom to throw candy at the bar-mitzvah boy when he completes his reading from the prescribed texts; in several cases families threw non-kosher candy. But no public announcement about this was made to the congregants, since it was felt that this would embarrass the non-religious family. Instead, the synagogue decided that in the future it would buy the candy itself for bar-mitzvah families.

In order to deal with the non-religious families who celebrate a bar-mitzvah in the synagogue, a contract was once written stipulating that the family was not to desecrate Shabbat. In addition, the family was to refrain from including information about the Saturday synagogue service on invitations to an evening celebration. The purpose was to discourage guests from riding to the synagogue. Current board members are unclear who drew up the contract or when it was first written, or even whether it was ever officially approved by the board (let alone sponsored by it). They are sure, however, that it was never presented to bar-mitzvah families as a precondition for holding the bar-mitzvah service.

G) Yom Kippur

The Day of Atonement is "observed" among non-religious children in Sira by bicycling and skateboarding on the car-free streets. While the religious feel that this undermines the sanctity of the day, almost nothing is done to curb the behavior. (There was one exception to this in 1981, when the rabbi had circulars posted in some buildings asking people not to ride bicycles.) In fact, the people who seem most disturbed by this behavior are the religiously "traditional" group. Secular Jews are indifferent, and the religious have no expectations from the non-religious. The religiously traditional have a more emotional, sentimental approach to those rituals and holidays which they do observe.

H) Building-related Issues

Some issues which have not arisen also merit comment. For example, religious residents do not use the elevator on Shabbat, nor do they turn on hall lights (which remain lit, once pressed, for thirty seconds). Nevertheless, they do not seek to have their monthly maintenance fees reduced because of this, although they are technically supporting the infringement of Shabbat. Nor do the religious residents ask for special consideration of their particular needs by utilizing, for example, special time-clocks for hall lights to keep them on for fixed periods on Shabbat or to keep the electrically operated entrance door open on a regular basis.

Tolerance by the Non-religious Residents

There are few opportunities for the non-religious residents to reciprocate the tolerance which the religious display toward them. One occasion is Sukkot, the Feast of Booths. Many religious residents build outdoor booths in the parking-lots adjacent to their buildings. This makes it more difficult to park during the eight-day holiday.

There have never been any complaints about this. Similarly, residents who have installed their own light fixtures (connected to their own electric meters) to overcome the problem of dark halls on Saturdays have never been asked to remove them, regardless of how unsightly some of these fixtures are.

The synagogue is located in the midst of the residential area. Neighbors suffer from the noise emanating from inside the synagogue, but especially from the noise outside the synagogue where many of the congregants' children play. Nevertheless, the neighbors accept this situation without complaint.

Residential Proximity and Social Segregation

One might expect that the tolerance of the religious residents would be attributable to the strong interpersonal relationships that have developed between themselves and non-religious Jews. In fact the relations between the two groups are not quite so simple. This section describes the contacts that the groups have with one another. It is followed by a consideration of additional factors leading to tolerance and unity in Sira.

Socializing patterns in Sira are largely separated along religious lines. Religious residents find their friends among other religious people, and secular residents say that their primary friends are also secular. Residents were questioned about their "neighboring" activities: this includes minor requests for assistance such as borrowing food products or leaving a key for a child, as well as visiting with other persons and going shopping with them. Neighboring is usually restricted to persons who are of a similar religious level. Non-religious persons seek assistance only from other non-religious persons and religious persons ask only religious persons for help, even when this entails the inconvenience of having to rely on someone in a different building.

The religiously segregated neighboring patterns of Sira adults affect most social activities as well. There are formal and informal activities throughout the week, such as a choir and study classes, that are unofficially closed to non-religious residents. While a few religious women take part in a local aerobics class, they mainly socialize among themselves after the class. The religious men have formed their own weekly basketball game rather than take part in the game open to all neighborhood residents. A meeting in 1988 open to all residents for the election of a Neighborhood Committee to lobby municipal and national government offices for better services attracted about two hundred persons. No religious residents attended, and the eleven-person committee did not include any religious ones.

Social segregation along religious lines is most clearly evident on Shabbat. Since the religious do not travel on that day, they must spend Shabbat within the confines of the neighborhood. Many congregate in the local park after Saturday-morning prayers, especially young families with small children; almost no non-religious people mix with them there. Other religious families entertain at home at that time, and the guests are invariably other religious people. Friday-night gatherings in the homes of the non-religious are also totally segregated.

Religious families occasionally organize weekend trips. One popular activity is to spend a weekend at a Nature Preserve Authority field school. Some of the schools are specially reserved for religious families on certain weekends, and families from all over Israel participate in such programs. Religious services and Shabbat meals are combined with lectures about the nature preserve, and several hikes to nearby locations are undertaken during the day. (Non-religious hikers who are surprised to see religious hikers on Shabbat occasionally ask them how they got there.) This program enables religious families to take a Saturday hike without violating religious commandments concerning travel.

Even the children are affected by the pattern of social segregation. Religious and non-religious children attend separate schools and belong to different youth movements. However, this separation is not complete. Many children attend university-sponsored or other extracurricular programs. While religious children generally plan to attend with at least one other religious child, the programs are religiously integrated. Thus the children develop at least passive friendship patterns with one another. The presence of the "other group" is acknowledged, although few intense relationships form as a result of this contact. The salience of the religious difference between the groups is seen when children use the religious (or non-religious) identity of each group to describe who they are talking about in the other group ("that religious kid" or "that non-religious kid"). The attitude that most children express is that the children in the other group are "o.k., although we don't have much to do with them."

In sum, the religious and non-religious residents consciously limit their primary relationships to persons of similar levels of religiosity.

Fifty-seven percent of the religious residents and 69 percent of the secular residents who were formally interviewed said that they have no close contact with members of the opposite group at all. Interaction across religious lines is generally found only at the level of secondary, or formal, relationships. This type of contact is not infrequent, however: two-thirds of the religious residents say they come into contact with non-religious persons on a daily basis. Since there are many more non-religious than religious Jews, the fact that only a third of the secular say they come into daily contact with religious persons is not surprising.

Discussion

The religious residents of Sira are a special group in that they have chosen to reside in a predominantly non-religious neighborhood. They prefer exposure to non-religious styles of life over living in a religiously segregated community isolated from the non-religious. They would probably prefer public observance of Shabbat. But they are no less anxious to affirm their identity as non-hyphenated Israelis who take full part in general societal affairs.

The desire of the religious to live in Sira is related to their perception that religious neighborhoods are inhabited by people who have a much more parochial orientation toward Judaism than they do. In one sense, they have more in common with the non-religious residents of Sira than they do with religious separatists. However, this also indicates that their own religion is much more privatized. It is just one element of their lives, and not necessarily the dominant one.

The religious background of the religious residents in Sira has had an impact on this attitude. These persons are all graduates of the state religious schools or moderate yeshiva high schools. Almost none of the men attended yeshivot after high school or fulfilled their military requirement while studying in *hesder* yeshivot (institutes that combine talmud study with military service). The religious residents generally support the middle-of-the-road National Religious Party, which, historically, has sought compromise and mutual understanding between religious and non-religious factions in the state.

In addition, religious and secular residents of Sira share a similar orientation toward Jewish/Israeli society on a cultural-symbolic level. For example, when asked in the formal survey whether they see themselves as more Jewish or more Israeli, most of the religious and the secular respondents said that they viewed themselves as equally Jewish and Israeli. Other questions in the survey dealt with the manner in which they perceived Israeli holidays, values, and institutions, such as the kibbutz, the supreme court, and the army. The responses of the religious and secular respondents basically overlap, reflecting a similar orientation toward Israeli customs and norms. Religious Jews of Sira, in other words, are living among people whose attitudes and whose perceptions of Israeli society are similar to their own. Their reluctance to impose behavioral demands on persons who are so like themselves is understandable. This, in turn, means that their nationalistic orientation leads them to alter their religious priorities. The unity of the Jewish people is no less important than the Jewish religion. Religious priorities do not take precedence over Jewish unity.

The tolerance of the religious Jews of Sira is further reinforced by the residential pattern of Sira. Residential proximity, even in the absence of close social contact, leads to a measure of empathy and understanding for the non-religious. A statement made by a religious resident captures this particular effect.

> It's easy from afar to tell somebody what he should or should not do. But you just can't do that when you live next door to the person—to tell someone to observe Shabbat because I want to keep Shabbat. I mean, when you think about it, it's not quite fair, let alone practical.

It is in this connection that the non-religious bar-mitzvah celebration is particularly significant. This specific case illustrates the attitude of the religious toward the non-religious. The religious welcome the participation of the non-religious, but no effort is made to encourage the bar-mitzvah or his family to embrace Orthodoxy or increase their level of religious observance. Instead, the prevailing sentiment is "we are all Jews, no matter what anyone does."

While the religious residents live in proximity to non-religious Jews, they nevertheless maintain a socially significant distance from them. The relationship between the groups is essentially limited to formal situations. They come into contact with one another at work; they make use of the same physical facilities, such as neighborhood stores and shops. Interaction between religious and non-religious Jews takes place on safe, neutral ground. Social norms in those situations generally preclude interaction of a more intimate nature that could lead to more serious tension. Social visits in homes, for example, entail drinks and meals: non-religious persons might well be offended when persons refuse to eat in their homes or to drink their wine for religious reasons. The exchange of opinions about attitudes that are religiously charged is also avoided by limiting personal encounters.

While proximity leads to tolerance, it does appear to exact a price from the religious. As noted, the religious residents in Sira have "privatized" their religion and limited it to certain practices and spheres of their lives. Judaism, however, is not a privatized religion, at least not as Orthodox leaders understand it. It makes demands in all areas of one's life. The religious residents of Sira not only confine their religion to their private life but they are not very religiously devout. The synagogue, for example, is well attended only on weekends, and then only by the men. Many women do not even use the recently constructed *mikva* (ritual bath), despite the requirements of religious law. Indeed, there were no local demands for a *mikva* in Sira prior to its construction by Tel Aviv's religious council.

The benefits of residential integration for unity and tolerance are clear. The question is whether this pattern of integration can continue. Will parents who do not perform all of the religious rituals required by Judaism be successful in fostering a similar pattern in their children, or will the children opt for a more or less intensive level of religious life? Many parents of teenage children are concerned about this question. A primary consideration in deciding which high school their children should attend is whether it will encourage them to become more or less religious than they are. Several of the older children who attended less religious schools have ceased being religious. On the other hand, several of the older children who attended more religious schools have since married and moved to religiously homogeneous neighborhoods. The question, then, is whether Sira residents are a one-generation phenomenon. The next generation of religious Jews may be less tolerant of non-religious practices.

The impact of residential proximity on the non-religious residents in Sira is much more limited, since the religious have made few demands on them. In addition, the small proportion of religious people in the neighborhood makes them less visible. Many are hardly aware of their existence. Nevertheless, whether independently or because of the pressure of religious residents, many non-religious residents adopt a basically traditional orientation toward religion. Hence they do not behave in a manner that Sira's religious residents might find intolerable. There is no general disregard of Yom Kippur as a holy day, stores are not open on Shabbat, pork products are not displayed openly, and demands are not heard to move the synagogue out of the residential area. Ten percent of the secular residents report that they recite kiddush on Shabbat eve; 32 percent fast on Yom Kippur; 22 percent maintain a kosher home; and 32 percent light Shabbat candles.

However, there are differences between "first-generation" and "second-generation" secular Jews that suggest potential problems. Secular persons who report they were raised in religious or traditional homes are designated as first-generation secular Jews; second-generation secularists are those who report that they were raised in secular homes. About sixty percent of the secular residents in Sira can be characterized as belonging to this first generation. Among them, over forty percent maintain a kosher home, as opposed to three percent of the second-generation secular, seventy percent fast on Yom Kippur as opposed to eighteen percent of the second generation, and fifty percent light Shabbat candles as opposed to twenty percent of the second generation.

Differences between these generations also emerge in their value orientations. While 53 percent of the second-generation secular emphasize their Israeli over their Jewish identity, the corresponding figure for the first generation is 27 percent. Similar differences are found with respect to other attitudes. In other words, many religious and non-religious Jews do share a common orientation to Jewish Israeli society. This limits potential conflict. They may disagree over specific issues—for example, opening movie theaters on Shabbat—but they share a whole world of common values. The first-generation secular Jews, together with those who identify themselves as religiously traditional, retain an emotional orientation toward religion, although they may not observe most of the ritual requirements. The orientation of the second secular generation appears to be more ideological. They not only reject religious demands because they conflict with their life-style, but as a matter of principle. When asked what problems Israel faces today, eleven percent complained of religious coercion—none of the first secular generation mentioned this. The question that bears examining in the future is whether the process of polarization that threatens the middle-of-the-road religious group will also affect future generations of non-religious Jews, as their familiarity with religion grows increasingly remote.

Asher Cohen

7

Political Partners

Relations between Religious and Non-Religious in One Political Party

THE POLITICAL PARTY Tehiya (Revival) was formed in the wake of the peace agreement signed by Israel and Egypt in 1978. The Party's founders came from the activist (hawkish) sections of Israel's three major political camps: the labor movement, the nationalist Likud Party, and the national-religious (religious Zionist) movement. Its first test at the polls came during the election campaign for the Tenth Knesset (Israel's parliament) in the summer of 1981. The main ideological plank in the Party's platform centered on the demand for Israeli sovereignty over the Greater Land of Israel, which meant, at the very least, the retention of all territory captured in the Six-Day War. The party announced its vigorous opposition to the Camp David Agreement, which required Israel to withdraw from Sinai and abandon the Jewish settlements established there.

Most of Tehiya's founders had worked together to advance the ideal of a Greater Israel prior to the formation of the new Party. Following the Six-Day War, in 1967, they joined the Movement for the Greater Land of Israel—an organization founded to propagate the position that Israel must not surrender the newly acquired territory. A few of these same individuals, the religious in particular, were active in the founding of Gush Emunim (Bloc of the Faithful), to which the non-religious nationalists extended their sympathy, their political, and often their financial support as well. Gush Emunim was created in 1974 for the purpose of establishing Jewish settlements on the West Bank. Neither the Movement for the Greater Land of Israel nor Gush Emunim, however, were political parties. Both are better characterized as pressure groups which enjoyed a great deal of support from the National Religious Party and the Likud, as well as the support of a smaller group within the Labor Party.

The peace treaty with Egypt provided the impetus for the establishment of an independent political party. Israel had in fact agreed to the principle of "territories in exchange for peace"—the absolute antithesis of the cry "af sha'al" ('not an inch'), the slogan of the supporters of the Greater Land of Israel. The disappointment was all the more bitter because the peace treaty was negotiated by a Likud-led government which had heretofore stood for the position of *af sha'al.*

Our concern in this chapter is with a second principle, ideological as well as pragmatic, which governed the thinking of the Party's founders. We refer to the idea of *holkhim b'yahad* ("going together"), a conception that pointed to the importance of cooperation between religious and non-religious Jews. Tehiya set great store by this conception. It claimed that it was unique in raising the idea of a partnership between the religious and non-religious to the level of an ideological principle guiding its activities. It is this idea, and its implementation, which we wish to examine.

Is Tehiya Really a Mixed Party?

In a brochure published during the 1981 election campaign entitled "Going Together," the Party projected itself in the following way:

> Who is going with whom? "Religious" and "non-religious," from the yeshivot and the suburbs, from the workers' settlements and religious ones. . . . We have decided to remove the barriers that have been erected between the camps, and form one movement—the Tehiya Movement. We know how revolutionary this is in view of the generally accepted division between religious and non-religious parties. That is why many who privately support our idea are hesitant about marching along this new path. . . .

The creation of a truly mixed (religious–non-religious) party is, indeed, a novelty in Israeli politics. (One other party, Tami, which lasted only two elections, might have also claimed to be a mixed party. But Tami's composition—overwhelmingly Sephardic—and the behavior of its religious activists—religiously traditional rather than rigorously Orthodox—was quite different from that of the Tehiya.) The religious parties label themselves as religious and devote their major efforts to the defense of religious interests. All their candidates are religious, as are the vast majority of their voters. Although the other parties do not label themselves as non-religious, they are considered as such by the Israeli public for several reasons: their candidates, with minor exceptions, are non-religious; the bulk of their supporters are non-religious; and if they are not anti-religious, the subject of religion is a minor issue in the party platform.

The idea of cooperation between religious and non-religious is not new, least of all to the national-religious public. That public, represented primarily by the National Religious Party (NRP), always supported cooperation with non-religious parties—but the idea of a partnership was conceived in terms of inter-party cooperation. The NRP's notion of cooperation and compromise meant partnership with other parties at the organizational rather than the individual level.

The partnership which Tehiya projected was, therefore, a new idea. This is reflected in the composition of its list of candidates for the Knesset. The list was intended from the outset to reflect the principle of partnership. About two-thirds of the candidates were non-religious, about one-third religious. Of the three Tehiya candidates elected to the Knesset in 1981, two were non-religious and one was religious. In elections to the Eleventh Knesset in 1984, five Tehiya candidates won seats. Three non-religious and two religious. The original list of party candidates had included four non-religious and only one religious candidate in the top five positions. However, before the list was actually submitted to the Central Election Committee, Party leaders had second thoughts. The four-to-one ratio was considered inimical to the idea of "going together" and to the Party's image. In last-minute consultations, one of the non-religious candidates among the top five was replaced by a religious candidate, Gershon Shafat, a leader of Gush Emunim. In 1988 the top two candidates on the list were non-religious and the next two religious. However, only the first three obtained seats.

"Going Together" – Who is Going with Whom?

A look at the composition of active Party members indicates Tehiya's particular achievement in bringing its religious and non-religious together. If the religious element in the movement were composed of those whose attitude towards *halakha* (religious Law) was moderate or permissive, if the religious constituents were liberal in observance of the religious commandments, then the partnership could be readily understood. Similarly, if the non-religious element in the movement were composed of those considered "traditional" rather than secular, i.e. those sympathetic to the practice of Jewish traditions or customs, the partnership would also seem more natural. (This, for example, had been the case with Tami). The closer the positions of the two sectors of the movement were to one another in religious matters, the easier it would be to understand the partnership. But this explanation would not hold for Tehiya's members, least of all for its leaders. The head of Tehiya, Professor Yuval Neeman, is secular rather than traditional in his private life. Many of the movement's supporters belong to collective settlements – kibbutzim and moshavim – affiliated with the Labor movement, where their private lives are totally non-religious. On the other hand, the religious members of Tehiya come from circles identified with the strictest adherence to Jewish law. Many of them are graduates of the Yeshiva (Talmudic academy) Merkaz Harav, an institution led (until his death in 1982) by Rabbi Zvi Yehuda Kook. Their position tends to nationalist as well as religious extremes. Religious personalities associated with Tehiya included Hanan Porat, Benny Katsover, Menahem Felix, and Rabbis Eliezer Waldman and Moshe Levinger, individuals who are uncompromising in their adherence to religious law.

Reservations on the part of religious leaders were expressed from the very outset. Religious Jews, their politically active leaders in particular, perceive of themselves as a social minority struggling to transform Israel into a Jewish state as they understand this term. Their goal is a "Torah State," although they may differ over the specific meaning of the term and the methods for its achievement. But in no case are they content with merely preserving their own religious freedom or being guaranteed their right to live the kind of religious life they prefer. The decision to form a joint party with non-religious was therefore not one to be taken lightly. It was clear to everyone that the decision would entail compromises and would certainly create many practical problems.

Following the initial exploratory discussions, leaders of Gush Emunim and some of the non-religious involved in the formation of Tehiya consulted Rav Zvi Yehuda Kook on the legitimacy of a mixed party. His agreement was probably a necessary condition, as far as the religious participants were concerned. Rav Kook is reported to have said: "For the sake of the Land of Israel we must go together." The reply was ambiguous; it did not answer the questions of whether or not a mixed party was legitimate or desirable. Some of the participants asked the question again, stressing the potential problems that could arise from the envisaged partnership. Rav Kook responded in exactly the same words, "for the sake of the Land of Israel, we must go together." When he repeated the same formula a third time those present understood that this was the only reply they would receive from him. To many, including some of his closest disciples, the reply was interpreted as encouraging the formation of Tehiya. Others, however, chose to continue their support for the National Religious Party.

Two men who were remarkably similar in their backgrounds followed the two different paths. Rabbi Haim Druckman and Rabbi Eliezer Waldman are both products of Bnei Akiva (the religious Zionist youth movement), students of Rav Zvi Yehuda Kook and graduates of Merkaz Harav, members of the inner leadership of Gush Emunim, and heads of yeshivot *hesder* (Talmudic academies in which students intersperse their study with army service). Rabbi Waldman affiliated with the Tehiya Party, quickly emerged as one of its leaders, and was elected to the Knesset in 1984. Rabbi Druckman remained at first in the National Religious Party, was elected to the Knesset in 1981, and when he resigned from the NRP formed a new religious party rather than affiliate with Tehiya.

It would be wrong to assume that the religious members were the only ones to have reservations or, as we shall see, experience problems in cooperating in the partnership. The non-religious had their doubts about the feasibility of a mixed party as well. They feared that Tehiya would become in effect a religious party with some non-religious candidates.

Conflicts, Crises, and Compromises— The Political Aspect of the Partnership

Tehiya presented its point of view on religious issues in a 1981 campaign brochure, "Going Together." The front of the brochure portrayed two heads. One covered by a knitted skullcap, symbol of the younger generation of religious Zionists, the other bare-headed, symbol of the non-religious. The language of the brochure, like that of other Party statements, avoids terms that appear one-sided. It reflects a preference for phrases that unite rather than divide.

> Where do we come from?—We are one nation—we have one country—we all have a common heritage. And where are we headed?—Towards the same goals—the redemption of the whole nation of Israel in the whole Land of Israel—drawing people closer together in love—the united return to the heritage of Israel.

The desire to find a formula that would appeal to both religious and non-religious is very apparent. In this and other literature, terms such as "Israel's heritage," "tradition," "returning to one's origin," or "common roots" are employed, whereas perculiarly religious expressions such as *"halakha,"* "religion," or "repentance" (i.e. becoming Orthodox) are only invoked in special circumstances.

On the subject of religious legislation, Tehiya upheld the principle of the "status quo." The guiding principle behind agreements concerning religious legislation in Israel has been the "status quo." This refers to a rather amorphous understanding that legislation on religious matters would more or less maintain conditions as they existed when the State was founded. It is a mechanism whereby political parties acknowledged the limits of the demands they could make on one another.

As a consequence of the dynamic nature of the Israeli economy, new technologies, and changing styles of life, disagreements arose over the interpretation of the "status quo." It is not surprising, therefore, that in spite of the existence of this principle, the subject of religious legislation continually recurs. Furthermore, the "status quo" was never satisfactory to the ultra-Orthodox, represented at best a necessary evil to the religious Zionist leaders, and has been the subject of increasing attack from secularists. To Tehiya, however, it seems to offer the only practical solution. According to its platform:

> The Party accepts all the laws and statutes passed on the topics of Torah and the State since the founding of the State until today. . . . Any further attempt at legislation . . . will be carefully considered by the movement on its merits, with consultations with the experts on the subjects, among them men of Torah and *halakha,* in an effort to reach a united front.

It is important to observe that Tehiya, committed to the ideal of a mixed party, found no better way to resolve the problem of religious legislation than by appeal to the "status quo." Both religious and non-religious, even within the Party, remain sharply divided over the issue of religious legislation. Appealing to the "status quo," therefore, bypasses further controversy despite the increasing dissatisfaction which both religious and non-religious have expressed with the principle. Perhaps the "status quo" does remain the only possible solution in Israel's present circumstances.

The marked differences over religious issues within Tehiya, however, point to the importance which a partnership between religious and non-religious assumed for the Party. "Going Together" is secondary to the main ideal of a Greater Land of Israel. "Going Together" by itself would never have provided the impetus to form a mixed political party. Nonetheless, Tehiya's founders chose to present it as an ideological principle and not a matter of convenience. They might have constructed the Party as a kind of confederation in which all sides would agree to the principle of a Greater Israel but each would retain its independence on the subject of religion and state. The decision to create a party with one voice on religious issues suggests that all sides believed that such an effort was valuable in and of itself. This, as we have already indicated, required compromises from both sides.

On the religious side, two important concessions led to a significant measure of unease within the religious-Zionist community. The first was the dominance of the non-religious in the composition of the Party leadership. In the 1981 elections, three members of the Party were elected: two non-religious—Yuval Neeman and Geula Cohen, in the top two positions—and Hanan Porat, the religious representative, in the third position. In the 1984 elections to the Eleventh Knesset, a total of five members were elected. Three non-religious—Yuval Neeman, Refael Eitan, and Geula Cohen, in the top three spots; and two religious, Rabbi Eliezer Waldman and Gershon Shafat, in the fourth and fifth positions. In 1988 two non-religious—Yuval Neeman and Geula Cohen—and one religious candidate—Rabbi Eliezer Waldman—were elected.

This apparent imbalance provided an important propaganda weapon to Tehiya's competitors in the religious community. One of the questions most frequently heard from the religious public in campaign meetings organized by the Party was, "if we are speaking of a genuine partnership, why is the number two position in the list not held by a religious member?" The National Religious Party seized upon this to buttress its claim that Tehiya was not a mixed party but a non-religious party with religious candidates.

The second concession by the religious members of Tehiya, as already indicated, was in their attitude toward religious legislation. Party leaders agreed that they would not initiate religious legislation and established certain rules of conduct for the eventuality of other parties doing so. This represents a significant concession by the religious relative to their own accepted norms of political behavior. The religious parties in Israel, conscious of their minority position, have sought to achieve their objectives by means of coalition agreements. These agreements were themselves the outcome of compromises which the religious parties hoped were only temporary. Their strategy in the field of religious legislation was to push the non-religious parties as far as they could and acknowledge whatever was achieved as an absolute minimum.

That is why the decision to affiliate as active partners in a party which eschewed any initiative in proposing religious legislation represented a major concession. We can only account for it by assuming that these religious representatives viewed the question of Greater Israel as so burning and vital an issue that it overrode other considerations. But this in turn created potential difficulties for Tehiya among religious nationalist voters. The National Religious Party repeatedly stressed that only a religious party can seriously deal with religious matters and that any support for other parties (the barb was aimed primarily at Tehiya) would prejudice the chances of success in this field.

The non-religious sector of the Party made concessions as well. In the brochure "Going Together" the Party expressed its attitude toward religious legislation in the following manner:

> The movement will oppose any change in these laws [meaning religious legislation already enacted] and any proposed legislation which would damage the unity of the people and its Jewish character. The movement therefore supports "conversion according to the *halakha*," and the law against fraud in Kashrut . . . will work toward strengthening the teaching of the Jewish heritage, the Torah, and Jewish creativity in every generation in all educational institutions . . . , recognizing that this education guarantees the preservation of our uniqueness as the chosen people. . . . The movement views Torah study in general, and within the framework of yeshivot in particular, as a national service of great value to the nation and the State. . . . Therefore, the

> movement will work to support Torah institutions in general, and will especially develop yeshivot which are loyal to the State . . . [and] will propose legislation which will achieve a fitting official status for them.

The above could have served as a policy statement of the National Religious Party. Most remarkable is Tehiya's promise to support legislation which would translate these principles into law, particularly the "Who is a Jew?" amendment to the Law of Return. The religious parties have sought to amend the law to exclude non-Orthodox converts. Now, for the first time in Israeli politics, the platform of a party the majority of whose members and leaders were non-religious included a demand for the amendment.

The commitment to proposed legislation which would grant official status and recognition to yeshivot and to Torah study was also unique in light of the movement's composition. In the discussion of the social make-up of the movement we indicated that one segment came from backgrounds in the Labor movement and working settlements. These individuals are strongly "secular," antagonistic to the imposition of religion in public life and thoroughly non-religious in the conduct of their own lives. This is particularly true of those who come from kibbutzim. Yet kibbutz members of the Labor movement not only gave their support to the platform; some of them even helped in its formulation.

Gershon Shafat's description of meetings in which he participated prior to the establishment of the Party illustrates this point. "Many of them learned that the religious do not have horns," is the way he characterized these early discussions.

While the concessions which the religious made to non-religious elements in Tehiya created difficulty in campaigning among religious voters, the concessions which the non-religious made to the religious were a source of strength. Religious activists within Tehiya claimed that the support of Yuval Neeman and people like him for "conversion in accordance with *halakha*" and other religious legislation was a significant achievement.

Concessions and compromises did not suffice to resolve all the problems. Hanan Porat, the leader of the Party's religious faction, resigned from Tehiya in 1983. Porat justified his resignation by the absence of "soul" the absence of "an atmosphere of Torah" within the movement. His former colleagues in Tehiya explain his resignation as a result of his exaggerated expectations from Tehiya and his subsequent disappointment. They believe that he had nurtured the hope that the close working relationship with the non-religious in the Party would draw them closer to traditional Jewish values and religion. When he realized that this was not happening, at least not to the degree he hoped, he abandoned the idea of a mixed party, resigned from Tehiya, and formed a new religious movement. This then merged with the group established by Haim Druckman (a development to which we will return) in time for the 1984 election. In 1988 their party was absorbed by the National Religious Party. The lack of widespread support from the religious-Zionist public was an added disappointment to Porat. The National Religious Party lost six seats in the 1981 election, but most of the votes lost did not go to Tehiya. The Party's own estimate is that less than one of the seats which Tehiya won in 1981 was attributable to the support of religious voters. It is clear that, in spite of wide support for the notion of a Greater Land of Israel among religious Zionists, most of them, at least those who were most sympathetic to Gush Emunim, were not prepared, or not yet prepared, to support any but a religious party.

Hanan Porat's resignation dealt a severe blow to Tehiya's image and caused a great deal of soul-searching among religious Party activists. How could the Party claim to stand for a new *modus vivendi* between the religious and non-religious when the most prominent religious leader within the Party had lost confidence in it?

Challenges to the vision of a new type of party did not come exclusively from the religious side. Refael Eitan, who had been chief-of-staff of the Israeli army during the war in Lebanon, embarked on a political career when his term as head of the army ended. He formed a party of his own, Tzomet ("Crossroad"), which from the outset embraced the notion of a Greater Land of Israel. He and his supporters joined Tehiya in time for the 1984 election campaign and Eitan was slated in the number two position, after Yuval Neeman, on Tehiya's list of Knesset candidates. But his strongly secularist views brought him into conflict with the official Party line on two occasions.

The first was his vote on a proposed law extending prohibitions on raising and selling pigs. Tehiya supported this legislation. In the 1960s a law banning the raising of pigs in most of Israel had been passed with the support of Herut, the most nationalist party at that time. In Knesset debates Herut spokesman evoked national memories recalling the Jews' particular revulsion for the pig. It came as no surprise that Tehiya supported an extension of the earlier legislation. The Party might have done so even without the urging of their religious constituents. Nevertheless, Refael Eitan voted against the legislation. His own values and his loyalty to his friends and supporters in the Labor settlements overcame his commitment to support the Party's position. One respondent explained Eitan's decision as follows: "He couldn't do it to his friends in Mizra." Mizra is more than the name of a settlement with a major food-processing plant for pig meat. In Israeli society it has become the very symbol of non-kosher food.

The second occasion on which Eitan broke Party ranks was the vote on the proposed amendment to the "Who is a Jew?" law. Whereas the other four Tehiya M.K.s voted in favor, in accordance with the Party platform, Eitan abstained on one occasion and cast a negative ballot on the other.

In addition, Eitan and his supporters demanded greater internal democracy in the choice of Party candidates for the Knesset. It appears that Eitan's supporters were among the leading opponents to the over-representation of the religious on the Party's Knesset list. Party chairman Yuval Neeman raised the delicate issue of balance versus democratization in a personal letter to the Party Council during the crisis precipitated by Eitan's demands:

> In my capacity as chairman I attempt to maintain the internal balance between the different groups, the former members of the historical camps: those which are called "national," "labor," and "religious" . . . My insistence on freezing the places of the first five (the rule that two of the top five representatives on the list would be religious) . . . is intended to prevent a clash over an explosive issue. . . .

Neeman understood that full democratization would upset the balance between the components of the party and destroy the notion of "going together." In 1987, Eitan came to the conclusion that the concessions expected from him in the Tehiya Party were more than he was prepared to make. He resigned, and formed a one-man faction in the Knesset. In 1988 he founded a separate party, Tzomet, which won two Knesset seats.

These crises illustrate the potential for friction that exists among groups which are, in many important respects, ideologically aligned. It suggests how much greater the potential for friction must be in Israeli society at large. On the other hand, the majority of Party supporters continued to support the conception of a mixed party despite the compromises it entailed. A consistent trend toward greater understanding between the factions is apparent within Tehiya. Each side has become increasingly sensitive to the "red lines" of the other, but beyond this each side increasingly looks for ways in which it can accommodate the other. Two examples illustrate this point.

In recent years, the city of Jerusalem has witnessed political and even physical clashes over the opening of public facilities on the Sabbath, places of entertainment in particular. Most religious bitterly oppose this breach of the "status quo," especially in Jerusalem, where the religious constitute a significant proportion of the population, and which they maintain has a special sanctity. Tehiya Knesset member Geula Cohen is avowedly non-religious and an outspoken opponent of religious coercion. Hence there was particular significance in her newspaper article on the topic of clashes between religious and non-religious in Jerusalem. The article, entitled "Shabbat Shalom?" ("A Sabbath of Peace?") admonished the secularists for their insistence that places of entertainment and leisure in Jerusalem be opened on the Sabbath. She stressed the necessity of maintaining the status quo, and claimed that any changes required the agreement of all parties concerned. Finally, she distinguished between Tel Aviv, where in her opinion a certain permissiveness in Sabbath observance was understandable, and Jerusalem, where it was not. She concluded by saying: "To struggle against coercion, therefore, whether religious or anti-religious, in Jerusalem—yes: but to force Tel Aviv upon Jerusalem—no!"

From the other side, a religious Knesset member of Tehiya, on at least one occasion, supported the demands of the non-religious against the opposition of the religious. Gershon Shafat has indicated his support for the construction of a sports stadium in Jerusalem. Professional soccer teams have always played in Jerusalem on the Sabbath. Until a few years ago games were played in the old Y.M.C.A. stadium. In 1985 Jerusalem's "home" ground was moved to Tel Aviv because of the deteriorated condition of the field, and plans were undertaken to construct a modern stadium. Religious groups opposed the new stadium: they claimed that since games would be played there on Saturday it would lead to widespread violation of Sabbath laws.

Gershon Shafat, in an interview, expressed his support for the stadium project, and promised he would vote for it when the topic came up for discussion in the appropriate Knesset committee. He based his position on his commitment to the principle of the status quo. The sole reason for discontinuing the games on the Sabbath in Jerusalem, he noted, was that the field was unsuitable. Therefore, the construction of a new stadium and renewal of games merely constituted a return to the *status quo ante.* "The religious must understand that they ought not, and it is not worth their while, to undermine the status quo, just as they would not want the reverse to occur," Shafat explained.

This behavior is quite exceptional in Israeli politics. Non-religious M.K.s have been known to support religious positions as the result of political arrangements. Virtually unheard-of is the case when a religious M.K. supports a position which the religious parties view as anti-religious. The fact that Shafat supports such a position, and this even though no pressure was brought to bear on him by his non-religious colleagues within Tehiya, is an indication of how accommodating religious and non-religious have become of one another within Tehiya. It might not be stretching a point to argue that both Geula Cohen and Gershon Shafat adopted the positions they did as a consequence of their experience within the Party.

"Going Together"—Some Social and Personal Aspects

So far we have dealt with the public and political aspects of the creation of a mixed party. We turn now to a no less interesting and perhaps no less important aspect of Tehiya's activity—the implications of cooperation in the political realm for values and behavior in the private religious realm. Many of the examples and incidents cited here were observed in the Petah Tikva branch of the Party. Petah Tikva was deemed an ideal branch for intensive observation. It is small enough for it to be possible to examine the range of interpersonal relations between a variety of members, yet large enough to assure a relatively heterogeneous membership in terms of educational and social background and religious or non-religious identity.

The very existence of intensive contacts between religious and non-religious, outside of work, is the first point worth noting. Such contacts are unusual in Israeli society. This is somewhat less true among the Sephardic Jews, but Tehiya is overwhelmingly Ashkenazic in its composition. Because of the sparsity of contact, each side forms warped images of the other based on oversimplifications and stereotypes. Social contact, in particular, can become a mechanism through which each side can learn to appreciate the point of view of the other. If the gulf were wide enough, social isolation could, it is true, serve to prevent clashes. In Tehiya, however, the central theme of "Going together" has created a positive ambience for contact at the personal level. No instance was reported in which contact between religious and non-religious resulted in heightened tension, but many cases were observed or described in which improved relations resulted from extended contact.

The first positive result of meetings between religious and non-religious is to dispel popular myths about the other side. The following anecdote about Tehiya's leader, Yuval Neeman, illustrates the point. In an attempt to discredit Tehiya among religious voters in one of the election campaigns, the National Religious Party quoted him as having said, "In the matter of religion, I am like Shulamit Aloni." (Shulamit Aloni, leader of the Citizens Rights Movement, is perceived as the leading antagonist of the religious parties). Neeman may never have actually said this, but it is generally accepted as reflecting a point of view he once held. Tehiya's publicists seized upon the NRP charges to demonstrate the merits of the religious–non-religious partnership. If even someone as antagonistic to religion as Yuval Neeman was once presumed to have been could change his views as a result of associations with religious Jews in Tehiya, then the Party surely deserved the support of religious voters.

Many anecdotes illustrate how social contact resulted in heightened consideration for one another's sensitivities. Three Party members from the Petah Tikva branch, one religious and two non-religious, were returning together from a meeting in Tel Aviv. The non-religious wanted to stop at a restaurant on the way. Their religious colleague said that since he was not hungry he would wait for them in the car. They parked at a non-kosher restaurant, but on leaving the car the two non-religious members recalled that their choice of restaurant precluded their religious colleague from joining them. They returned to the car and there then ensued an interesting discussion, almost an argument, between the three of them. The religious member insisted that it was the right of the non-religious to eat in a kosher restaurant; this was a private matter involving their individual way of life. The non-religious stubbornly refused, out of consideration for the sensitivities of their religious friend, even though he insisted he was not hungry and under no circumstances wanted anything to eat.

In another incident, a member invited a key Party official to attend the ceremony and festive meal that followed the circumcision of his son. A majority of the guests were religious and the circumcision took place at a religious venue. Many non-religious, in such situations, cover their heads, if only because of the religious nature of the ceremony. In this case, however, the Party official indicated that he preferred to eat without covering his head, apparently as a matter of principle. Nevertheless, he first inquired of his host if his doing so would upset him; and the host assured his guest that he was free to do as he wished. In general, religious Party members are very careful not to make requests or even allusions that their non-religious colleagues might interpret as lack of respect for a non-religious life-style. The non-religious, in turn, often show deference bordering on the excessive for the sensitivities of their religious colleagues.

A good example of the curious interplay that takes place in this connection is the matter of securing a *minyan,* a minimum number of ten males required for the recitation of certain prayers. Many religious Jews make a practice of always praying with a *minyan,* an act which is deemed of greater merit than praying alone. This can create a problem when the time comes to recite the afternoon and evening prayers and the religious Jew finds himself in a situation where there are fewer than ten religious males present. It is not uncommon, under these circumstances, for non-religious men who may be present to be requested to join religious Jews in order to constitute a *minyan.* Our observations in Tehiya's Petah Tikva branch yielded some interesting results. On the one hand, religious members are very careful not to exert any pressure in this matter, out of sensitivity toward the views of their non-religious colleagues; on the other hand, in many instances the non-religious hurry to join a *minyan* even when not asked. Moreover, the non-religious even join the prayers when there is a *minyan* without them. This is all the more significant since some of these non-religious are overtly secular rather than "traditional" in their own self-definition and behavior.

Increasing the awareness of Jewish values among the non-religious and raising their level of knowledge about the tradition is a byproduct of "going together." Following a casual discussion among Party members on a religious topic one non-religious member was heard to observe that he was "ashamed at how little [he] knows."

There are also examples, although these are less common, of non-religious members altering their religious orientation in significant ways. In a few cases, non-religious have become Orthodox. This is especially interesting since, as we have already indicated, Party mores discourage any attempts to influence someone to change his private behavior. It is precisely the emphasis on respect for one's fellow-man and his views and life-style that precludes the movement from engaging in or encouraging such activity. Nevertheless, such changes occur.

Such a "conversion" is likely to take place in stages. The non-religious member may become especially close to a religious member and seek to learn more about his religious way of life. He may spend a Sabbath with his religious colleague and gradually increase the level of his religious observance before he decides to "convert" to an Orthodox way of life. Such instances are rare, however, which demonstrates that social contacts do not necessarily lead to changes in religious behavior. And instances of religious becoming less religious are unknown.

More common than "conversion" to Orthodoxy is the adoption of certain aspects of traditional Judaism. This may take the form of making the home kosher or accepting certain restrictions connected with Sabbath observance. Non-religious members who heretofore defined themselves as secularists may now begin thinking of themselves as traditional, or, if previously traditional, they may strengthen their level of observance. Here too, different stages may be identified. The first stage is generally learning more about religion and religious values without any change in religious observance. Then may come a decision to observe some, though not necessarily all, of the rules of kashrut (such as acquiring two sets of dishes, one for meat and one for milk, or exercising greater care in the products served in one's home, or refraining from eating non-kosher foods outside the home); or some, though again not necessarily all, restrictions associated with Sabbath observance (such as preparing a more elaborate meal, or refraining from travel, or occasional attendance at a synagogue). Especially interesting, because of the difficulty involved, are the cases of kibbutz members, including a prominent party leader, who now maintain kosher kitchens and enroll their children in programs of religious education.

Nevertheless, most cases of social contact, regardless of their intensity, do not lead to altered levels of religious observance. This is especially significant since the nationalist ideology and commitments of Tehiya's members should make them especially receptive to the Jewish tradition and the observance of Jewish custom. In spite of this and of the close cooperation at the personal level between religious and non-religious, changes in life-style are relatively infrequent. Furthermore, as we have already noted, they are all in one direction. Religious do not become less religious. What does take place, from one end to the other of the spectrum of religiosity, is a growth in tolerance, in mutual understanding, and in genuine respect for a different point of view.

"Going Together"—Success or Failure?

Did the notion of "Going Together" succeed? Is there some lesson to be derived from Tehiya's experience in improving relations between religious and non-religious Jews in Israel? One measure of the Party's success is its ability to attract electoral support and to spread its ideas among the public. Another is the extent to which the program improved relations between religious and non-religious within the Party itself.

The answer to the question of the importance of "Going Together" in engendering electoral support is not an easy one. Examining its success is complicated by the fact that the partnership did not constitute the main plank of the Party's platform. The question is further complicated by the brevity of the time-span in which Tehiya has existed. It has only contested three elections.

The election returns and survey data give no answer to the question of whether the creation of a mixed party increased the level of the Party's support among the non-religious. Data relating to the religious voter are more revealing. In the 1981 Knesset elections the National Religious Party lost six of the twelve seats it had previously held. Survey data and political scientists' estimates suggest that three of these seats went to the Likud, two to Tami (a party which defined itself as Sephardic and religiously traditional rather than rigorously religious), and one seat, at most, to Tehiya.

The readiness of a large section of the religious-Zionist public to shift its support to non-religious or quasi-religious parties other than Tehiya has been interpreted as failure on its part. But this judgment, we believe, is unfair. The 1981 elections were peculiar in two respects. First, the ethnic issue surfaced with special intensity, and this may help explain the support for Tami (which diminished in the following election). Secondly, the balance between the two major sectors in Israeli politics, nationalist and labor, was evenly weighed. It is not, therefore, surprising that many voters who left the NRP because it was insufficiently militant in its nationalist policies gave their support to the Likud out of the fear that, if Labor won more votes than Likud, they would lead the next government. In addition, the National Religious Party slated Rabbi Haim Druckman—one of the leaders of Gush Emunim—to demonstrate its own fidelity to a Greater Land of Israel. Finally, Tehiya was contesting its first election. Hence, there is some justice to the argument advanced by the religious activists in Tehiya that they faced peculiar obstacles in winning the religious voter to their party just then. At the very least, they argued, the religious voter needed time to digest the notion of a mixed party.

The results of the 1984 election support the claim that the 1981 result was by no means a failure. A new religious party was formed to contest this election—Morasha ("Heritage")—under the leadership of Haim Druckman. Druckman had withdrawn from the National Religious Party because its program was insufficiently nationalist. Morasha was indistinguishable from Tehiya in its commitment to the Greater Land of Israel concept, and presented itself as an alternative strictly religious party. Hanan Porat, whose resignation from Tehiya was discussed above, also joined Morasha. The establishment of Morasha reflects the reservations felt by some national-religious leaders about too close a partnership with the non-religious. Some argued that the concessions demanded in such a partnership were unacceptable. Nevertheless, Tehiya increased its total number of seats from three to five. Survey data indicates that religious voters accounted for two of these seats, at least double the number they provided in 1981. Although Morasha also won two seats, at least one of them came from their alliance with the non-Zionist Agudat Israel Worker's movement. In other words, increasing numbers of religious voters who were committed to the Greater Land of Israel concept supported Tehiya, despite Hanan Porat's resignation and despite Morasha's campaign.

Prior to the 1988 elections, straw polls among religious high school students showed more support for Tehiya than any other political party, religious or non-religious. To everyone's surprise Tehiya lost two seats in the election, but not to other religious parties. It appears that most religious voters who abandoned Tehiya voted, instead, for a new right-wing party, Moledet (Homeland), that favors the transfer of West Bank Arabs to neighboring Arab states. Moledet ran a single issue campaign but was perceived as sympathetic to religion. Tehiya lost a number of non-religious voters to Refael Eitan's strictly secular Tzomet party. In other words, if there was any disenchantment with Tehiya's "going together" it came from non-religious rather than religious supporters.

The Party's success in effecting a partnership within the movement itself is beyond doubt. Hanan Porat's resignation in 1983 and Refael Eitan's challenge to the over-representation of the religious leaders within the Party both threatened the basis of the partnership. But the storms were weathered, demonstrating the inner strength of the members' convictions that theirs was the right path. The picture that emerges is one of increased understanding, mutual consideration and respect. The religious conceded on the matter of initiating legislation in the religious sphere and conceded to the dominance of the non-religious leadership. The non-religious acknowledged the "red lines" of the religious members and the topics of special concern to them. The sections of the platform concerned with religion and state demonstrate significant concessions on the part of the non-religious. Indeed, religious members were never asked to compromise on what they defined as religious principle. Neither in the platform itself, or in any of its parliamentary activity, did Tehiya do anything which might have involved their religious constituents in a violation of religious principle. The Party certainly does not represent or support secularist ideology or principles. The non-religious constituents of the party are not principled or ideological secularists, a point to which we return in our concluding section. The secularism of Tehiya activists is a way of life, not a conception of life.

Summary

To what extent can our findings with respect to Tehiya be generalized to all of Israeli society? Party loyalists claim that their achievements are replicable. They maintain that Tehiya represents a breakthrough in relations between religious and non-religious which in the course of time will extend to more and more levels of society.

The results of this study point to less sanguine conclusions. Tehiya's success was facilitated by a rather special set of conditions. The partnership arose out of a commitment by groups of religious and non-religious Jews to the Greater Land of Israel, and out of the sense of both groups that cooperation was essential to achieve their goals. By its very nature, a nationalist ideology can unite factions which are otherwise very different from each other. The religious nationalists who formed Tehiya define their nationalism in religious terms. Secular nationalists as highly committed as those of Tehiya also find it relatively easy to compromise their secularism for the sake of national ideas. "Going together" was a secondary objective. It is important to recall that religious and non-religious Jews shared the goal of a Greater Land of Israel without combining to form a political party until the late seventies. It was the trauma they experienced at the signing of the peace agreement with Egypt in 1978 which resulted in the formation of the Party.

It is difficult to envisage a mixed left of center party. Secularism tends to be a matter of principle to most people on the Israeli left, not simply a matter of life-style or convenience. They are, therefore, less likely to compromise with the religious left, a group which is in any event so small that it hardly merits anyone's compromise. In anticipation of the 1988 elections the NRP adopted a platform that closely resembled that of Tehiya on the issue of Israeli-Arab relations. This led a group of religious "moderates" to form a new slightly dovish party, Meimad. Meimad also espoused greater cooperation between religious and non-religious but the latter had no representation within the party leadership or in the formation of party policy.

For those at the center of the political spectrum, a mixed party also seems unlikely. The center, like all centers, lacks the powerful commitments of the extremes. Its members, be they religious or non-religious, have no compelling ideology in the sphere of economics, or security, or foreign policy, which would lead them to compromise their views on religion and state.

The Tehiya experiment may not be replicable, but there is much that can be learned from it. Each side must avoid raising issues on which no agreement can be achieved. Each side must understand the other's sensitivities and the red lines beyond which it cannot compromise. Each side must acknowledge that it has something to learn from the other and each must learn to carry on without its own extremists, regardless of how attractive they may be as persons or how capable as leaders.

Tamar Hermann and David Newman

8

The Dove and the Skullcap

Secular and Religious Divergence in the Israeli Peace Camp

POLITICAL ALLIANCES between secular and religious Jews on the political right have been markedly successful in the past two decades. This is especially true within Gush Emunim (Block of the Faithful), the leading ultra-nationalist extra-parliamentary group, and Tehiya (see the chapter in this volume). At the other end of the political spectrum, within what is referred to as the "peace camp," the situation is different. Although this camp contains both religious and non-religious groups, they exist as separate entities. This paper is concerned with the nature of the relationship between the religious peace organization and the secular peace movement, with special attention to the factors causing mutual estrangement.

Interestingly, those groups most concerned with the search for a non-violent solution to the Jewish Arab conflict in the 1930s and 1940s—Brit Shalom and Ihud—included a disproportionately large number of religious, at least non-secular, Jews. The leaders of Brit Shalom, an organization which was active from 1925 to 1933, included the essayist and journalist Rabbi Binyamin (Yehoshua Radler-Feldman),

Professor Shmuel Hugo Bergman, Professor Ernest Akiba Simon, Professor Gershom Sholem, and Nathan Hofshi, the founder of the Palestinian branch of the War Resisters International. All defined themselves as religious "believers" and some, though not all, were observant of Jewish law.

In Ihud, which was founded in 1942 through the initiative of Martin Buber and Judah L. Magnes and was in many respects a continuation of Brit Shalom, the religious element was even more pronounced. Magnes, early in his career, had served as a Reform rabbi in the United States; and Moshe Una, a leader of the religious kibbutz movement and a strictly observant Jew, was also active in Ihud's formation. At one stage Magnes, representing Ihud, held talks with Rav Amram Blau, the ultra-Orthodox leader, about the possibility of his participation. But because Ihud defined itself as Zionist, Blau contented himself with a proclamation of support for its positions, particularly those related to some form of bi-national arrangement under the supervision of the Mandate.

Magnes and Buber argued for a compromise settlement with the Arabs and the avoidance of any bloodshed beyond that necessitated by self-defense. But they, and other "religious" members of Ihud, were far from representative of the tendencies that then prevailed within the religious establishment and among the religious public. They were strongly influenced by the liberal humanism then current in the West and in Central Europe. Nevertheless, they grounded their conceptions on what they perceived as the spirit of Judaism. As Magnes wrote in his essay "Like All the Nations":

> Despite the fact that the conquest and retention of the Land through warfare was perhaps suitable to the needs of the people of Israel in the time of Joshua, it is certainly not suitable to the desires of simple Jews or the lengthy moral tradition of Judaism.

In his 1938 article, "On Betrayal," Buber harshly condemned Jewish reprisals against civilian Arab populations:

> This was betrayal. Rip the mask from its face and encounter its features: betrayal of Jews, of Judaism, and of humanity.

But despite the presence of many religious believers among them, and despite their repeated insistence that their universal humanitarian concerns were a consequence of Judaism's focus on the sanctity of human life, neither Brit Shalom nor Ihud saw themselves, or were seen by others, as religious peace groups. Some of their members were avowedly secular and addressed their appeals to the general public without recourse to a specifically Jewish message. Their platform included no theological references, and they made no efforts to achieve a broader legitimation through halakhic arguments. The framework of their discussion was secular, albeit with limited references to religious concepts.

With the exception of specifically religious groups, much the same was true of mainstream Zionism until 1967. Even though religion was the fiber which strengthened the tie between sections of the nation and the land, there was no attempt to rely upon Jewish sources in the pursuit of one policy or another. Jews in Israel saw themselves besieged by a hostile population. Their physical survival was threatened, and the struggle to survive does not require elaborate ethical justifications. Moreover, Mapai, the dominant political party, set the framework for political discussions, and there were no religious Jews in leadership positions in any non-religious party, including, of course, Mapai itself. Even among religious-Zionists who sometimes relied on sacred text to buttress their position, there was a sense that clear rabbinic guidance on such matters was absent, and the texts that were invoked pointed to general tendencies rather than halakhic obligations. In fact, even if religious-Zionists had wanted to rely on a specific rabbinic mandate, no clear-cut doctrine addressing itself to contemporary political questions was available.

The Israeli victory in the Six-Day War produced a marked change. Halakhic questions were raised concerning the right of Israel to withdraw from the territories acquired in that war. The right wing succeeded in acquiring legitimacy for its slogan, "not one inch," by grounding its claims in religious as well as historical and security justifications. The Labor party and its socialist secular orientation were considerably weakened by these and other currents, while the influence of its religious coalition partners increased. One result of this realignment was that religious arguments and religious perceptions were now considered relevant to the resolution of political questions, especially questions relating to the Israeli–Arab conflict. This attitude became more pronounced with the appearance of Gush Emunim in 1974.

The changes resulted in a new division within the religious-Zionist (national-religious) public. On one side were those who sympathized with the ultra-nationalist-messianic interpretation of Rabbi Zvi

Yehudah Kook and his followers. They viewed the achievements of the Six-Day War as the fulfillment of God's promise. Hence the territories acquired in the War had been "liberated" and were not subject to negotiation. On the other side were those who, while agreeing that the hand of God was to be seen in the victory in the Six-Day War, rejected the notion that withdrawal from any of the territory which Israel had acquired was impossible. The second group, a minority among religious Jews, are only prepared to maintain Israeli occupation should the Arabs refuse to negotiate a peace agreement, and are prepared to withdraw from them in return for a peace agreement. In other words, the territories are perceived as an instrument through which Israel is strengthened but not as an end in themselves.

As indicated above, religious Jews who oppose any territorial compromise have established a broad and stable base for cooperation with secular Jews of similar orientation. No such political alliance has been formed at the dovish end of the political spectrum. Spokesmen for the religious and some of the non-religious movements occasionally appear on the same platform, but beyond this there is little cooperation or coordination of activities. What factors have contributed to the ideological and operational estrangement between religious and secular politicians in the peace camp? What obstacles have prevented greater cooperation between religious and secular doves? To answer this question we must examine the ideology and structure of each of these groups.

Oz v'Shalom and Netivot Shalom

There is only one religious peace organization today, resulting from the merger of two groups, Oz v'Shalom ("Strength and Peace") and Netivot Shalom ("Paths of Peace"). These two groups united in 1985 and adopted the name of Oz v'Shalom—Netivot Shalom (hereafter referred to as Oz/Netivot). The combined name is retained for sentimental reasons rather than as an indication of continued division. The claim that the two organizations now constitute one united front is supported by Oz/Netivot's own publicity brochures, which no longer mention the separate origins of the two groups. The organization has about 1,500 dues-paying members and estimates that it has an equal number of passive supporters.

Oz v'Shalom was founded in 1975 in response to the success of ultra-nationalist currents within the religious community. The major ultra-nationalist movement, Gush Emunim, was founded in 1974 and succeeded in establishing several settlements in Judea and Samaria. Its style was caustic and confrontational. Oz v'Shalom not only objected to the ideology and policies of Gush Emunim but chose a markedly different *modus operandus,* much closer to the personal proclivities of its own founders. Most of them were religiously observant intellectuals, many of them academics, centered in Jerusalem. A disproportionately large number were immigrants or the children of immigrants from Germany or English-speaking countries. Many were identified politically with the moderate and older elements of the National Religious Party. Their initial intention was to establish an ideological circle rather than a political movement. Early activities focused on analytic discussions, expressions of opinions on current events, and the publication of semi-academic critiques of Gush Emunim's ideology and its supporters' activities. Educational activities were generally limited to meetings in private homes and occasional public lectures. At the same time, appeals were made to young people through B'nai Akiva, the religious-Zionist youth movement, which at that time was more open to diverse views on issues of foreign policy and security. (According to the educational coordinator of Oz/Netivot, the leadership of B'nai Akiva has adopted a much more right-wing line since then and will no longer permit Oz/Netivot spokesmen to appear before its members.)

Jewish communities in the West, especially in the United States, responded sympathetically to the message of Oz v'Shalom and provided some financial support. The movement maintained ties with Jewish organizations abroad, including the Jewish Fellowship of Reconciliation, an organization of pacifists which advocates resistance to army service. Appeals for funds met with a positive response not only from some religious circles but also from within the Reform and Conservative movements. Fearing that close connections with such groups would antagonize the Orthodox, the movement played down these ties and restricted these contacts to the leadership level.

Within Israel, its success was far more limited. Four factors contributed to the organization's inability to strike roots and attract wider support: the absence of any strong current advocating nonviolence within the Jewish tradition; a general move to the right in the religious camp since 1967; the pronounced intellectual characteristics of the founders and members of Oz v'Shalom, which nonmembers saw as elitist and exclusive; and the leftist label applied to it ever since its inception. Additionally, the fact that the leadership avoided undertaking practical political activities or establishing ties with political parties prevented it from attracting any media attention, through which it might have reached potential supporters. Thus, despite its aspirations, Oz v'Shalom remained an isolated minority within the religious community. For reasons which we will discuss later, the secular peace camp was neither interested in nor capable of responding to its message.

Significant reinforcements were added to the small religious peace camp with the outbreak of the war in Lebanon in 1982. Most of the founders of the new group of religious doves, Netivot Shalom, were students or graduates of *hesder* yeshivot (advanced schools of Talmudic study which alternate army duty with academic study over a four- or five-year period). Interest in forming such a group initially arose in response to the violent struggle conducted by the settlers in Yamit against the Israeli army during the final evacuation of Sinai in 1981 in accordance with the Camp David agreement. But Netivot Shalom was only officially established following the Sabra and Shatila massacres and the siege of Beirut. According to a report of its founding conference, these events aroused:

> . . . a sharp conflict between the values of peace and the matter of *Eretz Yisrael* [the Land of Israel]. . . . Then we understood that, with all our love for the Land of Israel, the time had come to cry out that the sanctity of human life takes precedence over the wholeness of the land.

The evacuation, the offensive war, the events of Beirut, and the heavy cost in blood paid by the *hesder* yeshiva soldiers—most of whom served in armored units where casualty rates were particularly high—all contributed to the feeling that the time had come to seek an alternative message within the religious camp. Such an alternative, it was believed, might help to lower the level of support for the war in Lebanon and prevent unnecessary bloodshed in the future.

Netivot Shalom was founded under the spiritual guidance of Rabbis Yehudah Amital and Aharon Lichtenstein. The two rabbis were joint heads of Yeshivat Har Etzion-Alon Shvut, a yeshiva established in territory captured by Israel during the Six-Day War. The members of the new movement were drawn from different socio-demographic segments of the religious population than the members of Oz v'Shalom. They were younger, the majority were native-born Israelis, and most were highly educated Jewishly (though not necessarily academically). Many of them felt closer, in style and behavior, to the younger elements within Gush Emunim, despite the fact that these elements tended to be further to the right. Rabbi Amital himself had until then been considered among the associates of Rav Zvi Yehudah Kook.

A number of factors explain the initial preference of these young people for an independent organization rather than affiliation with Oz v'Shalom. They were not only different in socio-demographic respects, but also far less alienated than the members of Oz v'Shalom from the currents which already dominated the national-religious camp. At least initially, they located themselves to the right of Oz v'Shalom on the political map. They were not, to use their own expression, "Peace Now with *kippot.*" They objected to the leftist, academic, image associated with Oz v'Shalom, which had become, in their opinion, a major obstacle to the recruitment of a mass following. The tactical style of the new group was also different. It was far more activist and focused on protests such as public demonstrations and petitions. Even the self-definition of Netivot Shalom—as a movement of Torah, Zionism, and peace—was more overtly religious. This time the goal was to produce a mass movement within the religious camp and to avoid, so far as possible, intellectual elitism. From the very beginning this goal had a decisive influence on the structure of the movement, constraining it to be less internally complex and more goal-oriented.

Despite their differences, the merger of the two movements proceeded rather smoothly. In retrospect it appears to have been an inevitable consequence of organizational imperatives. Neither organization was very large, and combining office staffs would be far more efficient. Oz v'Shalom lacked "simple foot soldiers." As noted earlier, most of its members were older and held senior positions, particularly in academic life. While prepared to carry the burden of intellectual debate, they were unable to carry out the tasks involved in organizing protests and demonstrations. More significantly, none of the Oz v'Shalom leaders had sufficient religious authority to impress the wider religious public. Netivot Shalom brought to the united movement the prestige of Rabbis Amital and Lichtenstein. Netivot Shalom, for its part, required the intellectual and verbal talents that Oz v'Shalom could provide. No less important, it needed the older organization's access to the support and financial assistance of Diaspora Jews. As time passed it had become clear that there was a considerable degree of overlap between the sympathizers of the two movements. It was senseless to emphasize small disagreements in the face of the shared opposition to and competition from right-wing groups for the attention and commitment of the national-religious public. Since the merger of the two groups into one organization, the minor differences that once existed seem to have faded.

From a structural perspective, Oz/Netivot is an extra-parliamentary movement. At the head of the movement stands a small secretariat meeting at irregular intervals. In practice, the secretariat is composed of six or seven members, half of whom are at the moment former leaders of Oz v'Shalom and three of Netivot Shalom, although there is no formal requirement to this effect. Below this level there is an expanded secretariat which generally meets monthly. The latter is composed of the secretariat members, leading activists of the two original movements, and heads of all committees (about 30 members). Continuous organizational activity is carried on through committees on education, special projects, youth, college students, foreign contacts, civil rights, meetings with Arabs, and publications. The level of committee activity, which tends to be low, varies primarily with the level of personal involvement of the committee head. The movement maintains a paid staff of two administrators who serve as activity coordinators (for foreign and local activities) and a secretary. Funds are derived from contributions (particularly from the United States) and membership dues. The office of Oz/Netivot is located at a strategically important site for a protest movement, in the Rehavia neighborhood of Jerusalem, just a few steps from the prime minister's residence. This choice location for demonstration purposes not only is helpful to Oz/Netivot, but allows it to provide occasional logistical assistance to other peace groups.

Divisive Factors Originating in the Secular Camp

This assistance notwithstanding, cooperation with secular peace groups on broader issues is minimal. Two major factors account for this. The first is a structural one. Two contradictory tendencies exist in the secular camp. On the one hand, a high degree of fragmentation among different groups, and on the other hand a measure of unity under the umbrella of one organization with a pluralistic orientation—Shalom Akhshav (Peace Now). Both tendencies have had a marked impact on the integration of Oz/Netivot within the peace camp as a whole.

There are roughly 45 different groups and movements which could ideologically be classified as comprising the peace camp. Their memberships vary from a few dozen to hundreds, and in the case of Peace Now even thousands, of supporters. This extreme fragmentation is primarily a consequence of the individualism of the majority of the activists, who prefer stressing nuances of ideology rather than struggling to set up a wider, more inclusive, and probably more effective framework. While the variety of ideas and organizational frameworks does indeed create obstacles to focused political pressure, it also maximizes the potential for "self-expression." This is apparently of particular importance to the type of individual attracted to the Israeli peace movement. It encourages the activists to remain within the ranks and strengthens their feelings of belonging.

Most of the small peace groups are by nature exclusive, even if they do not define themselves as such. A large proportion of the membership of many of these groups (such as the Red Line or The Twenty-First Year) had been active in Peace Now but left because of dissatisfaction, seeking either a clearer ideological framework or a sharper and more intense level of participation than what was offered by Peace Now. The trend toward greater exclusiveness expresses itself both in appeals directed to specific segments of the population (two groups, for example—The East Toward Peace and The Eastern Front—direct their appeals exclusively toward Sephardim), or in demands that members commit themselves to extremely high levels of activity and obligations. For example, the Yesh G'vul (There is a Boundary) movement is organized around the principle of refusal to perform army services in Lebanon or the occupied territories. Members of The Twenty-First Year commit themselves, among other things, to boycott goods produced by Jewish settlements in the territories and refrain from entering the territories for the purchase of products or leisure-time activity. Given these centrifugal pressures within the peace camp as a whole, the failure of a religious group to join one or more of these other groups so as to establish a wider, more pluralistic, structure is in no way exceptional. There is no external pressure on Oz/Netivot to fit itself into a more permanent relationship with these other equally small, if not smaller, movements. Its right to its own identity and program is unquestioned.

On the other hand, the largest, best known, and most influential of the peace movements, Peace Now, has made a determined effort to overcome this centrifugal tendency. Since its founding in 1978, it has offered a broad inclusive program, directed at the general population. It makes no extraordinary demands on its members, whether in terms of time, of material resources, of effort, or of socially costly acts of protest. It does expect its supporters to participate in mass protests in order to demonstrate its wide base of support and to strengthen its hand in negotiations within the Israeli political system. Its leadership makes no secret of its desire to set up a roof organization to include the widest possible range of ideologies and programs. Peace Now demonstrations are notable for their variety of signs and slogans, and for the participation of individuals who identify with many different political parties and who hold conflicting opinions on subjects beyond the one which has brought them temporarily together—peace. Even in dealing with issues central to the peace movement, Peace Now displays a marked pluralism, particularly with respect to tactics. Its general slogan calls for a just peace in the Middle East and a willingness to negotiate and surrender territory. Controversial questions, such as whether or not to negotiate with the PLO, or the future status of Jerusalem, are left open. One exception is Peace Now's adamant objection to any refusal to perform army service in the occupied territories. Although Peace Now does have a hard core of activists upon whom it depends in organizing its demonstrations and other activities, it has no formal membership and does not collect membership dues. Projects are funded through voluntary contributions. There are no clear procedures for selection of the leadership, no rules for decision-making, and no paid employees.

Peace Now has not entirely succeeded in its goal of projecting itself as an all-inclusive peace movement. Some of its leaders believe that efforts to achieve the goal have exacted too high a price. Its difficulties are a warning and a cause of anxiety to every peace group which has considered shifting to a more inclusive style or integrating itself with Peace Now. This is especially true of Oz/Netivot. First, despite its intensive efforts to widen its appeal, Peace Now continues to attract only a narrow range of supporters. Socio-demographically, the overwhelming majority of its activists and supporters are drawn from the secular, Ashkenazi, middle-class, urban, intellectual segment of the population between the ages of twenty-five and forty-five. A second important group of supporters come from kibbutzim, especially the kibbutzim of Hashomer Hatzair associated with the left-wing Zionist Mapam party. Sephardim, residents of development towns, and blue-collar workers have not only failed to show interest, but often display an ethnic and class-based antagonism to the movement. Religious circles have special reason for skepticism over Peace Now's self-proclaimed inclusive policy. A large proportion of the leadership of Peace Now identifies with Ratz (the Citizens Rights

Movement), which they consider the most anti-religious of all Israeli parties. The massive involvement of people from Mapam and Hashomer Hatzair supporters in Peace Now is a further deterrent to the involvement of religious Jews.

While the political goals of the movement are limited to foreign affairs and security, in no way touching on religious issues, religion is involved at a practical level. The majority of the founders and participants of Peace Now come from secular kibbutzim or other social groups whose perspectives are in polar opposition to those of the religious, and the movement is unwilling to make any effort to change its secular image. For example, it is unwilling to time its demonstrations to avoid violating the Sabbath. Leaders of Peace Now are aware of the fact that they are, in practice, excluding religious Jews from involvement. They argue that the broader interests of the peace camp require such a policy and contend that integration of the religious into a joint secular-religious framework will deter a number of religious people and ultimately reduce the overall number of the latter who identify with the peace camp. A different line of argument is that accommodation to the needs of the religious would require significant and undesirable change in the nature of Peace Now and deter a number of secular Jews who now identify with the group.

A second, no less important, obstacle to any willingness on the part of the secular peace camp to integrate the religious movement is the absence of any tradition of integrated secular-religious movements in Israel. Britain and the United States have for years had peace movements which include both secular and religious sub-units. For example, the Campaign for Nuclear Disarmament has a sub-unit of religiously committed members known as the Christian CND. Such an organization would be unprecedented in Israel, where secular-religious divisions cast their shadow over many other issues of ideological import. During the period of the *yishuv* (prior to the establishment of the State), it was clear that Hapoel Hamizrahi, the religious-Zionist labor party, was more closely identified with the petit-bourgeois but religious Mizrahi Party than with the socialist labor movement, with which it shared a common socio-economic perspective. (Indeed, Hapoel Hamizrahi and Mizrahi eventually merged to form the National Religious Party.) This traditional division characterizes the Israeli political system in general and is not peculiar to the peace movement. It is of special consequence when it comes to considering the integration of religious groups within an extra-parliamentary movement which is predominantly secular and under no pressure, unlike a political party, to compromise its ideological position in order to achieve the material benefits to be derived from a coalition agreement.

The estrangement between the religious and secular groups in the peace movement is also an outcome of the universalist orientation of the secular groups as contrasted with the particularistic, albeit not necessarily chauvinistic, orientation of Oz/Netivot. All the secular groups accept the notion of equality among individuals and nations as axiomatic. All would reject the concept "chosen people," but this conception is basic to the ideology of Oz/Netivot, even though Oz/Netivot interprets "chosenness" to mean that Jews have greater moral obligations rather than greater privileges.

The centrifugal pressures which result from an insistence on ideological purity have occasionally given way to compromise and cooperation for tactical purposes between the religious and secular camps. Joint demonstrations were held under the slogan "bring the soldiers back home" during the Lebanon war, especially in 1984 while a successful "Peace Succah" was constructed by Oz/Netivot together with East to Peace, a secular group with a relatively positive attitude to religion, in 1986–87. Anything beyond such *ad hoc* cooperation apparently requires ideological compromises which neither side is prepared to undertake. Should they do so, the consequent blurring of ideology would probably result in loss of support among that public to which the original message was addressed.

The secular majority in the peace camp displays complete indifference to the subject of religion or of the importance of incorporating religious values in its program. Peace Now, the most inclusive of all the peace groups, is representative of the entire movement in its indifference to absorbing religious members. Ideologically and socially it is rooted in secular Zionism and sees no relevance in ancient Jewish history. Its membership is apathetic both to Judaism and to the Jewish establishment. A close examination of most of the peace groups' publications since 1967 reveals an absence of references to the subject aside from minimal lip service. Perhaps more significantly, on only two occasions did Peace Now attempt to give a Jewish flavor to its message. In one instance it claimed that, since Judaism was by nature pluralistic, the position of Gush Emunim was religiously no more justifiable than that of Peace Now. According to a Peace Now publication:

> In basing its rigid nationalist stance on religion, on the tradition of Israel, [Gush Emunim] conceals the pluralism of Judaism and exploits

> religion and culture for the sake of short-term policies over which there is sharp controversy within both Israel and the entire Jewish people.

Another publication sought to answer the charge that Peace Now was against religion. Expressing itself in a question-and-answer format, the publication asks: "Is it true that Peace Now is a secular movement which is basically opposed to religious observances?" Its answer is:

> Members of religious settlements, the Oz v'Shalom movement, and graduates of yeshivot march with us. The [religious] ruling by Rabbi Ovadiah Yosef that love of one's fellow Jew is preferable to love of territory, along with the rulings of other great rabbis, agree with our position. We are in agreement with normative Judaism, while Gush Emunim is sectarian in its singular stress on territory in its hierarchy of values.

Peace Now has never been critical of Judaism. Its criticism of Gush Emunim implies that it is that organization, rather than Peace Now, which adopts a position at variance with the Jewish tradition. But overall, the references to Judaism are as mentioned above, few and far between.

The easiest and simplest explanation for this indifference is that religion or Judaism is deemed irrelevant to the burning issues of foreign policy and security. But the major opponents of the peace movement legitimate their positions in religious terms (as do Gush Emunim or Meir Kahana and his followers), or at least utilize religious arguments. So the indifference of the peace groups to the religious issue is not so easily explained. The major reason for this "willful indifference" is probably the fear of worsening the already weak legitimacy of the peace movement in the public's eye. This is especially true for such groups as East Toward Peace, which direct their appeals at segments of the population (such as the Sephardim) who are both suspicious of the peace movement and positive in their approach to tradition. Yet even such groups completely avoid raising religious questions, for fear of becoming involved in theological arguments with which they are unequipped to deal. There is good reason for this: most of the country's rabbinic authorities are closer to the hawkish than the dovish camp. Similarly, there is fear of challenging a central element in the national consensus. One can thus understand why Peace Now is reluctant to assert its claim to legitimacy by locating itself within a pluralistic Judaism, and why it avoids attacking Gush Emunim in any manner which could be construed as an attack on religion itself.

There may be an additional reason which is somewhat more speculative but nevertheless deserves mention. Secular peace groups, including Peace Now, may ignore the religious doves in order to clarify the nature of the distinctions between "those who are with us" and "those who are against us." It is easier to describe the characteristics of a given collectivity if one can do so on the basis of an already existing stereotype. In the case of the peace groups, the religious settler in the territories—bearded, wearing a crocheted *kippa,* armed with an Uzi submachine gun—is the stereotype of the hawkish nationalist enemy. This open identification between religion and ultra-nationalism is very useful to groups such as Peace Now in mobilizing support, particularly when the enthusiastic young public to which they appeal is relatively uninterested in wider public legitimation or in national unity. From this perspective, it is clear why any emphasis on the existence of a religious peace camp is liable to be dysfunctional: religious doves, members of Netivot Shalom in particular, are too similar in external appearance to members of Gush Emunim. Were Oz/Netivot to be projected as an ally, it would blur the boundaries between friend and foe. As will be discussed later, a similar calculation affects the policies of Oz/Netivot itself in its relationship to secular peace groups.

Divisive Factors which Originate among the Religious Groups

The secular peace camp is not enthusiastic at the idea of the practical integration of the religious movement into its ranks, although it has no objection to the participation of religious individuals. For its part, Oz/Netivot displays only a limited willingness to join an umbrella organization of peace groups. This is partially because of the limited legitimacy afforded the movement by the national-religious public, which makes it wary of any activity which might offend this sector of the population. In addition to the national-religious public's reluctance to accept the ideology of Oz/Netivot, other factors have also handicapped it. First of all, both Oz v'Shalom and Netivot Shalom originated as responses to the religious ultra-nationalists, Gush

Emunim in particular. Insofar as they were responding to the initiatives of others, they were not in a position to choose the issues for debate. As a result, publicity focused on the negative aspect of their message—their rejection of, and opposition to, religious-messianic Zionism. The groups' long-range goal, the development of an alternative conception of Judaism, attracted much less notice. Secondly, in comparison to Gush Emunim's pioneering image, expressed in its establishment of new settlements and through large-scale publicity, Oz/Netivot—despite its sensitivity to this danger—often appears as an organization mired in endless discussions. At one stage, the movement attempted to emulate the activist and constructive image of Gush Emunim by organizing a settlement in Galilee, but this attempt failed. On the other hand, even when a group of activists did succeed in a settlement effort in a development town, as they did in Yeruham, it received virtually no attention from the media and thereafter had no public effect.

Peace Now and its more radical allies in the secular peace camp have been stigmatized in the eyes of the national-religious public as saboteurs opposed to national aspirations. Since this was the public to which Oz/Netivot hoped to appeal, it quite reasonably avoided any proximity to the secularists or any activity which might have associated it with them. As Rabbi Amital admitted: "Many rabbis and Torah scholars fear to express themselves freely in public in apprehension of the labels with which they might be stigmatized." Dr. Michael Lerner, editor of the liberal Jewish quarterly *Tikkun*, comments: "We can't leave the work in the hands of Peace Now because a significant segment of [our] public cannot identify with the elitist and secular culture which characterizes the Labor Party and Peace Now."

In a conference which Netivot Shalom organized following the arrest of a group of Jewish terrorists, the distinguished senior professor of Judaica at the Hebrew University, Ephraim Urbach, was quoted as saying:

> I am not among those who call for "peace now" for the same reason as I do not call for "the Messiah now." "Now" is rash, and we as a people cannot permit ourselves to indulge in self-delusions.

In an article condemning the messianic tendencies of the Jewish ultra-nationalists, Professor Mordechai Breuer, one of the original leaders of Oz v'Shalom, claims that they are like Peace Now in their haste to arrive at an "end of days." "Against the movement for 'peace now' is arrayed a movement demanding 'salvation now'," he wrote.

At the simplest and most practical level, as noted above, the absence of more religious Jews at Peace Now demonstrations is a result of the fact that they usually begin shortly before or after the Sabbath ends. Someone who doesn't live in the immediate vicinity would have to violate the Sabbath to reach the demonstration before it was over. According to respondents, some religious Jews interpret this to mean that their presence is not welcome and refrain from attending even when they can do so without violating the Sabbath. But the leaders of Oz/Netivot are disturbed by the low turn-out of religious demonstrators, and some of them make special efforts to be present in order to demonstrate religious support for the peace message. (Professor Uriel Simon refers to them as the *mahleket kiddush Hashem,* the "sanctification of the Name of God department.") They do not view the scheduling as a deliberate provocation or as an open attempt on the part of the Peace Now leadership to distance itself from the religious public. Such scheduling, they have been told, takes into account the needs of the group's single largest and most important bloc of supporters—members of kibbutzim. Timing a demonstration for later would prevent members of the more distant kibbutzim from participating, since they would arrive home very late at night and they generally rise early on weekday mornings. No less important, a demonstration which began late would miss coverage by camera crews filming for the 9 p.m. news broadcast.

For tactical reasons the members of Oz/Netivot opted from the beginning to concentrate their educational activities on the religious public. It is operationally difficult to appeal to different publics simultaneously. Moreover, they feel themselves to be an inherent part of the religious population, with a special obligation to transmit their message to them. In order to reach this sector, most of whose members were not enthusiastic about Oz/Netivot ideas, they had to stress the religious character of the organization and the fact that it drew upon halakhic sources. As Professor Simon comments:

> As a result of this [growth of ultra-nationalism in the religious public], the desire for peace was presented as a weakness of the "secular-leftist" public, a result of the simple and ignorant Jew's yearning for comfort and personal security. Even other commandments, such as the sanctity of human life that was created in the image of God or the command to

> love the resident alien, were given narrow halakhic interpretations and rejected as "secular-humanistic values."

Because of this, spokesmen for Oz/Netivot minimize arguments based on authorities external to Judaism or even ideas taken from non-religious Zionist sources. In addition, Oz/Netivot is anxious to improve the image of Judaism in the eyes of the secular public. They seek to demonstrate that the religious ultra-nationalists have distorted Judaism, and that this distortion must be balanced by an alternative moderate and no less religious message. However, relying exclusively on Jewish and halakhic authorities and eschewing universalist arguments estranges them from the secular audience whom they also seek to influence.

According to the world-view of Oz/Netivot, peace constitutes a supreme religious value. The religious emphasis is evident in the names which each of the two religious peace groups chose for themselves. The name Oz v'Shalom ("strength and peace") is taken from the verse, "God will give His people strength, He will bless His people with peace," recited three times a day by the observant Jew. Netivot Shalom ("paths of peace") selected its name from the verse in Proverbs which reads, "Your way is the way of pleasantness, and all Your paths are those of peace." This selection is not accidental. It is the result of an effort to distinguish the peace groups from the religious ultra-nationalists. Peace is linked to strength in order to reinforce the notion that Israel's security is a function of its capacity to make peace and not its military superiority. The term "paths of peace" was selected in order to point out that the path of belief and observance of the commandments is not necessarily characterized by the obligatory and uncompromising rigidity associated with the principles of Gush Emunim and its supporters.

Gush Emunim legitimates its message on the basis of sacred texts and rabbinic interpretations. Many in Oz/Netivot feel that the only way to rebut their arguments is through the use of the same kind of arguments. Most of the religious population were educated in the national-religious school system. The language of the Bible and even the Talmud is understood, and citing proof texts from these sources is a standard form of argumentation. For example, Rabbi Pinhas Lederman, a leader of Oz/Netivot, stresses that, contrary to the usual assumption, territorial compromises are well anchored in Jewish law as a means of settling arguments and building a just world.

Particular importance is attributed to the statement of Israel's former chief rabbi, Ovadiah Yosef:

> If by returning territory to them we can avoid the danger of war and there is a good possibility of permanent peace, it would seem that all agree that it is permitted to return territory from the land of Israel in exchange for such a goal. Saving lives is more important.

The movement's literature frequently cites the blessing which appears at the end of the Eighteen Benedictions in which not only is the desire for peace stressed, but God is portrayed as the source of peace. To strengthen this argument, much use is made of a commentary which explains God's opposition to David's building the Temple, "because you spilled much blood on the ground before you." In addition, proof texts from such medieval commentators as Maimonides and Nahmanides, upon which the religious ultra-nationalists rely, are reinterpreted in support of Oz/Netivot's position. Spokesmen and leaders of Oz/Netivot are not averse to offering pragmatic arguments—for example, the argument that constant wars weaken the endurance of the people, particularly the secular public. But even when they do, the religious element is often introduced. Thus Rabbi Amital suggests:

> In my opinion every war weakens the Zionist commitment of the masses of Israeli Jews, and I mean by this particularly those Jews who lack belief in God's guidance of the process of the return to Zion in our time. . . . Each war introduces doubts in their minds as to the justice of the way and causes them to go wild in the stock exchange in an attempt to escape from the problems which threaten Jewish survival in the country, strengthens anti-Semitism in the world, and weakens the attachment of Diaspora Jews to Judaism.

Rabbi Lichtenstein adds the argument that the use of violence strengthens the tendency to see force as the natural and preferred way to settle complex problems. It encourges the delusion of total and independent sovereignty and ignores the elementary principle that "Not by force will man conquer." Once again, although the argument is political and pragmatic, a religious proof text is added.

Not only is the mode of communication uniquely adapted to the religious community, but special attention is also paid to those who are selected to communicate the message. Most rabbinic authorities outside the *haredi* camp (and the latter carry little weight in this matter) have lent their support, if not their leadership, to the ultranationalists. This includes the present chief rabbis of Israel and the heads of most of the *hesder* yeshivot. This is an important factor in the battle for the sympathy of the national-religious public. Oz/Netivot has sought rabbis of equal stature but with a more moderate political outlook in support of its political stance. Its efforts have not been very fruitful. Aside from Rabbis Lichtenstein and Amital, only a few authorities have responded, such as Rabbi Emanuel Rackman of Bar-Ilan University and Rabbi Immanuel Jakabovits, Chief Rabbi of British Jewry. Both these have publicly expressed opinions which are close to the movement, although they are not affiliated with it. Oz/Netivot has been forced to face the fact that it is unable to muster much rabbinical support for its ideology, and one encounters expressions such as "There *is* an alternative Jewish stance, and it makes no difference if it is supported by two rabbis or three thousand," apologetics that sound rather feeble.

Nevertheless, the search for rabbinic authority, the fear of adopting a more radical posture lest the movement lose the cooperation of even its present few rabbinic sympathizers, and especially the emphasis on religious sources and proof texts, make it difficult for Oz/Netivot to reach its secondary public—the secular sector. The latter is bored with and uninterested in the "war of citations" which the movement wages against Gush Emunim and its sympathizers and is unimpressed with how many rabbis do or do not support Oz/Netivot. Debates conducted in the Gush's messianic jargon appear to nonbelievers as too sectarian. Indeed, some members of Oz/Netivot believe that excessive concentration on this style is counterproductive, and that the group should shift to another strategy. Michael Lerner comments:

> Our goal should be to transform Netivot Shalom/Oz v'Shalom into organizations which can build a wide public movement on behalf of peace. We cannot leave the work of enlarging the ranks [of the peace movement] to Peace Now. We should cut back on the "war of verses" and on the efforts made to convince the supporters of the National Religious Party of the legitimacy of our cause. Instead of this, we should focus our appeal on the general Israeli public. . . . We must shift to a new possible constituency. [At this point he specifies four such: the traditional, the secular, Conservative, and Reform.]

However, both the original Oz v'Shalom and the present united movement continue to be guided by their initial reservations concerning the advisability of associating with the Conservative and Reform movements. The official explanation, as expressed in the movement's information leaflet, is the need to preserve carefully the group's character as a movement of observant Jews, in the Orthodox/halakhic sense.

Oz/Netivot seeks to appeal to the religious public by scheduling activities at times which have a special significance for the observant. Thus protest demonstrations may be called on, for example, the Fast of Esther, or public forums during the intermediary days of Succot. Sabbaths and holy days are avoided, lest the sanctity of the day be violated. For a number of years, the movement has arranged a week of events during Succot, under the title "Succah of Peace," which permits the religious to participate in events inside a succah. There is also a monthly meeting called the *Bet Midrash l'Shalom* ("The House of Study for Peace"). Leaders of secular peace groups do not find these tinges of ritualism attractive. Indeed, some believe that they also contribute to the alienation of secular peace groups and prevent them from initiating cooperative efforts with the religious movement.

It is clear that Oz/Netivot is more firmly anchored in the religious camp, with all that this implies, than in the peace camp. Professor Simon points out that all of religious Zionism, including his group, is founded on the same system of loyalties: to the Torah of Israel, the people of Israel, the land of Israel, and the State of Israel. According to Simon, the central problem which divides religious-Zionists is the differing emphasis given to the various elements, and not any qualitative difference in ideas among them. He notes with sorrow that secular Zionists feel no obligation toward Judaism, viewing it at most as a contribution to Jewish survival but not as a source of authority.

Unlike the secular Zionists, Oz/Netivot is part of the religious-Zionist camp which sees the entire Land of Israel as the territory promised by God to the Jewish people.

> The Land of Israel stood, and still stands, at the center of the consciousness and hopes of the Jewish people. Consciousness does not lend itself to division, even when concrete historical reality does not permit complete fulfillment and total realization . . .

writes Aviezer Ravitsky. The disagreement between the religious peace group and Gush Emunim is not over basic principles but rather the applicable meaning of the idea of "the wholeness of the land" and its place in the order of priorities at the present time. This is quite at variance with the stance of the secular peace camp, and efforts to paper over these differences are not likely to succeed. Religious authorities such as Rabbi Amital are almost apologetic about the nature of the movement's allies. "Peace is a value in and of itself," he says, "and does not cease to be a value because of the use to which it is put by different groups for political ends."

Other differences of some ideological significance divide Oz/Netivot from all the secular peace groups. Mention has already been made of the secular rejection of the Jews as a "chosen people" with all that this implies for the ideology of each side. In addition, unlike the secular peace groups, which view peace as primarily a contractual political arrangement, the religious tend to see it metaphysically. Peace implies "the end of days" when "the wolf will dwell with the lamb." Not surprisingly, therefore, the literature of Oz/Netivot is rather skeptical about the possibilities for a true peace with the Arabs, envisioning at best a truce or cessation of hostilities. As Rabbi Amital writes, "We don't delude ourselves about the probability of true peace with an Arab country in the near future." Under these circumstances, the proposal that Israel make territorial concession sounds rather dubious. The movement's halakhically based approach to non-Jewish residents is not based on a recognition of equal rights, but is rather a consequence of moral demands directed to a Jewish audience in general and especially to a religious audience. Nowhere in its literature does the movement accord the Palestinians national rights, or indicate a willingness to partition the land as a consequence of such rights—a theme which appears repeatedly in the literature of the secular peace groups.

Despite all the efforts made by Oz/Netivot to develop a religious argumentation, its appeal to the religious public has remained marginal. Its interpretation is generally viewed as a deviation from authentic Torah and *halakhah*. It has been suggested that this lack of success is a consequence of the contrasting styles of Gush Emunim and Oz/Netivot. The latter are characterized by "intellectualism, moderation, awareness of complexity, obfuscation, and a tendency to criticism." Gush Emunim's style, on the other hand, is marked by a "lack of ambivalence, which tends to identify the sacred with an empirical social order." Indeed, Gush Emunim describes its opponents as those who are too easily influenced by academic encounters with ideas and values which are foreign to Judaism. Oz/Netivot also aroused the antagonism of the religious public when on two occasions it demonstrated in front of the offices of the Chief Rabbinate; once when the chief rabbis announced their support for clemency for accused Jewish terrorists and once when the chief rabbis announced their opposition to an international conference on the Middle East.

Summary and Conclusions

Oz/Netivot is in a no-man's-land situated between the national-religious camp, which it unsuccessfully aspires to influence, and the secular peace camp, from which it is alienated. The very factors which might help it gain a measure of legitimacy in the eyes of one camp are those which would deprive it of legitimacy in the eyes of the other. The ultra-nationalist religious are ready to challenge Oz/Netivot's interpretation of sacred texts; the secular branch of the peace movement fails to see the significance of sacred text as constituting *the* source of political and moral authority. Beyond this, the secular peace camp sees the religious group as marginal and unimportant within the religious camp, unable to bring a significant number of supporters to any merger. They see no reason, therefore, to compromise their own style in order to accommodate their religious allies. Within the religious community the low esteem of Oz/Netivot became even more evident in early 1988. Rabbi Amital and a small group of friends announced they would establish a new moderate/centrist religious party—Meimad—following their disappointment at the National Religious Party's move to the right. Amital's party eschewed the formal cooperation of Oz/Netivot lest such a union damage its chances for attracting religious voters.

To sum up, the relationship between Oz/Netivot and the non-religious peace movement is an ambivalent one. Each side is pleased by the other's existence, since every addition to the peace camp is welcomed. But even here, as in so many other areas, despite the similarity in the practical policies which each side favors, the relationship between the two is influenced by the different structures of political thought that characterize the religious and secular segments of Israeli society. This finds expression in the way each side conveys its message, but primarily in the different network of loyalties, commitments, and sense of belonging that each one shares. It is therefore no surprise that each side prefers to retain its separate existence, despite the benefits of efficiency that might accrue from increased cooperation.

Leonard Weller and Sonia Topper Weller

9

Strange Bedfellows

A Study of Mixed Religious Marriages

THIS IS A STUDY of marriages between religious and non-religious partners—mixed marriages. Our primary interest is to explore how the partners cope with the problems that their marriage raises.

A mixed marriage raises at least three kinds of problems. First, it places a disproportionate burden on one partner. If the religious partner compromises, he or she is violating religious standards, which, because they are religious, carry an aura of sanctity that do not extend to non-religious standards. To choose an obvious example, the kitchen in the home must be kosher. The religious partner, after all, is forbidden by religious law from eating non-kosher food or even food cooked in utensils that were previously used in the preparation of non-kosher food. The non-religious partner, on the other hand, cannot claim any special sanctity for non-kosher food. And so it seems reasonable to both parties that the non-religious partner compromise. The problem arises when this is what, of necessity, happens on issue after issue. Pressure is placed on the non-religious partner to make the most compromises. And, as we shall see in the examples that follow, this places a strain on the non-religious partner that, in some cases, leads him or her to sense a loss of identity and, in other cases, leads to behavior that can only be understood as the assertion of that identity.

A second kind of problem arises from the all-encompassing nature of Jewish law. The areas of potential disagreement affect virtually every aspect of the marriage. There are three areas of Jewish law that, according to our respondents, most directly impinge on marital life: laws concerning the Sabbath, laws concerning diet (kashrut), and laws of family purity (*taharat hamishpakhah*). There are numerous Sabbath laws, but those that most immediately affect the lives of our mixed marriage respondents are restrictions on cooking, riding in automobiles, and using electric lights and appliances (radio, television, stereo, etc.).

These restrictions affect family life in many ways. One cannot travel to visit friends and family. Even inviting them to one's own home is forbidden, if they have to travel on the Shabbat to get there, since it causes them to sin. Adina, one of our respondents, puts it this way:

> I feel very lonely and cut off from all of my family who live in Haifa. Saturday is the only day we have off and I never can visit them. We can't have them visit us because my husband won't allow anyone to come here by car.

A traditional Saturday pastime for secular Israelis is a trip to the beach and the non-religious partner resents being deprived of this. Yossi solves his problem by taking the children to the sea every Saturday without his religious wife. But this creates problems of its own.

The Friday night film on television is a major form of family entertainment in many non-religious homes. Some of our non-religious respondents complained of an "invasion of privacy" when the religious spouse objected to viewing television. As Nava said, "If I can't go out at least I should be able to use one finger to put on a switch in my home—can you honestly tell me that's work?"

Saturday, which is supposed to be the day of rest and family togetherness, becomes a day of tension for some mixed couples. Ziva reported: "He drives me crazy to have everything ready before Shabbat—and he himself doesn't help. Sometimes I feel like spiting him by deliberately not having the food cooked on time."

Kashrut restrictions result in the unwillingness of religious Jews to eat in the homes of non-religious Jews unless special precautions are taken. Since much of our social life revolves around eating, the effect of kashrut observance on socializing between religious and non-religious, is clear. Outside Israel, many religious Jews will eat in homes of non-religious, even non-Jewish friends. They may bring their own food, or they may tell their hosts exactly what food they can prepare and how it should be served—generally on throw-away utensils. In Israel, eating at the homes of non-religious friends is much less common than in the United States. Perhaps this is just another aspect of Israeli lack of tolerance. The point is that the non-religious partner is effectively prevented, or at least restrained, from maintaining his or her non-religious friendships. "When our friends have a potluck supper," says David, "Pnina will eat only the food she brings. It's very awkward and embarrassing."

Several of the non-religious were annoyed by some aspects of the kashrut laws within the home. A few spoke of drinking coffee with milk after meat meals. Yaffa said, "Dan lets me. . . ." Raya said, "I try not to let the children see me. Why make problems?" Sabina does it openly, "To make my point that there are differences of opinion and both are valid."

Family purity laws—taharat hamishpakhah—prohibit sexual intercourse for at least twelve days during every menstrual cycle. At the end of this period, the woman immerses herself in a ritual bath called the *mikveh.* Infraction of this law is regarded as a serious sin and applies equally to both partners.

Imagine the reaction of a non-religious person to the demand by his or her spouse to adhere to these family purity laws. It almost resulted in divorce in one case where the husband, newly religious, demanded this of his secular wife. Another couple abstained from sexual relationships for three years because the wife refused to go to mikveh. They finally divorced, and the partner we interviewed attributed the divorce to this issue. According to another respondent, her husband's insistence on observing family purity laws is particularly difficult for her "because I have my greatest sexual and psychological needs then and the bastard refuses to even hold me."

The third problem, which places a particular strain on mixed marriages, results from the fact that Israelis are not very tolerant of other people's beliefs. So the position of a mixed family, especially one with children, is difficult whether they choose to locate themselves in a religious or a non-religious community. "Mixed" or religiously neutral communities hardly exist and recent years have witnessed a growing polarization of religious and non-religious. Even non-*haredi* moderate religious children attend separate, state supported schools. There are religious kindergartens and nursery schools. The religious community looks askance at the mixed family. Our own sense is that, in the eyes of the religious Jews, the mixed family unit is perceived as non-religious and perhaps even as threatening. Indeed, two couples reported that their religious neighbors would not eat in their home. "This grieves me," said Ziva, "as I go to great lengths to keep my house kosher." They also claimed that invitations to Saturday *kiddush* (literally, the benediction over the wine following Saturday morning services, in practice, a major form of socializing for most religious couples), were infrequent because the mixed couples were perceived as non-religious. Dalia, who is non-religious, complained to us that, "this is just unfair. I stopped traveling on Saturday. I keep a kosher home. I do everything I can to make Shabbat nice."

Moshe relates another example of the religious community's lack of tolerance:

> When we first arrived in the country, twenty years ago, the community in which we lived did not have a religious school. My wife (non-religious) opposed sending the children to a religious school because it meant they would have to travel long distances. Several years later, my wife agreed to send our oldest son to a religious high school, for she realized that it was untenable for a religious child to attend a non-religious school. When I phoned the high school principal where we wanted to enroll my child, he asked the name of the school he was presently attending. I told him the name and after a pause he said, "I am sorry but there is no more room." What happened was that the principal realized that my son was a transfer pupil from a non-religious school and therefore refused to admit him—this, in spite of the fact that I had identified myself as a professor at a religious university.

There are many other laws regulating aspects of daily living that can and do affect the relationship between the religious spouse and the non-religious spouse. We cite some of these, all taken from our interviews.

> All right, so I agree and don't go to the beach on Saturday. But, when we go during the week, my wife wants to go to the women's beach and sends my son and me to the beach for men. Doesn't she realize that this is supposed to be a family thing?

> I still can't believe it. My wife and I went with our children to a Luna Park located on the outskirts of B'nai B'rak. Well, there were certain times for men and certain times for women.

> I can't bear the heat. I'd love to wear sleeveless blouses and shorts but my husband insists on "modest" dress.
>
> I would go to synagogue if only I could sit with my husband and family, and I wouldn't have to sit behind the *mehitzah.* [A barrier that separates men and women in an Orthodox synagogue.] I refuse to be degraded by the mehitzah.

Our overall objective is to examine how these families adjust. We were also interested in the following questions:

- How extensively did couples who were mixed at the time of marriage discuss their differences before the marriage?
- What were the specific compromises of the religious spouse and the non-religious spouse?
- What changes took place in the patterns of compromise during the course of the marriage?
- To what extent did religious differences lead to serious marital conflict?
- Based on the premise that the two important areas of religious behavior, diet and family purity, affect the woman more than the man, is it easier for a religious woman to be married to a non-religious man than the reverse?

Method

This study is based entirely on personal interviews. In order to locate a large number of respondents, we began by interviewing mixed couples we knew and by asking other acquaintances if they could identify such couples for us. Some were startled by the question. They were certain that there were no such couples or, at most, that there were only a handful. One person said, "I didn't know that such a creature exists." A few acquaintances did suggest names, sometimes immediately, sometimes by phoning us a week later.

Most of those whom we approached for names of mixed couples felt that we were dealing with a most-sensitive topic and wondered if we should "bother those people." For example, one friend suggested four names, but his wife forbad us to contact two of them because she thought the subject was too emotion-laden for them. Someone else at first suggested three names but then said that he preferred that we should not contact the third couple unless we were in desperate need of people, "as they might feel insulted." A woman who serves as an informal leader in her religious community said that she knew four such families, but then decided not to give us their names since they would be harmed by the interviewing. In general, we found that our religious acquaintances were more aware of mixed couples than our non-religious acquaintances. This may be due to the fact that religious people are more often part of some kind of community network—one that is generally centered around the synagogue—and this network provides them with information about the existence of such couples who become an obvious topic of interest. On the other hand, we suspect that even the religious substantially underestimate the number of such couples, a point to which we shall return.

Mixed couples, for purposes of this study, were defined as husband and wife, between whom there were significant religious differences at the time they married or any time thereafter. A marriage was categorized as mixed only if it was identified in that way by others and if the partners admitted to this definition. Our respondents included couples who began their marriage with religious differences and couples between whom differences developed after they were married. We avoided seeking respondents among the *baalei tshuvah* schools (schools for penitents, i.e., men or women raised in non-religious environments who seek to become religious), for we felt they represented a very special case. However, when we discovered that some of our respondents were baalei tshuvah, we did not exclude them.

The very nature of our selection process made our sample unrepresentative in many ways. The two instances that deserve special mention are, first, the underrepresentation of mixed couples who are not involved in synagogue life—especially couples who were mixed at one time and then became religiously homogeneous by virtue of the religious partner's becoming non-religious. The second underrepresentation is of mixed marriages that ended in divorce, whether the issue that led to the break-up was or was not religious differences. We have examples of both these types of mixed marriages, but we don't believe that their proportion within our sample reflects their actual proportion among mixed couples in the general population.

The couples we interviewed were scattered throughout the country. We have respondents who live in Eilat, Jerusalem, and Haifa, but most are from the Tel Aviv metropolitan area. With one exception, interviews were conducted in the home of the respondents and the average interview time was one hour. We are ourselves a mixed couple, so the religious partner interviewed the religious respondent and the non-religious partner interviewed the non-religious respondent.

We feel confident that we achieved excellent rapport with our respondents and that their replies were open and candid. Our subjective feeling in this regard was supported by the willingness of virtually all the religious respondents to admit to serious transgressions of Jewish Law. Three couples mentioned that, when they first agreed to be interviewed, they were uncertain if they would respond as honestly as they eventually did.

We gathered data on thirty family units. In twenty cases, we interviewed both husband and wife, and in ten cases, we were only able to talk to one partner. This was due to a number of factors. In one instance, the husband was unaware of the wife's non-religious behavior, so we obviously could not interview him. In another instance, the family lived in a remote area, and we interviewed the husband while he was in Tel Aviv. One family was leaving for an extended trip abroad the day after the interview, and only one partner had time to see us. In one case, a partner was no longer alive. In another case, the wife agreed to be interviewed on condition that we did not speak with her husband. Five partners refused to be interviewed.

Those interviewed included couples of Ashkenazi (Western) origin and of mixed Ashkenazi-Sephardi origin. In only one case were both partners Sephardi. This imbalance is the result of our own network of acquaintances, and it does not reflect the incidence of mixed marriages among Ashkenazim and Sephardim. Indeed, it is very possible that the incidence is much higher among the Sephardim where religious Jews tend to be more tolerant about mixing with non-religious Jews and where the very categories of religious and non-religious are less rigid than among the Ashkenazim. True, the Sephardim have a stronger culture of male dominance, and it is very likely that a non-religious Sephardi woman will become religious for the sake of her religious partner. On the other hand, although we do not have the data to support this impression, we suspect that there is a very high incidence of mixed Sephardi couples where the wife is religious and the husband is not.

Respondents' ages varied from 23 to 77. Of the 50 respondents, 4 were between the ages of 21 and 30; 17, between the ages of 31 and 40; 11, between the ages of 41 and 50; 14 between the ages of 51 and 60; and 3, between the ages of 61 and 70; one respondent was over the age of 70.

Another characteristic of the sample that makes it unrepresentative is its social class composition; only four respondents could be classified as lower class.

Another limitation of the study is that of selectivity—do those who agree to be interviewed differ from the entire pool of mixed couples? We don't know, but we were pleasantly surprised by how few people refused to be interviewed. With the exception of the mixed couples whom we ourselves knew, other respondents were first contacted by our acquaintances who asked the mixed couples if they objected to being questioned. Whenever an acquaintance told us that they knew a mixed couple and would contact them for us, we always inquired as to the outcome. Ten of the sixty persons who were contacted refused to be interviewed. The refusal rate is relatively low, considering the sensitivity of the issue.

In Israel as in most societies, men are generally regarded as more closed than women. Indeed, a number of women who agreed to be interviewed were uncertain whether their husbands would likewise consent. They noted that their spouses were usually reluctant to discuss subjects of a personal nature. We found that men were no less agreeable than women to discuss the problems of a mixed marriage and the same number of men as women (five and five) refused to be interviewed.

During the open-ended interviews, we explored the following topics: how much religious education (if any) the respondent had; the religious atmosphere in the parental home and the religious education of siblings; participation in youth organizations; how the couple met and whether there were religious differences at that time; in the case of religious differences, whether the differences were discussed before marriage; specific religious observances (e.g., traveling, turning on television and answering the telephone on the Sabbath, and observing laws of family purity) and the compromises each spouse made in this regard; the educational system in which the children were enrolled; marital satisfaction and advice to a young couple in a similar situation.

Results

Conventional wisdom in Israel is that there are very few mixed couples and those there are result from one partner becoming a baal tshuva during the course of the marriage. This is not what we found—two-thirds of our couples began marriage as mixed couples.

We asked these couples if they had discussed their religious differences before marriage. Contrary to our expectation, that all would have had extensive discussions of the topic, half reported that they had hardly discussed the matter at all.

Aaron grew up in a small religious settlement. He met his wife, Rina, who had no religious background, in the army. Their marriage was contingent on her completely following a religious way of life. According to Aaron:

> We talked a lot. We had many discussions. I explained and she listened. I told her that a religious life means completely changing the way she now lives. It is not just refraining from travel on Shabbat. It means that she can't eat at her friends' homes. And she can't change her mind in another ten years. It is for all her life.

Ariela was born and raised in a non-religious kibbutz. She waited three years before agreeing to marry Aryeh because of their religious differences. Ariela says that they made an oral contract before marriage. We were surprised to hear the word *contract* because this is not an Israeli concept in regard to marriage. But the term seems appropriate in view of what Ariela told us:

> We had negotiations about how religious he would be and how non-religious I would be. We agreed that I could drive, visit friends, watch television on Saturday, and not attend mikveh. I agreed to keep kashrut, attend synagogue with him on the holidays, and not require him to go out with me on Saturday.

Among those couples who did not discuss their religious differences at all or who discussed them only superficially, there were two typical responses. One set of couples avoided specific issues. They satisfied themselves with a general understanding "to respect each other's way of life," as Moti put it. Others avoided the issue entirely, denying they ever had a serious discussion of the matter. As one respondent put it, "events just took over."

The interviews disclosed three basic ways in which mixed couples accommodated their differences. We will call the first type of accommodation, "separate and equal." In this type of accommodation, the non-religious person remains publicly non-religious and the religous partner remains publicly religious. Five families fell into this category.

We call the second type of accommodation, "compromise." The non-religious partner observes the proprieties of religious law in public but retains greater autonomy in the home. Thirteen of our thirty family units fell into this category.

The third type of accommodation, which we call, "change," is the most one-sided. It involves either the religious spouse becoming non-religious (there were five such instances) or the non-religious person becoming religious (there were six such instances). A final couple whom we interviewed consisted of a *haredi* woman married to an Orthodox but non-*haredi* man. The couple does not easily fit any of the three categories of accommodation and will be discussed at the conclusion.

Separate and Equal

The five non-religious respondents who fell into this category travel, use electricity, and (with one exception) write or work on Saturday. All eat non-kosher food outside the home. The interesting finding is that all of these respondents are men. In retrospect, this is not surprising. A separate and equal marriage could not be maintained with a non-religious wife who did not keep a kosher home.

In this case, it would appear that the non-religious spouses (all husbands) made very few compromises. What kinds of compromises do the religious partners (all of them women) make? None of them travel or cook on the Sabbath, but two of them use electricity and three do not observe the laws of family purity.

Yossi and Ora are an example of a couple who live separate and equal lives in relative satisfaction. Yossi married Ora knowing that she was religious. They spoke at length about the kinds of accommodations they would make. Yossi promised not to travel on Shabbat. Ora promised that she wouldn't object to his smoking, using electricity, and eating non-kosher food outside the home. For about four years, both partners explained, Yossi was sick every Saturday. Ora finally realized that the old accommodation was impossible, and they reached a new understanding. Now Yossi takes the children to the beach or to his parents on Saturday. Yossi regrets "that Ora will not go with me to parties on Friday nights. I often stay home rather than go alone," he says. The couple makes an effort never to use the word, *forbidden* with their children in connection with religion. The oldest child attends a non-religious school, while the others attend a school oriented toward Conservative Judaism. Yossi and Ora claim they are happier as the years go by.

In another case, the separate and equal relationship is less satisfying. In fact, Ada, a *hozeret bitshuva* (penitent) is quite unhappy with her husband's non-religious behavior. She has, over the years, become quite religiously observant. She does not use electricity or travel on Shabbat, keeps a kosher home, goes to mikveh, and avoids "mixed" swimming (men and women together at a pool or beach). Her husband refuses to cooperate, although he very begrudgingly accepts her insistence on observing laws of family purity. He sometimes makes kiddush, but there is no Shabbat atmosphere because he and the older children turn on the television and travel on Friday nights and Saturdays. The two older children attend non-religious schools and resent their mother trying to interfere with their way of life. In fact, they are ashamed of her. However, Ada refuses to acknowledge that her act of penitence has made her less happy personally. "All in all," she says, "I derive strength from the Torah and feel happier in that sense than I did before becoming religious."

Her husband refused to be interviewed.

Compromise

The compromise group is composed of thirteen families. Major compromises on the part of the non-religious partner include not traveling on Saturday or doing so infrequently or surreptitiously to avoid being seen by religious neighbors. Most of the non-religious spouses (ten out of thirteen) use electricity on Saturday and eight eat non-kosher food outside the home. Only four attend synagogue and only one of the six women goes to mikveh. None of the religious partners travel on Shabbat. One uses electricity and two out of seven religious women do not go to mikveh. It would appear, therefore, that most of the accommodations are made by the non-religious partner; we anticipated this fact at the beginning of the study.

The following cases illustrate the way in which couples who fall into the category of compromise accommodate their differences.

Binyamin and Sabina were both non-religious when they first married. They did, however, keep a kosher kitchen. Over the course of the next few years, Binyamin became increasingly religious and Sabina compromised in a few important areas. She does not travel on Shabbat, at least not if she thinks she may be seen, and she makes an effort not to be seen eating non-kosher food in public. She resents going to mikveh but does so because she fears that if she doesn't, Binyamin would insist on a divorce. Binyamin does not make an issue over the fact that she uses electricity and writes on Shabbat. He realizes that she eats non-kosher food and travels on Shabbat when away from home. Their three children, all religiously educated, are aware of the differences since Sabina has been quite vocal "about the religious nonsense" that she "has been forced to follow." One child is now non-religious. The couple have achieved a practical compromise and report they are happily married.

Soon after they met, Yigal and Shoshi knew that they wanted to get married, but they waited a year. Shoshi is religious and Yigal is not and they discussed at great length the accommodations each would have to make. Shoshi's parents tried to stop them. Yigal agreed to a kosher home and to send their future children to religious schools, and Shoshi agreed that he could continue to travel on Shabbat and work when necessary. "I thought I wouldn't miss the religious atmosphere of my parents' home," said Shoshi, "but I did—very much." About six years ago, Yigal stopped traveling and doing business on Saturday. "It was originally for the children's sake, but now I like having a day of rest," he noted. He has begun attending synagogue regularly and comments that he enjoys the social life surrounding the synagogue. When abroad, he travels on Saturdays and eats non-kosher food. His marriage, he says, is a happy one.

Zev and Raya describe themselves as happily married and seem to have an open, comfortable relationship. Raya consented to keep a kosher home, send their future children to religious schools, and not travel on Shabbat, in spite of her secular point of view. Zev agreed not to insist that his wife attend mikveh and to let Raya warm up food on Saturday for her non-religious friends. He also agreed to her eating non-kosher food at friends' homes. The house is almost completely wired with Sabbath clocks so that Raya does not need to use electricity. Only their oldest child, the couple told us, is aware of the mother's non-religious identity. The others are too young. Raya is very anxious to be part of the religious community, and is well-accepted. Only two of her closest friends know she is not religious.

Not all marriages of this type succeed. Avi and Ziva's marriage does not appear to be an especially happy one, and both admit moderate to low marital satisfaction. When first married, Ziva agreed to keep a kosher kitchen for the sake of relatives. Gradually, Avi became more religious while Ziva remained unchanged. When Avi inherited property in a religious neighborhood, they moved there. In order to please her husband and in the hope of becoming accepted by the neighbors, Ziva stopped traveling and watching television on Shabbat. Avi goes to synagogue. The children, however, do not attend religious schools. Contrary to whatever Ziva and Avi may have thought, this stigmatizes the family as non-religious in Israeli society. According to Ziva:

> It didn't matter how hard I tried, we weren't accepted as a religious family. No one asked us in for kiddush. The children had a difficult time too. Finally, I stopped worrying too much about what the neighbors will think and began hanging out my son's uniform on Shabbat—the only day possible. Now I wait for my husband to go to sleep Friday evening and then I turn on the television. The children and I are aligned against him and there is much bitterness and tension in the family, especially on Shabbat.

Change

This last type of accommodation is defined by the willingness of one partner to totally accommodate to the religious orientation of the other. Slightly more than one-third of our respondent couples belong to this category. In six cases, the non-religious spouse became religious and in five cases, the religious spouse became non-religious.

The now completely religious couples adhere to all religious observances about which we inquired, with the exception of family purity laws. Two of the five non-religious women who became religious do not go to mikveh. In both instances, they were not asked to do so by their religious husbands.

Although Leah was raised in a religious home, she had been living a "free, happy life" for three years before she met Yoram. She explained:

> He set all the rules which were to govern our life together and I agreed to everything. No more traveling on Shabbat, no lights or television or cooking on Shabbat. The children were to receive a religious education. Our life was to be beyond reproach. And so it is until this day.

Leah has very mixed feelings about the religious changes in her life, and she regards her married life as only moderately happy.

When Menahem and Sarah first met, both were non-religious. "His mother asked me to keep kosher and I agreed with no hesitations," said Sarah. "At that time we both traveled on Shabbat," she noted. Then Menahem became more and more religious. The children were sent to religious school. He demanded that Sarah observe the Sabbath. Terrible fights ensued. They contemplated divorce more than once. After much misery, Sarah agreed to do everything Menahem wanted, and since then, their life together is much easier. Menahem is quite happy with the situation. Sarah attests to moderate happiness. She says, "I'm religious in every way except in my mind where I'm free."

Our study includes five instances of the religious spouse becoming non-religious. Three of the five are women. They travel, work, and use electricity on the Sabbath. Two women, however, keep a kosher home and do not eat non-kosher food outside the home. All three women ceased being observant at the time of marriage or shortly thereafter. In the case of the two men, both remained religious for two years before changing their way of life.

Haim, according to his wife, Miriam, was totally non-religious before their marriage and Miriam was religious. She says:

> When we first married, we had no car and didn't travel on Saturday. When we finally bought a used car, I agreed to travel for the sake of *shalom bayit* [peace in the house]. I never went to mikveh. I would like to have gone but it would have caused a terrible fight.

Miriam still attempts to observe some Jewish laws. For example, without Haim's knowledge, she cleans the house thoroughly for Pesah.

Ilan, who had a Yeshiva education, married Nitza, a non-religious girl. Nitza agreed to keep a kosher kitchen and not travel on Shabbat. She refused to go with him to synagogue or to fast on Yom Kippur. When Ilan's mother died, two years after his marriage, he stopped being religious. Since that time, the couple reports they have led a happy, secular life. Their children, born after the change, have all received a secular education.

Discussion

The Incidence of Mixed Marriage

When we first began this study, we thought that there were relatively few mixed religious couples. All those with whom we discussed the project felt we would have trouble locating "so rare a breed." At the conclusion of each interview, we inquired as to whether our respondents knew of other mixed couples. Many of them did know of another couple, but none of these other couples were members of their communities. Some mixed couples were surprised to learn that there were any other marriages like theirs. Several suggested, only half jokingly, that we organize a support group.

We kept a record of every acquaintance whom we asked to suggest potential respondents. Fewer than half said they didn't know any mixed couples. Were they telling the truth? Some replied immediately in the negative, almost without thinking. Perhaps if they had thought a while, they would have realized that they do know some mixed couples. Perhaps they knew such couples but didn't want to bother them or to take the trouble of making the initial contact for us. We do not know. On the other hand, over half the people whom we asked for contacts did know at least one mixed couple; some knew more than one. Based solely on our investigation, we found that, on the average, each religious person we asked knew at least one mixed couple. But quite often, we discovered, only the mixed couple's closest friends knew that the couple was mixed. This was especially true among the compromisers—those couples whose non-religious partner, the woman, observes the amenities of religion in public. If the non-religious partner is a man, and does not wear a kippah, he is easily identifiable as non-religious. But if the compromiser is a woman, even religious neighbors are not aware that the couple is mixed. As we noted in the introduction, the non-religious in general seem less aware of the existence of mixed couples.

In no case did we identify more than one mixed couple in the same synagogue. The mixed couples to whom we were referred were members of synagogues throughout the country. Our sense is that excluding *haredi* neighborhoods and synagogues, there is, on the average, at least one mixed religious couple for every synagogue. But this may be a gross underestimation.

In our own synagogue of forty-five families, we know fifteen couples fairly well and the rest only casually. However, we are very friendly with the son of one of these couples. In discussing our study with him, quite by chance, he revealed that his parents were a mixed couple. In other words, there is at least one mixed couple of whom we were unaware in our rather small synagogue.

Is our synagogue representative? If so, then the number of mixed religious marriages is considerably higher than one per synagogue. In our own synagogue of forty-five families, there are at least four mixed couples, and there may be more.

Religion and Marital Satisfaction

We were surprised at the bitterness and resentment we uncovered among some of the non-religious spouses. Some of the bitterness is directed against the religious spouse, but in some instances, it was directed, or at least articulated, against the Jewish religion rather than the spouse.

One woman agreed, at marriage, to be observant. She told us that she has kept her agreement faithfully for twenty years but she also told us that she "does not want to talk about it, it is too painful. I want to keep it repressed." The bitterness of being forced to go to the mikveh, of not being able to spend a "normal" Shabbat with one's spouse and children and of constantly being told that you are forbidden to do something, is very real for many non-religious partners.

Many of the religious spouses yearn for the beauty and the atmosphere of the Shabbat and Holy Days, but many non-religious partners perceive religion as one prohibition after another. The religious spouses have failed to communicate a love for the life of Torah but have succeeded in imposing a series of prohibitions. It may be more difficult to communicate the former than the latter. Rabbis working with such couples would be well advised to emphasize the positive aspects of Judaism.

We asked our respondents to rate their marriage in terms of satisfaction on a scale of one to five. We did not find any sharp differences among our mixed couples in accordance with their type of accommodation. We did, however, find that most respondents felt they would be happier if their partners were of the same religious orientation. Ariela, a secular woman whose religious husband changed after two years of marriage, said, "Now I would give us a five on the happiness scale. A few years ago I would have said much less." Ada, a religious woman says sadly: "I really miss the Shabbat atmosphere—*zmirot* [Shabbat songs], some Torah. At my house everyone eats hurriedly and rushes away." Dov expresses loneliness: "It's a couple society and I'm the only one who comes to kiddush—alone. My wife doesn't invite people to our home nor does she go out with me on Shabbat. I respect her point of view, but it's really rather lonely."

Types of Accommodation

We found three major types of accommodation. We labeled them, first, separate and equal, where one spouse is religious and the other spouse is non-religious in his or her public behavior; second, compromise, where the non-religious spouse observes religious proprieties in public but remains non-religious in the privacy of the home; and third, change, where one partner adopts the other's religious orientation.

The separate and equal families face the greatest difficulty. From a psychological perspective, they may benefit from preservation of their identities, but they are bucking societal norms. In Israel, the religious and non-religious may work together but they live separate social lives. These families challenge the norms of a society that has little sympathy or understanding for such alliances.

When such couples have children, their difficulties are exacerbated. Sending the children to a religious school identifies the family as religious. With whom will the non-religious person go to the beach on Shabbat? Socializing at a Saturday kiddush really requires the presence of both partners. The continued absence of one of them will stigmatize the couple, and future invitations will not be forthcoming. The children may find themselves unwelcome in the homes of schoolmates. Parents of schoolmates will be reluctant to let their own children play in the home of a mixed couple.

If the couple sends the children to a non-religious school, then the religious person will be left home on Saturday when the non-religious partner goes out with the children. The stigma of being religious in a non-religious society is less oppressive than being non-religious in a religious society, but it means a lonely existence for the religious partner who must celebrate his or her religion without spouse or children, and it undoubtedly subjects the children to at least minor, if not major, discomforts that result from having idiosyncratic parents.

We assumed that our separate and equal families would be inherently unstable and that, at some point, especially if they have young children, one partner or another would become a compromiser, if not a changer, thereby permitting the family unit to locate itself within one type of community or another. But four of our five separate and equal couples avoided this difficult choice in a startling manner. They split their children by sending some to a religious school and some to a non-religious school. One parent explained this by claiming that, "we sent them to the best school in the neighborhood." That may be what the family believed they were doing. We have difficulty in accepting this as the only reason for their choice. The fifth family was instrumental in establishing a school oriented toward Conservative Judaism in the neighborhood because they felt that both they and their children would be most comfortable there. In other words, separate and equal couples resisted the obvious social pressure to force them into one camp or another. But, we must recall, they are the minority among the mixed couples we interviewed.

Rivkah and Shimon are a very special kind of separate and equal couple; one so special that we refrained from placing it into any category. Both are twenty-five-years old and totally observant, yet Rivkah seriously thinks of divorce because of their religious incompatibility. She comes from a *haredi* background and Shimon from a Bnai Akiva religious-Zionist one. They fell in love, and Rivkah married Shimon against the advice of a number of rabbis with whom she consulted.

Before marriage, the couple had many discussions about their religious differences. Shimon agreed not to go to the army and to study in a yeshiva. He refused, however, to dress in black. Rivkah acceded to Shimon's objections and didn't cut her hair and wear a wig.

Shimon is disturbed by the fact that he did not go to the army. He now wishes to volunteer, although he is married and the father of three children. He wants to leave his yeshiva, discontinue intensive Torah study, find a job, and stop depending upon his wife to support the family. Rivkah refuses to hear about this. They would not advise another couple in their circumstances to get married because "it is just too difficult to handle."

The compromisers are defined as mixed couples whose non-religious partner observes the religious proprieties in public but not all of them in private. The one accommodation common to all compromisers was the non-religious partner's use of electricity on Shabbat. The use of electricity has symbolic and practical significance. After all, one can avoid turning electrical switches on and off with relative ease. Electrical timers can be preset for almost all appliances.

Our explanation of why so many non-religious refuse to compromise in this area is that they are thereby asserting their identities, demonstrating that they have some control over their lives. One person stated this explicitly:

> Frankly, I could [avoid using electricity]. It would be somewhat bothersome. It would involve me in thinking out beforehand what television programs I want to watch and the time I want to go to sleep. I imagine that once I did this, there aren't too many differences between one Saturday and the next. But I just don't want to. I gave up enough by not traveling on Saturday. It's my home too and I want to do what I want. And besides, I'm not requiring her to turn on the lights.

Among the compromisers, the religious spouse is cognizant of the sacrifice made by the non-religious spouse and is tolerant of the use of electricity. A number of them join their non-religious partners in watching television on Friday night, something which they regard as a compromise on their part.

There are two categories of changers—one of religious partners who become non-religious and one of non-religious partners who become religious. We interviewed five couples in the first category and six in the second. As we indicated above, the incidence of the first category is probably understated because our network of contacts tended to be overrepresentative of religious people. In other words, we have an overrepresentation of mixed couples who are part of a religious community.

All the non-religious partners we interviewed, who agreed to be religious as a condition to marriage, have lived up to their commitments although some have specific grievances such as the limitations on visiting their relatives on Saturday. One is very resentful of this imposition.

Of the five religious partners who became non-religious, three, all women, did so at the time of the marriage or soon thereafter. This wasn't always spelled out as a condition for marriage, but both partners reported that they assumed it would happen. In the two cases of men who became non-religious, both had separate and equal marriages for two years before they changed. We do not know if their choice of a non-religious mate was related to a desire to unburden themselves of religious observance but one wife suggested this.

Among the eleven changers, eight were women. Our sample is too small for us to draw any conclusions but the disproportion does not surprise us. Israeli society is more traditional than society in the United States, and if one partner accommodates entirely to the other, it is likely to be the woman. In addition, five of the six non-religious spouses who became religious were women. We would point out that it is much easier for a non-religious woman to learn how to behave in a religious environment (she need only master technical rules of kashrut or family purity) than for the man to do so. A fairly high degree of bookish knowledge is required if he is to integrate himself into a religious environment.

The most complex case in our category of changers is the instance of a double change. Yaffa and Dan married with the general understanding that she would continue being religious and he would live a secular life. They really didn't talk much about the details. As Dan said, "Events just took over." The house was kosher. Yaffa didn't travel, use electricity, or cook on Shabbat. Dan accepted family purity laws. He went to soccer games on Saturdays and ate non-kosher food outside the house. As time passed, Yaffa became less and less observant. She began switching electricity on and off and even traveling on Shabbat. She says she didn't feel bad about it at all. At the same time, Dan began observing more and more religious laws. He stopped traveling on Shabbat, attended synagogue and now identifies himself as religious. But Dan is not as understanding as Yaffa had been. He insists on obedience of all the rules, except laws of family purity, and this only due to Yaffa's strenuous refusal to attend mikveh. Yaffa gave in to Dan for the sake of family harmony and their home is conducted in strict accordance with religious law. The children receive a religious education and all of them are religious. Yaffa speaks freely of her non-religious feelings and says:

> Dan's smart enough not to ask me what I do when I'm on my own away from home or on Shabbat mornings when he's at synagogue. The kids have known [about my religious orientation] for a few years.

We caution the reader against overgeneralizing from this study. We did not select a random sample of mixed couples. In only one case are both partners Sephardim. Only four couples are lower class. Had we turned to other people to suggest respondents, the findings could have been different. In addition, life is complex and marriages especially so, and each of the mixed marriages with which we dealt seemed like a world unto itself.

Nevertheless, we are left with two very striking and related findings from our study. First, the incidence of mixed marriage appears to be much more widespread than we had believed. Polarization between the religious and non-religious has always existed in Israel, but it appears to have heightened the last few years. It may very well be that it was easier thirty years ago for a mixed religious couple to get along than it is today. What is most remarkable, however, is that such marriages continue to be formed. Secondly, both partners to the marriage make at least minimal accommodations in virtually every case. On the other hand, in the majority of cases, they retain at least minimal loyalties to their previous religious (or non-religious) orientation.

Yisrael Wollman

10

A Meeting of the Hearts

Reducing Tensions between the Religious and the Non-Religious

Tensions between religious and non-religious, in particular between religious and secular, have risen in recent years. Are there any institutions devoted to the resolution of these tensions? This chapter is concerned with organizations, both governmental and non-governmental, that are concerned with these tensions and whose activity, directly or indirectly, seeks to reduce if not eliminate them.

One way to reduce these tensions is to bring religious and non-religious together in informal settings so that they can get to know one another as people. This may serve to demonstrate how much they share in common as well as what it is that separates them at an ideological or value level; it may also serve as a foundation upon which friendships can be built without regard to religious differences. This method, therefore, makes the encounter itself the goal.

A second method is to nurture the values which religious and non-religious Jews share, i.e. Jewish identity and commitment to the Jewish people and the land of Israel. This kind of activity, if successful, necessarily strengthens the non-religious Jew's understanding of and sympathy for the religious Jew, whose Jewish identity is almost by definition the stronger of the two. In other words, the path toward the goal of strengthening Jewish identity becomes the method whereby tensions are reduced.

Moreover, along this same path, religious Jews can be shown that a Jewish identity does exist among secular Jews. Since many religious Jews bear contempt if not hostility toward the non-religious, believing that the latter lack a Jewish identity and strong commitment to the Jewish people, such a program would also serve to reduce tensions. This variation of the Jewish-identity approach is hardly ever employed, however—the only experiment in this direction was one undertaken by the Torah Culture department of the Ministry of Education and Culture in a very limited manner. The reason for this is, no doubt, that almost all the efforts at reducing tension between religious and non-religious are undertaken by the religious and are directed primarily toward the non-religious.

A third method would be to emphasize the importance of pluralism, tolerance, mutual understanding, and a shared humanity, as rooted in the Jewish or the western humanistic tradition and as essential in the survival of any social system. In this method, striving toward the goal of strengthening humanism and universalistic norms becomes the method for reducing religious–secular tensions.

These methods are not mutually exclusive. Organized encounters between religious and non-religious can be based on methods two or three or both, or these methods can be utilized in the absence of encounters. Indeed, they tend to reinforce one another; as we shall see, however, some movements, such as the Sapir Center, emphasize the third approach, whereas others, such as El Ami, focus exclusively on the second and would probably be hostile to the third.

As a matter of fact, the second method is the most common. We will find that most organizations in Israel that concern themselves with reducing the levels of tension between religious and non-religious do so through the effort to strengthen Jewish identity. The reason is fairly simple: their major concern *is* Jewish identity, and reducing tensions is a by-product, or a secondary development, or at best a later one, in their programs.

However, not every organization with this purpose is entirely clear about which of the three methods or goals it most favors. In fact, in the case of at least one organization, Gesher, there are differences of opinion which have consequences for its policy.

This paper is not concerned with "penitential" organizations—groups whose goal is *l'hahzir bitshuvah,* to turn non-religious Jews into Jews who believe in God and observe Jewish law. Most of these organizations are run by *haredim* and have caused a great many problems for those with whom this paper deals. We will return to that topic in the final section.

The Organizations

There are three major organizations—Gesher, El Ami, and Shai—that function in the area we have described. However, there are a number of additional organizations, the largest of which we will briefly describe, that also devote their resources to the nurturing of Jewish identity, and to reducing secular–religious tensions either directly or as a by-product of their efforts in strengthening Jewish identity. Altogether these organizations involve tens of thousands of Israelis (primarily but not exclusively teenagers), employ on a full-time or part-time basis hundreds of staff members; and spend some three million dollars a year.

Gesher ("Bridge")

Gesher was founded in 1970, in the United States, by a group of young religious Jews concerned with the polarization between religious and secular in Israel. It is the only organization which was founded for the primary purpose of confronting and reducing this polarization. Most of its members were native-born Americans, graduates of Yeshiva University, who had spent varying periods of time in yeshivot or universities in Israel. They felt that the problem of secular–religious tension in Israel could only be resolved with the assistance of an outside group which was well funded but not involved in Israeli politics.

One of the members of the group, Dr. Daniel Tropper, whose field was Jewish history, settled in Israel in 1969, intending to join the faculty of Bar-Ilan University. For an interim period, as he thought, he undertook to establish the Gesher organization in Israel, and he became its director. He has continued to direct Gesher to the present time.

Among Gesher's leaders there are two different approaches to the group's goals, and this difference finds expression in its activities. One approach sees the search for unifying elements within the Jewish tradition as the movement's main purpose. This approach hopes to use elements within the tradition to further religious–secular understanding and cooperation. The second approach sees Gesher's main task as creating dialogue between groups whose world-views are foreign to each other, in the hope that such encounters will themselves help create a new socio-spiritual climate in Israel. This approach does not foresee the transmission of a "religious" message to "secular" Jews, but rather mutual stimulation and enrichment.

Tropper claims that the two approaches are not in conflict. They are, he believes, responses to two different problems. The first approach, which sees the group's activities as focused on Jewish identity, is a response to a problem shared by both religious and secular. "Many secular," he claims, "denigrate Jewish identity. And many religious have lost a wider Jewish perspective as they focus on narrow and excessively specific subjects." The attitude of each side, he believes, pushes the other to adopt an extremist position. "Correcting the misunderstandings of the religious is no less important than bringing the secular closer to Judaism," he observes. The second approach, which sees the encounter itself as the essence, answers another need: lack of understanding between the sides can induce extremism and create social problems. The two approaches, therefore, are really one. Resolution of the social problem is intimately linked to resolution of the spiritual one.

El Ami ("To My People")

The El Ami Movement was founded in May, 1983. Rabbi Yehoshua Zuckerman, a dominant personality in Jerusalem's Mercaz HaRav Kook Yeshiva, is the guiding figure in the organization. (The official head of the Executive Board is the Chief Rabbi of Israel, Rabbi Avraham Shapira, who also heads Mercaz HaRav.) According to Rav Zuckerman, El Ami's first goal is to spread the doctrine of Rabbi Abraham Isaac HaCohen Kook and his son, Rav Zvi Yehuda, and secondly, to unite the different types of Jews in Israel (by which he presumably means religious and non-religious), and create mutual understanding. This is to be achieved through eliminating ignorance and familiarizing the population with the Torah.

The official founding of this organization came soon after the Israeli withdrawal from Sinai. While the goals of El Ami are different than that of Gush Emunim, many of its activists were motivated by their experiences in the efforts to prevent the withdrawal. During the final four months of the evacuation, a group of students from

Mercaz HaRav manned the offices of the Movement to Stop the Withdrawal.

These students suggested the creation of an independent public information and education center. This new center would not deal with current events but systematically nurture an "awareness of the tie between the people of Israel and its land." Following the decline in the political ferment over the withdrawal from Yamit, the students pressured the leaders of Mercaz to found a permanent organization devoted to informal education. This, they argued, would strengthen the involvement of the Yeshiva and its sympathizers in Israeli society.

The first conference of El Ami activists was held in the summer of 1983. Various institutions, secular and religious, had been turning to students and graduates of Mercaz for assistance in conducting topical seminars, presenting lecturers, and organizing study groups. In the initial stage, El Ami's founders sought to consolidate these activities.

The historical context in which the movement was created is significant. National goals are interspersed with socio-religious ones. The main goal, according to Elisha Vishlizki, the movement's educational director, is to clarify to those who participate in the Zionist enterprise how much that enterprise is built upon a foundation of faith. In another formulation which according to Vishlizki parallels the first, "El Ami seeks to create an alternative to non-Zionist and anti-Zionist conceptions."

The Shai Institute

In 1982 Rabbi Israel Hess, a prominent figure in Mercaz HaRav circles who was then serving as campus rabbi at Bar-Ilan University, established a branch of the Meir Institute under the University's auspices. (The Meir Institute is a center for religious-Zionist education for penitents, run in the spirit of Mercaz HaRav.)

The founders noted that no other body in the Tel Aviv region was engaged in teaching basic Jewish concepts from a Zionist perspective to the secular public. The founders hoped to reach secular high-school and college students living in the area who were interested in acquiring Jewish knowledge and enriching their spiritual world in evening study. Many of these people were deterred from getting in touch with existing *haredi* bodies for fear of being "caught in the snares" of the penitential movement.

In 1984 the branch gained greater independence and changed its name to the Shai Institute of Jewish Learning. ("Shai" is an acronym of *shvut Yehuda,* "the return of Judea.") Avi Roth, a graduate of a *hesder* yeshiva, who had served until then as a lecturer in the Institute, was appointed director, the Institute's activities were broadened, and its emphasis changed.

Today the Institute is still located on the Bar-Ilan campus and utilizes its services. Bar-Ilan retains nominal supervision, and Rabbi Yitzhak Cohen, who heads Bar-Ilan's Torah Institute for Girls, also heads Shai's educational board. But in fact Shai enjoys a great deal of educational, organizational, and budgetary independence.

The Institutes for Jewish-Zionist Education

In the period after the Yom Kippur War, Israeli social commentators perceived an increasing sense of aimlessness among young people, a loss of values, and a weakened sense of basic Zionist purpose. This led, beginning in the late 1970s, to an increasing demand from high-school educators for educational material dealing with Jewish and Zionist identity.

In response, the Ministry of Education established an interdepartmental body called the Institutes for Jewish-Zionist Education. The Institutes were designed to work informally through unconventional educational activities. Their goals were defined as:

> Stimulating within the Jewish Israeli youngster an awareness of his Jewishness, and assisting him in examining what this Jewishness demands of him with respect to himself, his family, his society, his state, the Jewish people, and the minorities.

The Sapir Jewish Heritage Center

The Sapir Jewish Heritage Center, located in a dormitory building in the Jewish Quarter of Jerusalem, was erected in 1973 through the initiative of Rabbi Menahem HaCohen (a Labor party representative in the Knesset for many years and the rabbi of the General Federation of Labor). Its goal was to create an informal educational institution to teach Judaism from a humanistic perspective to young people and adults. Judaism was to be presented as a civilization with the human being at the center of its value system. The Sapir Center also sought to provide that public with the tools to enable it to cope with traditional Jewish texts and sources on its own. In the earliest stage, the founders also envisaged a kind of spiritual center which would produce theoretical publications.

These goals appear in different formulations in the Center's various publications. For example, in a folder mailed each year to secular-school principals, the primary goal is presented as "breaking down technical and psychological obstacles which limit access to Jewish cultural material by breaking the monopoly which a certain public has acquired on Jewish literature." This is a rather militant formulation, possibly designed to break down the psychological obstacles that a secular principal might experience on reading a letterhead emblazoned with the name "The Jewish Study Center."

Both ideologically and in its personnel, the Sapir Center is linked to the Labor Party. Rabbi HaCohen, who heads the Center's board, is a political figure, and most members of the board, as well as of the Friends of the Sapir Center (to be discussed below), identify with the moderate Zionist left. The Sapir Center, however, gets no subvention from the Labor Party, nor do politics enter into its educational activities or its administration. The link is expressed primarily in the type of groups that make use of its services: most identify with the labor movement.

Amiad

Amiad is an independent corporation established in 1982 with the manifest goal of acquainting the wider public in Israel with Judaism. In practice, though they never declared it publicly, the founders—among them prominent figures in the administration of Gesher and other religious-Zionist educational enterprises—sought to create a movement for penitents as a religious-Zionist counterweight to the *haredi* institutions then blossoming in Israel.

Dr. Daniel Tropper serves as general director of Amiad, but he is less intensively involved in this organization than in Gesher. Initially, Amiad's major activity was the organization of seminar weekends, study days, and classes aimed at those members of the secular public—particularly young couples—who were desirous of deepening their knowledge of Judaism, with the hope, at a later stage, of transforming their lives to ones of religious observance.

Two years after the movement's founding it became clear that there was less of an interest in the program than its founders expected. Amiad attributes the problem to the fears generated by the *haredi* penitential return movement and fanned by the press. The secular public refused to distinguish between types of institutions which sought to strengthen Jewish identity, and Amiad suffered from the general backlash.

For lack of an alternative, Amiad transferred its focus to traditional families who had a very low level of Jewish knowledge. Their goal was now to deepen their audience's knowledge of the Jewish tradition and particularly of Jewish thought. The form of the activities remained the same: weekends at a hotel, week-long vacations during the summer, and other such activities.

A year later, in 1986, Amiad was offered an opportunity to work with the secular public once more. The Ministry of Religion commissioned the organization to design a program for young couples about to marry. According to David Harnick, who coordinated the project on behalf of the movement, the goal was to transform the marriage into a Jewishly meaningful experience. There was also a belief that a sophisticated understanding of the meaning of the tie between the couple would stimulate them to explore other issues associated with a Jewish family life-style.

"We try," says Harnick, "to stimulate the young couple to think and become at least minimally aware of the Jewish approach to these subjects."

Other Institutions

The growing gap between the religious and secular publics in Israel, and the fact that this problem retains a high priority on the public agenda, mean that virtually every agency within Israel's educational system has been involved in efforts to cope with it. This often results in duplication, but sometimes one sees a vacuum being filled from an unexpected source.

The division of Torah Culture of the Ministry of Education, for example, turned its attention to the problem in 1987. It allocated a quarter-time position in order to try and tackle the subject from an unconventional angle: developing an awareness among the religious of the spiritual world of the avowedly secular. Advertisements were placed in the general press seeking lecturers with secular world-views prepared to appear before religious audiences.

At first, only one person responded to the advertisements. He was found suitable, and lectured once to twelfth-grade religious girls preparing for national service. Following additional publicity, some 20 more secularists were identified. They have been invited—not too frequently—to participate in study sessions organized by the Torah Culture department.

In 1987 the department organized a course, in cooperation with Bar-Ilan University, to prepare moderators on the topic of religious-secular relations. In 1988, however, the person responsible for all these programs found his position eliminated from the budget due to financial cut backs. As of this writing (1989), the Department offers some assistance to the Ministry of Education's Youth department in organizing encounters between religious and secular high school youth and has also sponsored a research study to test the effectiveness of these encounters in reducing tensions and creating mutual understanding.

Another young institution, which is taking its first steps, is "Maaleh: the Center for Religious Zionism." Maaleh was founded by the National Religious Party. It seeks to become a "body which directs and guides religious-Zionism." It sees its role as spreading religious-Zionism among the public, by various means. An unconventional house of study is planned, whose students will be involved in research in Jewish law and thought as applied to current events.

Maaleh is directed by Moti Shklar, a former director of the Golan House of Study and one of the leaders of Gesher. It falls within our purview only because of the motivation for its establishment. According to Shklar:

> We are trying to create instruments which will prevent religious-Zionism from going to extremes, to educate for complexity. Within the religious-Zionist public, radicalization in the *haredi* direction has taken place. On the other hand the phenomenon of secularization stemming from an absence of values and superficiality is also found. If we can't develop a more complex vision of reality, there won't be anyone in the future with whom the "opposing side" can meet and create a joint language.

Maaleh is also involved in organizing meetings among the "leaders and doers" of religious-Zionism and the central figures in the United Kibbutz Movement. The intention here is to initiate a dialogue between the leading ideological groups in Israeli society, those who influence a wide public, and various secondary groups.

Shorashim (Roots), under the directorship of Eleazar Shturm (an avowed secular Jew, though once a student at a *haredi* yeshiva), and Avraham Burg, a religious Jew who serves as a Labor party Knesset member, concentrates on activities of a completely different type.

Shorashim focuses primarily on organizing study days and educational weekends at hotels. The gatherings are widely advertised in the press and radio and the cost of the weekends is covered by participants' fees. The goal is to explore issues related to the Jewish people and Jewish thought through the ages with an open, critical approach, an approach in which the different currents in Judaism and Zionism are expressed.

Shorashim also organizes open discussion evenings once every few months, primarily in Jerusalem. Unlike the weekends, these events attract many young people. Shorashim also runs educational tours, led by academics, to Jewish locations abroad.

There are institutions called "houses of study" involved in programming Jewish identity. Their programs are considerably more modest than those mentioned here. Until 1984–1985, their activities were primarily focused on secular youth and various army units. All were caught up in a severe crisis as the public's anxiety rose over the wave of penitents. Schools stopped sending students to them and army units cut off all contact with them.

Today the majority of the activities of these houses of study (of which the most prominent are those of Hebron, the Golan, and Tel-Haim) focus on enrichment of religious high-school and yeshiva high-school students, on Jewish thought, and religious-Zionist identity.

"Malitz" (an acronym from the initials of the Institutes for Jewish-Zionist Education) is a sister organization to the institutes which operate within the framework of the Ministry of Education. Malitz, however, operates primarily with the adult public, with emphasis on new immigrants and delegations of Israelis being sent abroad. It also counsels activists in educational fields (community workers, delegates, rabbis, etc.) in teaching Jewish identity. Its goal is "to assist the participants to clarify their relationship to themselves as Jews, to their families, to their communities, to their cultures, to their traditions, and to the Jewish people and the land of Israel."

Another goal, unique to Malitz, is "to fertilize anew the pattern of relationships between Israel and the Diaspora, on a basis of mutual and realistic understanding of the two sides." It provides assistance for this purpose to Jewish organizations abroad.

Organizational Methods

All the organizations we have described devote most of their activity to working with youngsters below army age, although, almost all work with the I.D.F. as well. Indeed, the I.D.F. is an important source of funds and prestige for many of these organizations. In addition, almost all devote some program activity to adults.

The work with young people is built around principles of informal education. There are discussion groups, simulation games, films, light-and-sound programs, visits to synagogues, museums, and historical sites, and, less often, formal lectures. Most of the activity is for the intellectual elite from academic high schools. The organizations differ in their innovativeness and effectiveness. We will look more closely at Gesher's activities, because Gesher makes use of the most sophisticated educational techniques and thus, in some respects serves as a model for all the other groups in the field. We are, furthermore, particularly interested in Gesher because, unlike other groups, its original goal was to reduce the polarization of the religious and non-religious segments of Israeli society.

Gesher's main activity is the operation of seminars for religious and secular teenagers at the Gesher House in Safed. The seminars are generally four-day meetings (running from Wednesday through Saturday evening), in which youngsters meet from secular and religious high schools. The latter are regular religious high schools, high-school yeshivot (dormitory institutions for boys which stress Talmudic studies), and ulpanot (schools for girls modeled on yeshiva high schools). Students are recruited solely from the best schools. Since boys and girls participate together, a number of yeshiva high schools and ulpanot refuse, for reasons they describe as halakhic, to cooperate.

Gesher also runs seminars for secular students alone. In educational seminars known as "time tunnels," students from non-religious high schools analyze episodes in the Jewish people's past and apply the consequences to the present.

In all, about two thousand secular and religious students participate each year in Gesher activities. Its isolated location, on Mount Canaan in Safed, far from large cities and the center of the country, contributes to improving concentration, focusing discussion topics, and unifying the participants.

About fifty percent of Gesher's counselors are students from *hesder* yeshivot, and of these most are from the Har-Etzion Yeshiva in Gush Etzion. The majority of the other half are religious students, although there are a few secular counselors—mostly students at institutions such as the Kerem Seminar in Jerusalem or the Oranim Seminar, where secular-humanistic education is stressed.

Employing secular counselors is a source of controversy within Gesher, and the controversy is related to the different approaches to the movement's goals. In general, those who emphasize the goal of strengthening Jewish-religious identity disapprove of employing non-observant counselors. Supporters of the other approach, which stresses the importance of the encounter *per se* (the one which we referred to as the first method in the introduction), seek to increase the number of such counselors to the point where they equal the religious ones in number. Dr. Tropper is aware of the problem:

> In principle, I favor integrating secular counselors in our activities. It contributes equally to both sides—the religious and the secular. Of course, we are referring to counselors who have a positive attitude to Judaism regardless of how they define it. But there are two problems. The first is practical: employing secular counselors requires the agreement of the religious-Zionist community and, more particularly, of the heads of the institutions [with whom we work]. It's very important for Gesher's seminars to include participants from yeshiva high schools and ulpanot. They contribute a great deal to the other side and also learn much from them. If these institutions were to break off contact with us it would have a deleterious effect on our activities. I could fill the seminar without them, but the question is who would participate. Anxieties of religious parents and educators which take the form of "Gesher is too open an organization" endanger us. After all, Gesher was suspect in the eyes of the religious public from its very founding.

Another problem is the responsibility which Gesher bears to the parents and educators of the young people who attend its programs. According to Tropper:

> I have to be faithful to the parents who send me their children. I must return them home without damage to their basic world-view, whether it be religious or secular. From my own experience, I would say that the danger of religious influence on youth is less than the danger of secular influence. Within the religious community there is great sensitivity to this topic, and the fears have a well-established empirical basis. Many youngsters "take off their *kippot*" on reaching adulthood. Within the secular public, on the other hand, there is more hysteria over "penitential return" than the facts would warrant. Despite all this, the nature of Gesher's activities has been accepted with understanding. People see that everything is done with care and fairness.

At least until now, secular counselors have been integrated into the Gesher staff slowly and carefully. "We'll do this in stages," says Tropper, "experimentally and without raising fears, until the seminars' counselling staffs are fully integrated." In the meantime, the subject is tested in experimental seminars in which every discussion group has two counselors, one religious and one secular. In most cases this has been done in response to specific demands from principals of secular institutions and with the agreement of the principals of the participating religious institutions.

Gesher also operates encounters designed for graduates of the Safed seminars who express interest in such meetings. By 1988, two groups of "veterans" had met, in Jerusalem and Tel-Aviv, for two-week learning encounters under the guidance of the Gesher staff. Each was composed of about fifty young men and women, ages 17 and 18, religious and secular. Gesher promises to help these groups maintain contact during and after their army service. Members of the groups participate in outings and spend the high holy days together. In addition to staff, Gesher provides access to its facilities.

Since 1985 the movement has undertaken additional activities in new fields. First, it has organized study days on the subject of Jewish identity in secular high schools. The participating school will cancel its regular classes and the entire day will be devoted to lectures and discussions on Jewish identity under the guidance of the Gesher staff. This same type of activity is sometimes carried out with the participation of two schools—one religious and one secular: students will meet at least twice, exchanging roles of host and guest.

In 1988 Gesher organized three encounters between religious and secular teachers prior to an encounter between the students. The purpose of bringing the teachers together was to exchange opinions and lower their levels of anxiety. This also led to better preparation of the students, according to Tropper.

Gesher has also organized encounters between religious and nonreligious youth groups. One group would act as host to the other, and then for a second meeting roles would be exchanged. Activities included discussion groups and simulation games. Gesher also runs a seminar for the senior levels of these youth groups (eleventh- and twelfth-graders) at its Safed facility. Secular counselors participate in these seminars. Gesher has been invited by a number of youth movements to advise them on the subject of encounters between secular and religious youth.

And Gesher runs some special, one-time-only activities designed for youth. For example, it maintains a summer "house of study" designed for youngsters who have already participated in the movement's study days or seminars and are now interested in more intensive study. Another activity is its weekends for "youth seeking knowledge," designed for yeshiva high-school students who show an interest in broadening and deepening their knowledge of Jewish thought through unconventional means.

A standard feature in many of the encounters which Gesher sponsors is a humorous performance by its encounter administrator, Benjy Levin. Levin acts the role of four types of Jews—the secular, the *haredi,* the religious-Zionist, and the hippy—in an interview situation. The performance serves to dramatize value conflicts related to Jewish identity. The show, "Now with Benjy Levin," is extremely popular, and Levin has performed before audiences from kibbutzim and rural settlements, audiences of youth counselors, university lecturers, prisoners, teachers, senior army officers, and many others. It serves as the warm-up for an in-depth discussion on Jewish identity and is an integral part of Gesher's seminar programs.

Roughly seventy percent of the participants in the movement's activities are below army age. Recently, Gesher has invested efforts in programs designed for older groups. In 1988 two discussion groups for university students (one in Jerusalem and one in Tel Aviv) were established. There are about forty young people in each group, half of whom are religious and half secular.

In general, the participants in the movement's activities are evenly divided between religious and secular. According to the executive director, Dr. Tropper, during the bitter 1986 backlash aroused by the *haredi* community's penitential movement Gesher's programs were unaffected. But Tropper notes:

> The tremendous backlash in the secular public forced us to invest a lot of time and spiritual energy in running around explaining to it, proving to it, and persuading it that its fears were unwarranted. To our great good fortune, we work regularly with particular institutions and the principals know us. We were forced to strengthen our ties with them.

Gesher's efforts were assisted by a formal letter sent out to the schools by M.K. Nahman Raz, chairman of the Knesset's Committee on Education. The letter, which encouraged schools to establish ties with Gesher, contributed toward lessening fears.

Gesher runs a yearly program for its counselors. The program includes lectures and discussions on current events relevant to their work. The new counselors also learn group techniques, some of which have been pioneered by the organization itself. In addition,

Gesher runs a basic enrichment and learning encounter program for its counselors. These encounters, which include joint study and analysis of specific topics, are designed to create a staff able to think in sophisticated terms.

In the light of what Gesher's leaders perceived as growing tensions between religious and secular Jews, and between the political left and the political right, the organization has sought to reach an adult group which it felt had a central influence on public opinion: political leaders, writers, journalists, the heads of social movements, etc. Gesher has organized meetings between rabbis and religious intellectuals on the one hand (the Hagut group) and secular intellectuals on other. They also organized two encounters of three days' duration to which they invited secular and religious leaders in various professional fields. The purpose is to bring people who may be on different sides of a dispute in one setting to meet one another in an informal and personal manner in a different setting.

According to Dr. Tropper, the experimental project has run into difficulties and requires extraordinary organizational effort. "In general," he notes, "one could say that it is the secular who are uninterested in meeting with the religious. I find a much greater openness among the religious."

Gesher is trying to assist the religious community in structuring its relationship with the worlds of creativity, culture, and art. In the last two years it has organized a number of small encounters between secular authors and artists and religious intellectuals. During the intermediate days of Succot and Hannukah, in 1986, it made a noteworthy attempt to bring artists and religious scholars together before a general audience. In 1987 it organized a two-day-long seminar in a Jerusalem theater with the participation of authors, poets, top composers, and religious-Zionist rabbis. Those present participated in discussions and small creativity workshops, and viewed films and live performances on Jewish topics.

Initially, Gesher's organizers hoped to draw both a secular and a religious audience. As it turned out, most of the audience were religious. They now hope to set up small creativity workshops for young religious Jews.

Gesher's newest project is the creation of a Jerusalem Center House which will organize seminars in Jewish identity for secular Jews. This, it claims, is in response to a growing demand which it was unable to meet in the Safed Center. The Jerusalem Center will also serve as a special house of study in which young people may enrich their religious education using unconventional methods in studying traditional sources.

In 1987 Gesher closed one of its units, Jerusalem Productions, which had been engaged in the production of films. The unit was set up in 1982 with the intention of exploring the medium of television for Jewish educational purposes. Jerusalem Productions employed two professionals who, with outside assistance, experimented in producing popular films with Jewish content. The unit produced short films on the Sabbath and prayer, an English-speaking animated film on the holiday of Hannukah and its significance, a three-part series called "With Man" which dealt with value-conflict in Israeli society, and an animated film, "The Legend of the Hagaddah," on the exodus from Egypt as seen from a modern perspective. A number of the films were commercial successes, particularly in the United States.

According to Dr. Tropper, the unit was closed for two reasons. First, its activities were such a major drain on the budget that Gesher's ability to develop or even maintain its other programs was threatened. Equipment and materials were particularly costly. "Despite the success of the films we prepared," admits Tropper, "I still prefer the personal touch, intensive and face-to-face, over other means of education."

Another reason which contributed to the decision, according to Tropper, was "the feeling that a true success in transmitting a Jewish message in this medium will come only after reaching a 'critical mass,' using the very best material. A trickle has only marginal effect."

Gesher employs about sixty counselors on either a full-time or a special-contract basis. Its annual budget is roughly $500,000. A third of this is provided by assistance from various government offices, a third comes from contributions, from both Israel and abroad, and a final third is raised from participants in the organization's activities.

Summary

Each of the institutions we have listed, even the Sapir Center, represents a specific shading within the religious-Zionist public. That community, which looks so homogeneous at a superficial glance, is in reality composed of different ideological currents and subcurrents. In order to understand the movements and their relationships to their environment we must first understand why they were created.

All share certain characteristics. To begin with, all the movements (except Shorashim) were founded by religiously observant and Zionist Jews. This is not surprising. After all, in a society racked by tensions between the non-religious majority and the religious minority, it is the minority who have the more to lose. They are in a subordinate position, politically and economically and even socially, and it is in their interest to overcome the hostility of the non-religious public. Moti Shklar, who worked for years at Gesher and at the Golan House of Study and today heads the Center for Religious Zionism, adds this additional reason: religiously observant Israelis, he maintains, have a spiritual need to create encounters with the secular in order to accord legitimacy to themselves. For many years the religious in Israel were objects of scorn and ridicule; in some ways they still yearn for the approval of the non-religious.

Similarly unsurprising is the fact that it is the religious-Zionists rather than *haredim* who undertook the initiative in this regard. *Haredim* have difficulty in relating to, let alone working with, the non-religious public. They anticipate the hostility of the non-religious, indeed to some extent they thrive upon it, since it reinforces their own values, whereas this hostility undercuts some of the basic ideological premises of the religious-Zionists. Reducing polarization among Jews, especially within Israel, is a major religious *mitzvah* (mandate) in the catalogue of religious-Zionist *mitzvot.* Among the central ideas within each movement are notions such as "the unity of Israel," "heart to heart," and "all Jews are responsible for each other." These ideas are all perceived as religious imperatives.

Issues such as social awareness and responsibility for humanity are emphasized throughout the religious-Zionist educational system. The B'nai Akiva youth movement, in which most of the religious-Zionist activists were raised, has played a major role in nurturing these ideas.

All of the movements (except Gesher) were founded between 1973 and 1982, in the years after the Yom Kippur War, during which time the gaps between political and religious groups widened in Israel and problems of social and personal identity came to the fore. (Gesher was founded two years before the war, but its activities were significantly expanded afterwards.) The founders of the different organizations, graduates of higher yeshivot, attempted to act out the strong sense of mission which had been implanted in them. They sought to produce a more Jewish society in Israel.

Some of the characteristics which the founders share, however, contribute to the independence of their organizations. Many of the founders see themselves as unique. Each seems to think that only he lives in both the religious and the secular world and speaks the language of both, and therefore that only he and his movement are suited to bring the secular Jew closer to his Judaism.

The yeshivot which produced the founders of the movements also gave birth to decidedly different behavioral styles and even ideologies. One group was composed of former students of Rabbi Soloveichik in the United States; they were graduates of Yeshiva University and the founders of Gesher. They represent a tolerant orthodox style, intellectual and positive in its approach to world culture. They brought to Gesher's administration a mental style that was pragmatic and sophisticated. On the educational side they represented intellectual openness, which means an understanding of and sensitivity to the nature of secular society and the willingness to make an effort to adapt to it.

Gesher's pragmatic and sophisticated style is reflected in its system for selecting its staff and program. It may, however, account for the fact that it has met with opposition from the religious educational establishment. In some yeshiva high schools Gesher is still suspect because of its "extreme" liberalism, and some schools refuse to cooperate with it.

Gesher has been the subject of dispute in religious circles since its founding. Prominent activists have resigned. Some of them have charged that Gesher is a camouflaged missionary movement; others have argued that Gesher's religious values have taken second place—at best—to a spiritually barren concern with encounters between religious and secular youth.

El Ami's ideological character is reflected in the scholarly background of its founders and the timing of its establishment. It is the outgrowth of a public-relations movement concerned with fostering ties to the land of Israel at the time of the evacuation of Sinai, and was transformed into a movement to spread Judaism to the public on the basis of the principles of Mercaz HaRav Yeshiva. The organization's objectives as far as penitence is concerned are somewhat amorphous. The stress on nationalism and ties to the Land, the dominance of rabbis over organization policy, the opposition to activity involving mixing of the sexes, all represent an approach which has been widely accepted in Israel's religious-Zionist community. It is the dominant approach among the Gush Emunim settlers in Judea and Samaria, in most of the *hesder* yeshivot, and the religious-Zionist rabbinate.

The Sapir Center constitutes a third type in the range of movements surveyed in this chapter. Founded by Rabbi Menahem

HaCohen in 1973, it has a pronounced liberal-humanistic ideology and stands to the left of Gesher. In choosing between the value of study for the sake of furthering knowledge and enriching one's own moral values and study for the sake of changing attitudes and lifestyles, Sapir Center comes down firmly on the side of the former. Gesher is far more ambivalent in its attitude, and El Ami is closer to the latter approach.

One expression of its approach is the Sapir Center's appointment of a secular educational coordinator, who directs, as a matter of policy, a mixed staff of secular and religious counselors. Whereas Jewish identity in El Ami is understood to be linked intrinsically to the Land, at the Sapir Center it is linked to the centrality of man and the values of humanism. At the Sapir Center the specifically religious aspect of Judaism plays a marginal role in the program of study. The central aspect is the cultural-moral dimension. This approach is characteristic of groups of intellectuals and secular educators located in the academic world (the Oranim Seminar of the kibbutz movement and the Kerem Seminar in Jerusalem) and the settlement branch of the labor movement. It is also spiritually akin to the religious-Zionist humanist camp which finds expression in the Oz v'Shalom/Netivot Shalom movement.

The Shai Institute falls between Gesher and El Ami. The basic ideology which was and is taught there stems from Mercaz HaRav. Mercaz remains the spiritual home of a large proportion of the Institute's lecturers and counselors. On the other hand, it recruits staff from the entire range of religious-Zionism, nationalism is not the focus of its conceptions of Judaism and it is not committed to a dogmatic ideology.

The Zionist Institutes can be located between Gesher and the Sapir Center. The fact that they are part of a government ministry limits their goals. They may seek to nurture an interest and curiosity in the area of Jewish identity but must not espouse a particular version. They avoid activity that might lead to marked transformation in their students' perspectives. This approach, even if conducted under the best possible conditions, has the least chance of success. Lack of emotional involvement on the part of the educator limits the chances for the internalization of attitudes and values by the student.

The ineffectiveness of the Institutes, particularly the study days which used to be their specialty, is convenient for everybody. Teachers, parents, and even the Ministry of Education might feel threatened by a greater curiosity and involvement on the part of young people. The students, for their part, enjoy the vacation from academic routine during the two days of informal education. The Institutes' staff—civil servants with very low morale—make no effort to renew and update their material.

In general, attempts by the formal establishment to deal with religious–secular relations and Jewish identity have failed. The limited attempt by the Torah Culture division of the Ministry of Education to deal with the topic has been discontinued. The youth division of the Ministry, which once nurtured the Zionist Institutes, now recommends that schools turn for assistance to the other movements discussed in this study. Even the Ministry of Religion has learned that the success of an activity depends on the motivations of the people involved. Two Ministry activities which are fairly heavily funded have been turned over to El Ami (the Hearing Heart project) and to Amiad (the Living Together project). Governmental institutions face problems of low-status employees with inadequate salaries and poor morale: they tend, therefore, to be rather ineffective.

One found a general aura of crisis around groups engaged in confronting secular–religious tensions, which now appears to be coming to an end. The public's fear of the *haredi* penitential movement was the cause of the crisis. It was a death sentence for some of the independent movements working in the field. It seriously handicapped others. Some scrupulously refined their goals in order to convince potential participants that they were not penitential movements. Others simply changed the direction of their activities.

Public bodies which dealt with the question through their own initiative or as "buyers" of services provided by others suffered in their own way. The Ministry of Education was under fire on this issue, but the I.D.F. was the main target. Following sharp protests, whose echoes reached as far as the Knesset, the activities of non-Zionist *haredi* movements on I.D.F. bases were discontinued by order of the Minister of Defense, the Chief-of-Staff, and the commander of the Military Manpower division. As a result of this order, and because of the I.D.F's difficulty in distinguishing between the different religious movements, all activities of this nature were stopped—even those of the Zionists—except for those which only dealt with Jewish identity in a marginal way.

As we noted, the furor has abated since its peak in 1987. After quiet contacts between senior people in the security system, the commander of the I.D.F.'s Educational Office prepared a manifesto on activities concerning Jewish identity in the I.D.F. The paper recommends that the I.D.F. refrain from employing "secondary contractors" in teaching Judaism to its soldiers and rely instead on its own educational staff and on lecturers doing reserve army duty.

The paper does, however, stress the importance of:

> broadening perspectives on the subject of Judaism and strengthening understanding between soldiers of different opinions and attitudes, in order to encourage mutual respect and cooperation during army service and later. . .

a formula very close to the declared objectives of most of the movements surveyed in this study. In fact, the Chief Educational Officer has begun setting up courses, in-service training programs, and study days on this topic for officers. A program on Jewish identity scheduled to open at the Gesher House in Safed was to have been operated by a military educational unit with Gesher acting the role of silent partner, and it was eliminated for budgetary reasons alone.

There is, therefore, some renewal of cooperation between the I.D.F. and the religious-Zionist movements, but at a slow pace and with strict adherence to army guidelines.

Exercising hindsight, most of the people with whom I spoke are of the opinion that, whereas the *haredi* penitential movement may have transformed several thousand young people into God-fearing observant Jews, the backlash they aroused may have indirectly prevented many others from contacts with the world of Judaism.

As opposed to the *haredim,* most of the Zionist movements seek to develop a positive connection to Judaism on the part of the nonreligious public and are less concerned with individual behavior. They seek to create an awareness of Judaism, a curiosity about it, and to stimulate independent thought without mandatory prescriptions. The opposition which *haredi* activity engendered thus did more harm to the objectives of the Zionists than to the *haredim* themselves.

According to the leaders with whom we spoke, young Israelis are interested in their programs but it is difficult to secure their participation. Within the yeshivot there are still reservations about encounters with secular youth (especially if this involves mixing of sexes), but the major objection is on the secular side. Moti Shklar notes the lack of symmetry in participants' agreement to encounters. "The greater the response from our [the religious] side, the greater the resistance and the lower the response from their side," he says. But the resistance only precedes the encounter. "Someone who has already participated in one comes back for another and has an appetite for more."

Given the present social and political reality, the future of "heart-to-heart" activities in Israel is a gloomy one. Most of the current successes involve the shattering of stereotypes that many secular young people have of Judaism and stimulating them to additional thinking about values. They have had no impact on the anger that many of the secular public feel toward the nation's religious establishment—political and rabbinic—and had no softening effect on the rage directed against the self-segregated non-Zionist *haredi* community.

There are other problems. Involving the social elite of the young generation (primarily from the big cities and from workers' settlements) is essential, but another public has been left untouched. There is almost no involvement of young people from slums, from developing towns, from vocational schools, or from other non-elite segments of society. Shai's activity in this respect appears to be a notable exception.

The fact that the subject arouses the active interest of only one side—the religious—and only a passive interest, at best, from the secular, is another problem. This generates anxieties among the religious.

The movements discussed in this study, even if they were able to expand their activities, are not likely to resolve the growing gap between secular and religious Jews in Israel, though they do have a positive contribution to make. The problem can only be resolved through a transformation of the *image* of the rabbinical establishment; by the opening of additional centers equipped to deal with Jewish identity among young people from the lower classes; and by changes in the Ministry of Education's order of priorities, including the crystallization of a program to integrate the subject into existing school programs.

Despite this, the contributions of the movements discussed here are neither marginal nor simply a "drop in the ocean." They have introduced basic Jewish concepts to many secular youngsters and shattered their myths and stereotypes. Who knows what the situation in Israel today might be without the contribution of these organizations? Furthermore, they may have prepared the groundwork for better relations between religious and non-religious which might require new instruments or new conditions for its development.

Charles S. Liebman

11

Relations between *Dati* and *Non-Dati* Jews—Some Final Reflections

IT IS EASY to exaggerate the tensions between *dati* and non-*dati* Jews. This is what the Israeli public tends to do when a particular event, such as a controversy over the opening of a movie theater on Shabbat, gains media attention. But, as a number of authors point out, the vast majority of *dati* and non-*dati* Jews live in relative harmony, and most Israelis expect that this will continue to characterize their relations. The latest public-opinion study on the topic was conducted by the Israeli Institute of Applied Social Research on behalf of the Ministry of Religion in January and February of 1988. Their survey of a random sample of the adult urban Jewish population found that 85 percent believed that religious and secular Jews could live in harmony with one another. Only four percent were certain they could not. On the other hand, the same study found that 62 percent of the respondents felt that relations between the religious and secular sectors were a problematic issue in Israel. Bearing in mind, therefore, that we must not exaggerate the scope or intensity of the conflict, what do our case studies tell us about the nature of the problem, and what hints, if any, do they provide about possible resolutions? In the following discussion some additional material, not included in any of our case studies, is utilized where it seems particularly helpful to the analysis.

The *Issues* that Divide

What is the source of the tension between *dati* and non-*dati* Jews? Most observers have identified the tension in the opposing positions which the two camps adopt on issues of public observance. In the eyes of most *dati* Jews, even those most anxious to resolve tensions, the issues which divide them from non-*dati* Jews can be reduced to the question of whether public life, the Israeli "street," is to be conducted in accordance with the Jewish tradition. In other words, the major issue, as the *datiim* see it, is the extent to which Israel is a Jewish state not only by virtue of its population composition but by virtue of the manner in which it conducts its public life at both the symbolic and the practical level. Knesset legislation which defines who is a Jew (an issue to which we did not devote a case study) has become a key symbolic issue to many of them, and the opening of places of amusement on Shabbat is probably the key practical issue. To most non-*dati* Jews these tension-provoking issues can be summarized in terms of the extent to which individuals are to be free to lead the kinds of lives they wish or whether Israeli life is to be governed by Jewish law. In the words of Ben-Gurion, which are so often invoked by the opponents of any religious-based legislation, the choice is between a state governed by law and a state governed by *halakha*. These differences were expressed very clearly in our chapter on the controversy over the Petah Tikva cinema, and they repeat themselves over and over when spokesmen for each side present their points of view.

It is very important to understand what is and what is not at stake here. Note that *dati* spokesmen do not argue that every Jew must conduct his life in accordance with Jewish law. In this respect, analogies that some secularists in Israel draw between the demands of Muslim fundamentalists and those of Jewish extremists are erroneous. Muslin fundamentalists insist that it is the state's obligation to ensure that Muslims conduct their personal lives in accordance with Muslim law. Even when Muslim fundamentalists do not expect the state to favor Islam over other religions, as in Indonesia, fundamentalists have insisted that the state enforce Islamic law on those who are Muslims. But *haredim* in Israel make no such demand, and leading spokesmen for the religious-Zionists have time and again insisted that even if they were to constitute a majority in the Knesset they would never, on principle, raise such demands. It is a matter of record that the right of Jews to observe as much or as little as they want of Jewish law in their private domain has never been challenged by any religious party or group. There is a self-imposed limit, therefore, on the kinds of demands which the *dati* camp would impose on the non-*dati* Jew. And on the other side, there are few non-*dati* spokesmen, groups, or parties who would prefer to overturn the Jewish character of the State of Israel. In fact, according to legislation adopted by the Knesset in 1985, a political party is ineligible to participate in an election if its platform seeks to deny the Jewish character of the State of Israel. In 1988 a distinguished group of jurists submitted a proposed constitution for Israel. The proposed constitution was denounced by all the religious parties as dangerous to religion and inimical to religious interests. Nevertheless, even that constitution affirmed that Israel was a Jewish state, and its Jewish nature was embedded in a constitutional declaration. Libertarians may find the 1985 Knesset legislation and the proposed constitution offensive, but they do indicate how widespread is the public's acceptance of the principle that "the character of the society is and ought to be rooted in Judaism"! It is true that not every secularist is happy with this. But those who demur, have, at least until the present, stood at the margins of Israeli political life. This constitutes a self-imposed limit on the resistance of non-*dati* Jews to demands concerning the conduct of Israeli public life.

In summary, there is a consensus among Israelis that the individual ought to be free to practice or not practice the Jewish religion, and there is also a consensus that the state of Israel ought to reflect its Jewish nature. This consensus still allows a wide margin of difference between the *dati*, who feels that the Knesset can legitimately impose Jewish law upon all aspects of public life, and the secular Jew, who favors "separation of religion and state," i.e. no legislation based upon Jewish law whose consequence is to restrict the citizen in public or in private. But however wide the margin of difference, both sides can appeal to a common set of values as they seek to justify the legislation they favor or oppose. What we are saying, in other words, is that the consensus over religion and state in Israel is broad enough to allow each side to appeal to the other in the name of principles to which both sides adhere. Both parties can debate the issues of religion and state in Israel becaue of this common ground. There is a political language which both sides share and which, therefore, makes conflict resolution at this level possible though by no means inevitable. Finally, both sides, except at the margins, profess and probably believe in the principle of the unity of the Jewish people. In the case of some *dati* Jews, as we saw in Sira, this principle may override some aspects of Jewish law. Among other *dati* Jews, including some rabbis, this principle is actually embedded in their interpretation of *halakha*. It has led a few religious spokesmen (albeit a minority) to denounce demands for further religious legislation on religious as well as on practical grounds. According to Rav Yehudah Amital, who is mentioned in our chapters on the peace movements and on Tehiya, there is a priority in the rank ordering of Judaism's highest values: they are the people of Israel, the Torah of Israel, and the land of Israel, in that order. Among some secular Jews, as we saw in the chapters on Tehiya and the mixed settlements in Samaria, it has led to a recognition that, since *dati* Jews cannot be expected to compromise Jewish law, the burden of compromise is properly imposed on the non-*dati*.

There are, on the other hand, certain principles to which only one side is committed and the other opposed. Should they gain ascendancy they might exacerbate tensions to the point of violence, because they limit the possibility for meaningful debate. The *dati* Jews, religious-Zionists in particular, speak in terms of the establishment of a halakhic state. The claim of religious Zionism since its earliest years has been "the Land of Israel, for the People of Israel, in accordance with the Torah of Israel." Now religious-Zionists have never spelled out precisely what this claim entails, or how the state ruled in accordance with Torah to which religious-Zionists claim they aspire would look. But even if we grant religious-Zionists the benefit of the doubt and concede that the halakhic state to which they aspire would still provide the non-*dati* Jew (or even the non-Jew) with religious liberty, the non-*datiim* can hardly rest content. A state that is ruled in accordance with Torah or *halakha* seems quite incompatible with democracy and personal liberty. Surely, if the notions of Torah and *halakha* have any grounding in reality, if these are not purely symbolic words, then they suggest that some measure of authority will reside with the rabbis and scholars who are the authoritative interpreters of Jewish law. Even if one trusts that a state ruled in accordance with Torah allows for a legislature and executive elected by popular vote, there will be limitations on these bodies. At the very least they will not be permitted to enact legislation contrary to Jewish law, which in practice means legislation contrary to some rabbinic bodies' understanding of what constitutes Jewish law. It is fruitless for religious apologists to pretend that a state ruled in accordance with Torah is compatible with basic conceptions of democracy. No doubt legal terms lend themselves to a variety of interpretations and to manipulation. No doubt religious conceptions can be extended to the point where they appear to embrace everything that modern society affirms as good, right, fair, and humane. Such efforts abounded in Islam, Judaism, and Christianity in the last two centuries. But why should anyone believe that this is what those who affirm the desirability of a state governed in accordance with religious law have in mind, or that this is how such a state will be governed in practice?

It might be argued that this is not a real issue because, despite the fears that have been aroused in some of the more extreme secular circles, the eventuality of a religious majority in Israel with the power to impose such legislation is remote. But, as we saw in Chapter Three, some of the secular response to the outcome of the 1988 elections expressed just that fear. Indeed, in the weeks following the election, the religious parties spent a great deal of effort in reassuring Israelis that they had no intention of seeking new religious legislation—with three exceptions. They favored an amendment to the "who is a Jew?" law which would provide that only those who converted to Judaism in accordance with Jewish law would be recognized by the State of Israel as Jews. Secondly, in pursuit of the same objective, they announced their intention to insist that the authority of the rabbinical courts in matters of personal status be strengthened. Finally, they announced their demand for legislation that would have the effect of overturning a 1988 district-court decision that denied municipalities the authority to enact Sabbath ordinances. In other words, the religious parties sought to return to the municipalities the authority they were assumed to have had since the early years of statehood, *viz.* to decide whether places of public amusement would or would not be permitted to remain open on Shabbat.

The expression "the Land of Israel, for the People of Israel, in accordance with the Torah of Israel" is, we suggest, a slogan, a symbol of some ultimate wish, a utopian vision which no religious group seriously seeks to implement. But it is also true that religious-Zionists have refused to surrender the symbol, it still finds expression in their school curricula, and it frightens many secularists.

Among secular Jews, there is at least one principle that finds increasing support and that undermines the development of shared values and attempts at the reduction of tension. This refers to the demand for the establishment of a particular form of liberal democratic society: one in which all rights are located in the individual rather than in the society or the collective body of people who constitute the society. We identified this group in the Introduction as universal-secularists. Its views find prominent expression in the journal *Politika,* published by the Citizens Rights Movement. For example, in the December 1987 issue, political scientist Ze'ev Sternhall bewails the absence of western-style democracy in Israel. He defines this as a system of government which places the individual and not collective goals at the center of its concern. The problem in Israel, he says, is:

> understanding the essence of democracy. And democracy is first and foremost the expression of the rights of humans to be masters of themselves. Democracy is the expression of man's recognition that all sources of political, social, and moral authority inhere in man himself.

Israeli political culture, he suggests, rejects the basis of democratic thought—that "society and state exist in order to serve the individual. . . and are never ends in themselves." Sternhall traces Israel's collectivist culture to, among other elements, the Jewish tradition. Even the non-religious Zionists, he maintains, "never really freed themselves from the tradition of their father's home, and in one form or another they deferred to *Yisrael Saba* ['The term, literally Grandfather Israel, invokes the image of the traditional Jew and Judaism'].

This line of thought leads to the dejudaization of Israel. Its power, furthermore, resides in the fact that it does not explicitly demand that Israel cease to be a Jewish state. It need say nothing about the subject at all. Instead it appeals to another principle, one that does not seem far removed, at least at first glance, from notions of democracy and liberalism that virtually all Israelis share and which certainly accord with that trend in contemporary culture which places ultimate value on the well-being of the individual. It is in the name of this value that the universal-secularists attack the notion of "moral community," the notion that society exists for a purpose beyond the provision of services which individuals are unable to provide for themselves.

The conception of a "moral community" is the basic assumption not only of those who believe in a Jewish state but of those who believe in a Zionist state as well. To the extent that secularists adopt the position described above, the possibility for dialogue between them and non-*datiim* is severely limited. The only basis for negotiation remaining would be the privatization of religion and the securing of the narrow group interests of the *dati* community. In other words, this principle, at least by implication, requires *dati* Jews to reinterpret their tradition so that Judaism no longer speaks to the public aspects of life but only to the manner in which the individual conducts his private life. The alternative would be a condition of permanent conflict.

But this is not the present situation, nor is it a likely scenario as long as threats to Israel's security reinforce the Israeli's sense of being Jewish and his conception of the State of Israel as an extension of the Jewish community. Broad consensus and shared values with regard to the nature of religion and state continue to characterize Israeli society. This may account for the fact that, despite the frequent publicity given to tensions between the *dati* and non-*dati* populations, and despite the differences of opinion among Israelis on issues such as the opening of restaurants and theaters on Shabbat, issues are almost always resolved without resorting to violence. Even where some violence occurs, as our Petah Tikva study suggests, as soon as the issue itself subsides good feelings between *datiim* and non-*datiim* can be restored. But, as other attitude studies show, such incidents—especially when they multiply as they have in Jerusalem—also leave a permanent scar.

The *Style of Life* that Divides

Differences over issues are not the only source of tension between the *dati* and non-*dati* sectors. A second source of tension is the matter of life-style. A number of our studies are relevant in this regard. The study of *haredim* in Har Nof indicates how a demand to limit private transportation on Shabbat within neighborhoods arises as soon as *haredim* feel that *dati* Jews constitute a majority within an area. The value which they seek to uphold here is not the religious prohibition of riding on Shabbat, but the maintenance of a "Shabbat atmosphere" where they live. The demand is not confined to *haredim,* as our study of mixed settlements in Samaria and our study of mixed religious and nonreligious marriages indicate. Many, perhaps even most *dati* Jews take it for granted that the preservation of a Shabbat atmosphere in their neighborhoods overrides the value of an individual's freedom to travel on Shabbat on public thoroughfares in their vicinity.

An important study by Yosef Shilhav and Menachem Friedman, published by the Jerusalem Institute for Israel Studies, along with similar studies, indicates that much of the tension between religious and non-religious in Jerusalem stems from the expansion of *haredi* neighborhoods into areas that were heretofore non-religious, and the resentment by the non-*dati* Jews over what they perceive as unreasonable *haredi* demands or what they fear will become *haredi* demands. These include the prohibition of transportation within the neighborhood on Shabbat, insistence that women in the neighborhood dress in "modest" fashion, and objections to Friday-night parties in the homes of the non-*dati* residents which disturb the Shabbat atmosphere. The non-*dati* residents also find that living in the neighborhood of *dati* Jews exposes them to features of a style of life they may find unpleasant—for example, the home gatherings that are characteristic of *dati* Jews on holidays or in celebration of family events: these often include singing that the unsympathetic listener finds raucous and disturbing. The incidents of the burning of bus stops by a small group of *haredim* in 1985 and 1986 are further evidence here. The bus stops were destroyed because they carried advertisements which many *dati* Jews considered "pornographic" and which even by more liberal and tolerant standards could be labeled "sexually provocative." It is unlikely, however, that bus stops would have been burned had the advertisements not been posted in the vicinity of *haredi* neighborhoods.

In an era of population mobility, the question of what does or does not constitute a *haredi* or a *dati* neighborhood, in other words the question of whose "turf" this is, is not easily resolved in all cases. But it is this very mobility which throws people of differing life-styles together and exacerbates tensions. Indeed, one study of the residents of two non-*haredi* neighborhoods in Jerusalem indicates that non-*dati* Jews have far greater objection to the establishment of *haredi* institutions, be they synagogues, schools, or yeshivot (schools for the advanced study of sacred texts), in their own neighborhoods than they do to their establishment elsewhere in the city.

The differences over issues and life-styles are interrelated. For example, even groups who clamor for movie theaters to be opened on Shabbat concede that they should remain closed in *dati* neighborhoods. My own impression is that there are many *dati* Jews who would agree, albeit reluctantly, to opening places of amusement on Shabbat as long as they were not open in *dati* areas. But the issue of what is or is not a *dati* neighborhood is itself a matter of dispute. Indeed, this was a major point of contention in the argument over whether the Habimah theater in Tel Aviv could be used for public forums on Shabbat, a controversy to which we alluded in Chapter Four. But the interrelationship between issue and life-style is deeper. To the extent that *dati* and non-*dati* Jews find themselves deeply divided over issues, we may expect less tolerance over differences in life-style. And to the extent that life-style differences annoy and provoke each side at the more intimate level of home and neighborhood, we may expect a greater propensity to clash over public issues.

Nevertheless, even the problem of life-style differences as a source of tension must not be overstated. The Jewish population of Israel is not divided into two groups, religious extremists with one life-style and dejudaized secularists with a contrary one. Israeli life-styles range along a vast continuum with respect to "Jewishness." The extremists on both sides are minorities of the population who avoid contact with one another anyway. Instances of totally secular neighborhoods invaded by *haredi* extremists are the exception and not the rule. Generally, neighborhoods change through the penetration of families whose styles of life differ slightly rather than radically from those of the families already living there. In addition, the class factor is an important one. Life-styles are dictated by income, education, and ethnic origin as well as by religious orientation. The cost of homes in a neighborhood helps maintain a certain level of homogeneity, although there are many exceptions to this rule. Our study of the Sira neighborhood and of the mixed settlements in Judea and Samaria suggests that at least some *dati* Jews who move into predominantly secular communities are more than ready to "suffer" a life-style contrary to their own. In general we may assume that those prepared to move into neighborhoods whose way of life is different from their own are also prepared to tolerate this way of life and to accommodate their own behavior to the norms prevailing within their neighborhoods. Not that this always happens. In some places, Jerusalem being the most notable example, there have been many exceptions to the rule during the last ten years. But this may be the result of a peculiar set of circumstances and not of any long-term trend endemic to Israeli society. Nevertheless, the transformation of a homogeneous neighborhood into a mixed one should invite the attention and special concern of anyone anxious to reduce tensions between *dati* and non-*dati* Jews.

The question of army service is also a potentially explosive one which overlaps conflicts over issues and conflicts over life-style. Many Israelis, including many religious-Zionists, are upset by the fact that so many *haredim* do not perform regular army service. Although the issue cuts across religious-secular divisions, it is so central in the attitudes of non-*haredim* towards *haredim* and in *haredi* attitudes toward Israeli society that it deserves attention here.

Under Israeli law, men are exempt from army service as long as they are enrolled for full-time study in yeshivot. This has led to the exemption of many *haredim* from any army service. The vast majority of Israelis find this objectionable on symbolic grounds—not serving in the army is viewed as symbolic rejection of the State of Israel; as a matter of principle—why should some risk their lives while others do not? And as a matter of life-style—it places additional hardships on those who do serve, reservists in particular, whose service is lengthened because others refuse to undertake their share of the burden. It reinforces, in the eyes of many, the "otherness" of the *haredim,* and their unwillingness to integrate themselves into the society in which they live. The issue and life-style dimensions of the problem are of no less, indeed of even greater, centrality to the *haredim*. They view efforts to impose army service on their youth as a deliberate challenge to their central values, the primacy of Torah study, and their way of life. They also fear the impact of army service on the behavior of their own youth.

The subject of army service for *haredim* is too complex to be treated in summary form. There is a great deal of misinformation about how many *haredim* do and do not serve in the army and in what capacities and for what length of time they serve when they do. But a couple of points merit consideration in the context of this chapter. First, the issue of army service for *haredim* bubbles beneath the surface of Israeli society and is a continual irritant in relations between *haredim* and non-*haredim*. Nothing to be said here should be misunderstood to imply that the issue is not a real issue and that alleviation of tensions does not require consideration of how differences on this matter can be overcome. However, the fact of the matter is that the issue surfaces when groups on one of the sides are particularly anxious to mobilize their own side against the other. Thus, for example, during the 1988 election campaign, the issue of *haredi* army service was not raised by the secular parties. It was raised by the *haredi* parties, who warned the *haredi* public that unless the *haredi* parties were strengthened the law permitting exemptions for *haredi* students would be amended. On the other hand, immediately after the election, those forces in Israeli society that feared the formation of a government centered on the Likud and the religious parties placed full-page ads in the newspapers and organized mass public demonstrations to protest the exemptions given *haredim*. They felt that by reintroducing the issue at that time they would render such a coalition impossible.

The second point to be made here, with regard to this question, is that it is another indication of how divisive issues overlap divisive life-styles. *Haredim* are not the only group within Israeli society who benefit from exemptions for those in yeshivot. Not all yeshivot run under religious-Zionist auspices require their students to perform their army service during the period of their enrollment in the yeshiva. But no objections have been raised to these arrangements. Part of the reason may lie in the fact that, unlike the *haredim*, religious-Zionists are not viewed as radically "other," and so whatever resentment one may harbor about the "benefits" they enjoy in this respect is not reinforced by generalized hostility.

The *Expectations* that Divide

A number of chapters have referred to the importance of recent events in transforming the perceptions of both *dati* and non-*dati* Jews about the nature of their relationships and the future position of each sector in Israeli society. The chapter on the Petah Tikva cinema controversy makes this point explicitly, but it is also expressed in the chapters dealing with Tehiya, with organizations dedicated to easing tensions between *datiim* and non-*datiim*, and with the *haredi press*. Here we try to put the problem in a larger context and provide one especially illustrative example.

Dati Jews, as we noted, represent an estimated twenty percent of the Jewish population in Israel; the *haredim*, approximately five percent. The sum total of *dati* Jews, in other words, barely exceeds the number of Arab citizens of the State of Israel. But in many instances *dati* Jews, especially their leaders, think of themselves or behave as though they constituted a majority of the population. Religious symbols, as noted in the introductory chapter, increasingly penetrate Israeli society. The Israeli political elite increasingly appeal to religious symbols in their effort to mobilize the population. The rhetoric and symbolic behavior of Israel's two most recent prime ministers, Yitzhak Shamir and Shimon Peres, demonstrate the importance of these symbols. Both men are completely secular in their private lives. Yet Shamir peppers his speeches with such phrases as "with God's help" in discussing public policy. Peres, following his election as prime minister in 1984, went to the Western Wall, where in accordance with custom (superstition?) of many traditionally oriented Jews he placed a note between the stones presumably containing a request to God. Other political leaders in other societies also invoke the name of God or pretend to a level of religious observance that is inconsistent with the way they conduct their private lives, but in Israel this is a recent phenomenon and suggests the increased recognition of religion as an attribute of Israeli culture. We have already observed, in the Introduction, that ideological secularism has declined, and this means that religious interpretations of Judaism have become increasingly normative. Religious spokesmen have become the authoritative interpreters of Judaism, at least for the masses of Israeli Jews.

This, along with other developments, has instilled a sense of confidence in the religious segment of the population they did not have heretofore. This is a phenomenon that has been widely observed by students of Israeli life. It finds expression among social scientists, among literary figures such as Amos Oz or Gershon Shaked. It is reflected, at least indirectly, in a number of our case studies and most explicitly in Chapter Ten.

Religious parties, because of the developments already mentioned and because of the nature of the electoral system, have more political influence than they enjoyed in the past. Paradoxically, the political influence of the religious voter continued to grow even in the last decade, when the vote for religious parties, the religious-Zionist parties in particular, contracted. Indeed, the dramatic reduction in support for the party of religious-Zionism, the National Religious Party, whose representation dropped from twelve seats in 1977 to five in the last two elections, suggests that religious-Zionist voters no longer feel the need for a religious party to protect their interests. These voters feel free to vote for non-religious parties. Those parties, in turn, are increasingly likely to slate *dati* candidates and compete for the vote of the *dati* public. The *haredi* parties, on the other hand, demonstrated an ability to attract non-*dati* voters in 1988, further evidence of the legitimacy of religion in the eyes of at least one segment of the non-*dati* public.

Another reason for the confidence of the religious public lies in the mistaken belief that the proportion of religious Jews within the population is growing. We are not concerned with the accuracy of this perception or with its causes. The important point for our purposes is that this is how religious Jews currently see their position in Israeli society. This sense of confidence is reflected in the following passage, which we quote at some length because it not only conveys ideas but gives the reader a sense of the mentality of at least one important segment of the *dati* camp. It is taken from an interview with a *haredi* Jew in Jerusalem and was printed in the June 1987 issue of *Emdah*, a religious-Zionist publication.

> Why do you think Ben-Gurion agreed to exempt yeshiva students from his army? From an abundance of love of Torah? No! He thought to himself: let us leave them alone because whatever happens, they will disappear. . . . Little by little no *haredi* Judaism will be left. At the most a small group in B'nai B'rak [a Tel Aviv suburb in which religious Jews are concentrated] or Meah Shearim [an exclusively *haredi* neighborhood in Jerusalem] will remain.
>
> That is what he thought to himself. But see for yourself, God denied him his wish. Among the secularists there is a wife and child, and maybe a dog (he laughs), in every family. And among us, without an evil eye,. . . our neighborhoods are expanding more and more. . . . Look how many *baalei t'shuvah* there are around here. A little longer, with God's help, and Jerusalem will look like B'nai B'rak. For more than fifty years the Zionists ruled here, now the time for Jewish rule has come. For the time being at least, in Jerusalem. Among us, the children want to live near their parents and thus we continue to expand.
>
> We want to see a Jewish street. Without Sabbath desecration, without non-kosher food, without exaggerated permissiveness, without pornographic advertisements on bus stops. And this is coming to pass, thank God. [The respondent then goes on to cite a number of passages from sacred text to demonstrate that this process is inevitable.]

This triumphalism is reflected in the readiness of many *haredim* to demonstrate publicly and sometimes violently against the opening of movie houses and coffee shops on Shabbat, against certain types of archaeological excavations, and against advertisements they consider pornographic.

On the other hand, these developments in Israeli society which generate an unfounded confidence in the religious segment of the population have provoked a backlash among some secularists and led to the growth of anti-religious, almost anti-Jewish, tendencies. In the last two or three years there have been a growing number of demonstrations by secular Jews against the demands of the religious. There have been efforts, some of them successful, to overturn previous status-quo agreements on the closing of places of entertainment on Shabbat. (The "status-quo" refers to an understanding between the leaders of religious and secular parties that agreements previously made concerning the extent to which public life is or is not governed by religious law will not be changed without the consent of both sides.) For the first time in recent memory, anti-religious segments have initiated incidents of violence including desecration and burning of synagogues—though no one attributes these acts to more than a handful of extremists.

Secular-universalists, to whom we referred earlier in this chapter, are not only anti-religious, but often indifferent if not hostile to Judaism in almost any form. But many Israelis who are certainly not anti-religious, and still less hostile to Judaism, have aligned themselves with the secular-universalists because they fear what they perceive as the growth of the power of the religious segment and its intolerant attitude toward them. These attitudes, nurtured by many prominent intellectuals who express their fears in books and plays including apocalyptic visions of the day in which Khomeini-like rabbis would rule Israeli society, found dramatic expression following the 1988 elections.

There are a number of indications of a renewed aggressiveness on the part of the secularists, as our chapter on the *haredi* press demonstrates. Even a member of the *Jerusalem Post* editorial board urges secularists, since they have no other choice, to take to the streets in a fight "that the secular population should not fear" since "it needs a good dose of consciousness-raising." (December 4, 1987, p. 10). Heretofore, those who opposed the behavior of *dati* Jews, or who were critical of what they termed "religious coercion" or the aggressive posture of the *dati* public, were likely to distinguish *haredim* from religious-Zionists and blame the *haredim* for what they didn't like, even where the distinction was unjustified. Those who attacked *haredim* were likely to preface their attacks by exempting the religious-Zionists, or religious moderates. They don't always do so now, as we saw in Chapter Three. In the past year one increasingly heard charges against religious Jews in general, when the reference could have been limited to *haredim*. One also hears the charge that the more religious the society the less democratic it will be; and even, by inference, the more *Jewish* the society, the less democratic it will be. Such, for example, is the thrust of many articles in the semi-academic journal *Israeli Democracy*, published by the Israel–Diaspora Institute at Tel Aviv University, or in the major Israeli newspaper *Ha' Aretz*.

Little can be done about secular and religious extremists, since both thrive on tension and find their own world-views and beliefs reinforced by hostility between *datiim* and non-*datiim*. But since some and perhaps much of the support they receive stems from the mistaken expectations of each side, wide dissemination of information in popular form should reduce some of the support for the extremists. Moderates in the *dati* and non-*dati* sectors might also be encouraged to pursue a more aggressive policy in confronting the lies and misconceptions disseminated by the extremists on both sides.

Compromise and Accommodation

By compromise we mean the surrender of some value or principle or ideal for the sake of some other value or principle or ideal. By accommodation we mean adjustment by one side to the needs of another side without surrendering any value or principle or ideal. Reducing tensions between *dati* and non-*dati* Jews involves accommodations and perhaps compromises on the part, probably, of both sides. Indeed, compromise and accommodation by only one of the parties is unlikely to reduce tensions, since it would convey a message that one side is infinitely flexible, that both sides recognize that the demands of only one of the parties are justified, and that if further demands are made they will also be met.

The first stage in compromise or accommodation is to recognize the legitimacy of the other side. The effort required from the non-*dati* Jew in this regard may seem slight, but the principle is by no means self-evident, least of all to intellectuals. He or she is called upon to recognize that, however contemptuous one may feel toward religious beliefs and practices, however primitive, medieval, superstitious, and unworldly they may seem, religious beliefs and practices are central to the life of the religious Jew and therefore demand no less respect than any other set of beliefs and practices which are central to the lives of people with whom one wishes to live in harmony. No less important, the secularist must recognize that the attitudes and beliefs of the religious Jew include a societal component. They extend to convictions about the manner in which public life in Israel ought to be conducted. They are not to be understood as simply a desire to impose a way of life on the secular Jew which the latter finds repugnant, although that indeed may be their consequence.

Insofar as the *dati* is concerned, he or she may have special difficulty in internalizing the notion that, however proper it is to hope and pray for and believe in the ultimate "penitence" of the non-*dati*, relations between the *dati* and non-*dati* must be conducted at a level which accepts the secular way of life as a given. This may be achieved by reinterpreting secularism in religious terminology, thereby requiring religious accommodation rather than compromise, which is what Rabbi Abraham Isaac Hacohen Kook did. It may also be achieved by legitimating secularism in secularist terms, thereby requiring compromise and not simply accommodation, as the contemporary Jewish philosopher Eliezer Schweid urges. In practice it may also be achieved by eschewing any attempt to understand the nature of secularism, as most *dati* Jews do in their day-to-day contacts with the non-*datim*. This third method is only successful to the extent that people choose not to reflect on the kinds of lives they lead. Fortunately or unfortunately this is not true of all people, least of all the cultural elite whose contribution to the exacerbation or mitigation of tension is so crucial. The question of whether accommodation or compromise is a more desirable strategy for mitigating tensions is a question which we will only treat in passing.

The attitudinal and behavioral changes required of *dati* and non-*dati* Jews are viewed by some as compromises of religious principle or democratic-liberal faith, respectively—a surrender of elements of basic ideology and faith. Alternatively, one or both sides may legitimate accommodations by reinterpreting ideology, faith, or both, in a manner that allows for reducing tensions without surrendering principles. The first method, initially, appears ideal. It is the route which some *dati* Jews of Sira and the mixed settlements in Samaria, and to a certain extent the secular Jews of Tehiya, are taking. It is awkward to admit that one mode of tension-reduction results from compromising what is ostensibly basic principle. It may be equally awkward to acknowledge that tensions are also reduced by indifference to or ignorance of the practical implications of values and principles to which an individual claims to adhere. But this is the case. On the other hand, one cannot expect all secularists, and certainly not all religious Jews, to compromise basic principle, even if this would contribute to more harmonious relations. One may argue, of course, that this is what makes many pluralistic societies viable, but it is also what makes them weak, and unable to resist pressures from strongly committed advocates of particular causes within or without. One cannot dismiss the possibility that to conduct one's life in such a way is to encourage a kind of nihilism and normlessness and to discourage the forging of any commitment or the maintenance of any principle.

Concern with reducing tensions between *dati* and non-*dati* Jews, especially when it is formulated in terms of commitment to the value of unity of the Jewish people, need not involve Jews in compromise of principles. There are grave issues at stake not only in the conflict between religious and secular Jews but even and perhaps especially in the conflict between *haredim* and religious-Zionists. Each side perceives the other as fundamentally in error about the nature of Judaism. Insofar as *dati* Jews are concerned, this means misunderstanding if not distortion of the will of God. This is too serious a matter to allow for compromise. The solution, therefore, is not the resolution of differences but learning to live in one society despite these differences. This means either, as our study of Tehiya shows, emphasizing the values which both sides share; or, as our study of the peace movements shows, maintaining civil relations but separate structures when the shared values are not sufficient to overcome religious differences.

The alternative—and the two approaches are not necessarily mutually exclusive—is to encourage an understanding and interpretation of Judaism on the one hand and of secular, democratic liberalism on the other, which legitimates the kinds of accommodation which living peacefully in a Jewish state requires. Such a course of action suggests that each side has a stake in the kind of education and socialization process that takes place in the other. *Datiim* have every reason to be concerned with what is taught in secular schools or conveyed in the press and electronic media about the nature of democracy and liberalism, just as non-*datiim* have every reason to be concerned with what is taught in religious schools, preached in synagogues, and written in the religious press about the proper understanding of Judaism.

About the Contributors

Asher Cohen is a doctoral candidate at Bar-Ilan University writing on the meaning and consequences of the religious-Zionist demand for a state governed in accordance with Jewish law. He is also active in political life.

Naomi Gutkind-Golan is a member of the editorial staff and a feature writer for *Hatzoffe,* the daily newspaper of the National Religious Party. She is the editor of a number of books on Judaism.

Samuel C. Heilman, professor of sociology at Queens College and the Graduate Center of the City University of New York, was a visiting professor at the Hebrew University in 1988. He is the author of a number of studies on the religious life of Orthodox Jews. Co-author of *Cosmopolitans and Parochials: Modern Orthodox Jews in America* (University of Chicago Press, 1989), he is presently completing a manuscript on *haredim* in Israel.

Tamar Hermann is a doctoral candidate at Tel-Aviv University where she has just completed her dissertation on the ideology of the Israeli peace camp. She is co-author of *National Security and Public Opinion in Israel* (Westview Press, 1988).

Amnon Levi, the parliamentary reporter for the daily newspaper *Hadashot,* is the author of a best-selling book on the *haredim* published by Keter Books.

Charles S. Liebman, editor of the volume, is a professor of political science at Bar-Ilan University and the author of many studies dealing with religion and society among Jews in Israel and the United States. He is co-author of the forthcoming book, *Two Worlds of Judaism: The American and Israeli Experience* (Yale University Press).

David Newman is a senior lecturer in the Department of Geography at Ben-Gurion University. He is editor of *The Impact of Gush Emunim* (Croom-Helm) and co-author of *Between Village and Suburb: New Settlement Patterns in Israel* published in Hebrew by the Bialik Institute.

Ephraim Tabory is a senior lecturer in the Sociology Department of Bar-Ilan University and author of a number of studies on religion and society in Israel.

Leonard Weller is a professor of Sociology at Bar-Ilan University. He is the author of books and articles in the area of sociology and social psychology in Israeli society.

Sonia Topper Weller is the director of the municipal library of Kiryat Ono. She is co-author of a study of rehabilitation in Israel (with Leonard Weller).

Yisrael Wollman, an editor for the daily newspaper *Yediot Aharonot,* edits the religious-Zionist magazine *Emdah.*

Glossary of Hebrew Terms

Af sha'al. "Not an inch." Slogan of opponents to Israeli withdrawal from lands acquired by Israel in the Six-Day War of 1967.

Agudat Israel. Predominantly Ashkenazic *haredi* political party.

Ahi. Local *haredi* political group in Har Nof.

El Ami. "To My People." Founded in May, 1983, addresses religious/secular schism.

Amiad. Established in 1982 to acquaint general Israeli public with Judaism.

Ashkenazi (pl. Ashkenazim). Jews of European origin.

Az Nidberu. Paper of the Vishnitz *haredim.*

Baalei t'shuvah. Religious penitents—those raised in non-religious environments who have become religious.

Bet Midrash l'Shalom. "The House of Study for Peace." Monthly meeting held by Oz/Netivot.

B'nai Akiva. Religious-Zionist youth movement.

Ben Torah. One who is religiously observant and well-versed in the classical religious texts.

Dati (pl. datiim). Religious, (Orthodox) Jews.

Davar. Daily secular newspaper associated with *Histadrut* (General Federation of Labor).

Edah Haredit. A central organization of the *haredi* community in Jerusalem.

Emdah. Religious-Zionist publication.

Eretz Yisrael. "The Land of Israel."

Erev Shabbat. "Sabbath Eve"—commercial *haredi* newspaper.

Gesher. "Bridge." Movement founded in 1970 to ease religious/secular tensions.

Goy (pl. goyim). Gentile, or non-Jew.

Gush Emunim. "Bloc of the Faithful." Ultranationalist group created in 1974 to establish Jewish settlements on the West Bank.

Haaretz. Secular daily newspaper. Also, *Ha'aretz.*

Haedah. Publication of *Edah Haredit.*

Hahomah. Publication of extreme *haredi* group *Neturei Karta.*

Halakhah. Jewish law.

Hamahaneh Haharedi. Weekly paper of Belz *hasidim.*

Al Hamishmar. Secular daily newspaper.

Hamodia. A daily *haredi* newspaper, organ of Agudat Israel.

Haredi (pl. haredim). Literally, "fearful," from the scriptural reference to the righteous person who fears the word of God. Generally categorized by a strict interpretation of Jewish law, rejection of secular culture, and an ambivalent attitude toward the present State of Israel. Formerly a term for any Orthodox Jew, currently it means an "ultra-Orthodox" Jew. Broadly divided between *hasidim* and *misnagdim* (q.v.)

Hasid (pl. hasidim.) An adherent of a particular Jewish religious philosophy which emphasized the relationship with a *rebbe* (charismatic spiritual leader) to bring one closer to the Divine.

Hesder Yeshivot. A *yeshivah* which combines Talmudic studies with military service.

Hiloni. Secular or non-religious.

Holkhim b'yahad. "Going together." Concept of cooperation between religious and non-religious Jews.

Hozer biteshuva. (pl. Hozrim biteshuvah) Another term for one raised in a non-religious environment who has become observant.

Kashrut. (Kosher) Jewish dietary law.

Kfar Habad. Newspaper of Habad (Lubavitcher) *hasidim.*

Kiddush. Literally, the benediction over the wine on the Sabbath.

Kippa. (pl. kipot). A skullcap—worn as a religious symbol.

Kol Ha'Ir. Weekly secular newspaper.

Kooknikim. Followers of Rav Kook.

Kugel. Baked pudding-like casserole.

L'ma'an Har Nof. "For Har Nof." A list of Anglo-Saxon *haredim,* known locally as "the Boston list," which contested the local election in Har Nof in 1987.

Lo dati (pl. lo datiim). Those who are not religious. Also, *hiloni* (q.v.).

Maaleh. Educational center for religious Zionism.

Maariv. Secular daily newspaper. (Also, *Ma'ariv.*)

Mahleket Kiddush Hashem. "Sanctification of the Name of God Department." Reference to religious supporters of "Peace Now" who appear at demonstrations; often from *Oz/Netivot.*

MALITZ. Hebrew acronym for "Institutes for Jewish-Zionist Education." Teaches Jewish identity to adults.

Masorati (pl. masoratim). Traditional Jews, as opposed to "secular" or "religious" Jews in contemporary Israeli parlance.

Mehitzah. Separation of men from women in an Orthodox synagogue.

Mikvah (pl. mikvaot). A ritual bath, primarily used by women prior to resumption of sexual relations with their husbands after abstention during the menstrual cycle. Also, *mikva, mikveh.*

Minyan. Prayer service of at least ten adult males.

Mishkan. Biblical Hebrew term for "sanctuary." Modern Hebrew term for "official building," as in *mishkan Hanasi* (president's mansion) and *mishkan HaKnesset* (Knesset building).

Mishloah manot. Gifts of food exchanged during Purim.

Misnaged (pl. misnagdim). Literally, "opponent," originally defined those opposed to hasidism. Currently refers to religious, generally haredi ashkenazi Jews who are not hasidim.

Mitzvah (pl. mitzvot). Biblical or rabbinic commandment.

Morasha. "Heritage." A political party similar to Tehiya (q.v.), except that it is strictly religious.

Netivot Shalom. "Paths of Peace." Taken from the verse in Proverbs, "Your way is the way of pleasantness, and all Your paths are those of peace." More mass-movement oriented and more religious than *Oz v'Shalom,* and to its right politically. Founded in 1982, merged with *Oz v'Shalom* (q.v.) in 1985.

Neturei Karta. The haredi group that is most extreme in its hostility to the State of Israel.

Otiot. Weekly children's magazine.

Oz/Netivot. Short term for *Oz v'Shalom[n-]Netivot Shalom.* See under individual entries.

Oz v'Shalom. "Strength and Peace." Religious peace group, founded in 1975. Academic in nature. Merged with *Netivot Shalom* in 1985. Also, *Oz/Netivot, Oz v'Shalom[n-]Netivot Shalom.*

Oz v'Shalom[n-]Netivot Shalom. Official, full name of *Oz/Netivot.*

P'sak. Halachic judicial ruling on a contested matter.

Ratz. "Citizens Rights Movement." Anti-clerical political party.

Sephardi (pl. Sephardim). Broadly defined in Israel as Jews originating from Asia and Africa.

Shalom Akhshav. "Peace Now." Largest of the Israeli peace groups.

Shalom bayit. "Peace in the house," refers to domestic tranquility.

Shas. Sephardic *haredi* political party.

Shma Yisrael. "Hear, O Israel" Traditional prayer which declares the Oneness of God.

Shomer mitzvot. One who observes the commandments.

Shorashim. "Roots." Group founded to relieve tensions between religious and non-religious through educational weekends.

Taharat hamishpakhah. Laws of family purity; include a prohibition of sexual activities for at least twelve days during every menstrual cycle, and requiring the woman to immerse herself in a *mikva* (q.v.).

Talit. Prayer shawl. Also, *tallit.*

Tami. Political party; primarily Sephardic and religiously traditional.

Tehiya. "Revival." Political party formed in 1978 as a reaction to the peace agreement between Israel and Egypt. Primarily a "hawkish" party, wants to retain Israeli sovereignty over land captured in 1967. Unique because it is composed of both religious and non-religious members.

Tzitzit. Fringes on a four-cornered garment worn by Jewish males. Generally worn under a shirt. Also, *tsitsiot.*

Yarmulke. Skullcap. Same as *kippa.*

Yated Neeman. *Haredi* daily controlled by Rabbi Eliezer Shach.

Yediot Aharonot. Secular daily newspaper.

Yesh G'vul. "There Is a Boundary." Peace group whose members refuse to perform army service in Lebanon or occupied lands.

Yeshiva (pl. yeshivot). Academy for Talmudic study.

Yishuv. "Settlement." In contemporary parlance, refers to Israel before the establishment of the State in the twentieth century.

Yisrael Saba. Literally, "Grandfather Israel." The stereotype of the traditional Jew and Judaism.

Yom Hashishi. "Friday." Weekly commercial *haredi* newspaper.

Zmirot. Sabbath songs.